WRITING
THE
ROMANTIC
COMEDY

WRITING
THE
ROMANTIC
COMEDY

FROM "CUTE MEET" TO "JOYOUS DEFEAT": HOW TO WRITE SCREENPLAYS THAT SELL

BILLY MERNIT

Collins
An Imprint of HarperCollinsPublishers

HarperCollins books may be purchased for educational, business, or sales pro-
motional use. For information please write: Special Markets Department,
HarperCollins Publishers Inc., 10 East 53rd Street, New York, NY 10022.

First HarperResource paperback edition published 2001

The Library of Congress has cataloged the hardcover edition as follows:

Mernit, Billy.
    Writing the romantic comedy : from "cute meet" to "joyous defeat": how
to write screenplays that will sell / by Billy Mernit.
        p.   cm.
    Includes index.
    ISBN 0-06-019568-1
    1. Motion picture authorship.   2. Love in motion pictures.
3. Comedy films.   I. Title.
PN1996 .M49 2000
808.2'3—dc21   00-039727

ISBN 0-06-093503-0 (pbk.)
  07 08 09 RRD 10 9 8 7

TO: Claudia Nizza Mernit,
      who showed me how real life
      can be the best romantic comedy of all

FOR: My students, who asked me to do this

WITH THANKS TO:

Linda Venis and her stalwart staff at UCLA Extension, Stacey
Snider, Romy Kaufman and the Story Department gang at
Universal Studios, my agent Bonnie Nadell, Marion Maneker,
my editor Greg Chaput, Jay Adler, Lynda Nusser, Thomas Pope,
Cameron Crowe and Dick, Dee-Ann, John, Kathy, and Lucy
Mernit—a family of good-humored romantics who supported me
along the way.

Contents

PART IV: Completing Your Draft and After

Introduction

Three of the biggest box office successes of the past few years—*Shakespeare in Love, What Women Want,* and *Runaway Bride*—are among a slew of recent movies that demonstrate the remarkable staying power of romantic comedy, a genre that's been delighting mainstream audiences and challenging screenwriters since the silent era. As a Hollywood story analyst, I can attest to the fact that all the studios (and most major stars) are actively seeking romantic comedies. Savvy screenwriters are pitching romantic comedy projects, since such scripts showcase characterization and dialogue skills and can often lead to lucrative writing assignments, even if the movies themselves don't ultimately get made.

But hundreds of romantic comedies are rejected by the industry every month. Why? Because they're too formulaic in plot. Or they lack memorable characters. Or they don't speak to today's audiences in fresh, provocative ways, mistaking superficial silliness for the genuinely deep laughs that a well-crafted, deeply felt comedy should evoke. Evidently, a lot of would-be romantic comedy writers think that boy meets, loses, and gets girl is all you need to know.

But having personally "passed" on (said no to) countless romantic comedies in the past half dozen years and given a "consider" (a yes) to only a precious few, I know that there's a lot more to it than that.

A few years ago, being both a screenwriter and a longtime lover of the form, I offered to teach a course at the UCLA Extension Writers' Program in romantic comedy screenwriting. When my class was announced, registration closed in record time, with a waiting list as long as the class roster. Yet I couldn't find a single textbook in print that specifically spoke to the genre. A few history/analysis tomes study the Screwball Era and go no further—as if we'd stopped watching romantic comedies after World War II. Among the many how-to screenwriting books extant, no book currently exists that shows writers how to craft a successful romantic comedy.

Writing the Romantic Comedy was written to fill a gap. It's a complete romantic comedy screenwriting workshop in one book.

WHO THIS BOOK IS FOR

Novice screenwriters with embryonic ideas, intermediates who are stuck in a draft that needs help, and seasoned pros either new to this genre or searching for inspiration should all be able to find something useful between these covers—as should fans of the form who'd merely like to get an inside look at what makes it tick.

If you're just getting started, the book is ideally suited for guiding you toward the completion of a first draft. But if you've already got a draft that's been through some rewrites, this text can be a problem solver; it'll help you deconstruct, rethink, and perhaps reassemble your story. Getting back to basics is often the best way to discover where and how you may have gone off track (i.e., "What got me excited about this movie in the first place?").

The book is designed to get you through your process, following your romantic comedy idea from genesis, through character and story development, and into a completed draft. It features myriad examples from classic and contemporary romantic comedies, and it includes writing exercises that will spark inspiration and short-circuit potential mistakes.

HOW THE BOOK IS ORGANIZED

Part I ("Getting Started") starts with a chapter on the fundamentals of cinematic storytelling (those basic story components that make up a successful script in any genre): character, plot/structure, theme, imagery, dialogue, point of view, and world.

Our second chapter then defines just what a romantic comedy is. We focus on the dynamics of the "meet-lose-get" formula, analyzing how a romantic comedy story concept is dependent on strong inner conflicts for its protagonists and how it uses love as a catalyst or antagonistic force for plot development. It's also noted that the most successful contemporary romantic comedies are often those combining a traditional romantic comedy story with elements from another genre. The first group of writing exercises addresses how to develop a premise and story concept for your own project.

Chapter 3 maps out a thumbnail romantic comedy history, noting highlights, trends, and evolutions up to the millennial present. It cites classics, sleepers, and cross-genre romantic comedies in every decade.

Part II ("Into the Thick of It") begins with an in-depth analysis of romantic comedy characters. We explore what audiences look for in a romantic comedy lead, male and female, defining cultural biases and predilections. Chapter 4 examines how supporting characters function, identifying certain staples of the genre, such as the Bellamy (i.e., the wrong mate). A Case Study movie, *Tootsie* (the first of four such movies to be analyzed in depth), demonstrates how the many subplots of a story can stem

from character choices, and a writing exercise has you fill out
Q & A forms for your lead characters.

Chapter 5 discusses theme. The best romantic comedies are
shown to be *about* something. We analyze the Case Study movie,
When Harry Met Sally (which is motored by an axiomatic question
about the compatibility between men and women) to show how
having a workable theme can immeasurably deepen a script—
how theme can strengthen all plot and character choices. A writing exercise helps you find the thematic throughline in your
project.

"Structuring Conflict" (Chapter 6) looks at the process of developing an organic plot, identifying the so-called romantic comedy formula, a variation on a three-act construct that has seven
key beats. We examine how this traditional structure works and
look at ways it can be enlivened or tweaked. A writing exercise
helps you prepare a brief working outline of your project in
progress.

Chapter 7, on credibility, shows how an understanding of plot
logic techniques can make the fantastical seem real. It demonstrates how writers ground their comedy in serious rules, defining
various approaches that will help create a more believable story.
This chapter ends with a Starting-the-Draft Checklist exercise,
which reviews the material thus far and applies it to your project.

Part III ("The Finer Points") gets into more advanced issues
of screenplay craft. "The Art of Funny" (Chapter 8) maintains
that, though much of it's instinctual, there is a science of comedy
governed by fundamental truisms. We explore the use of reversals
(a crucial comedic concept), along with other techniques of
comedic writing. "Being Sexy" (Chapter 9) notes that many romantic comedies have run aground by losing sight of what's genuinely romantic and erotic. Basic principles (e.g., in a romantic
comedy, it's never *just* sex) and various approaches to the before,
during, and after phases of intimate encounters are demonstrated,
with examples from some influential films that should prove inspi-
rational.

Exploiting the many uses of dialogue is the thrust of Chapter 10. Writing visually is the theme of Chapter 11, in which we cite a number of techniques used to make storytelling more cinematic. The Case Study movie *Annie Hall* demonstrates imaginative visual writing, and writing exercises in both chapters enforce the concepts in dialogue and visual storytelling.

In Part IV ("Completing Your Draft and After"), Chapter 12, "Deepening Your Craft," introduces five craft enhancers that will strengthen your screenwriting skills. We look at what a first draft is really for and at the many hard choices (as well as imaginative leaps) called for in rewriting after that first draft is completed. We also examine the reader-friendly form, with an eye toward getting past the story analysts who serve as the business's first line of resistance to script submissions. A final writing exercise submits your draft to a rigorous checklist, reviewing all of the book's important points, to help guide you through the rewrite process.

Finally, Chapter 13 takes a look at romantic comedy's present and future. What is the genre up to now, and where do contemporary audiences seem to want it to go? Along with some insights from a prominent studio head, we offer some other specific suggestions on how to approach the market.

HOW TO GET THE MOST OUT OF THIS BOOK

To get the best results from your reading, (1) see the movies discussed, and (2) do the exercises.

Every Case Study in the book is available on video (some on DVD), as are all of the films quoted or cited. The clips introduced in every chapter aren't there merely to revisit favorite moments, they're provided to illustrate specific points, and quite often, context is crucial. Chapter 4's *Tootsie* discussion will mean a lot more to you if the viewing experience is fresh in your mind. So even if you've seen a given movie before, you'll reap much more from your reading if you watch the video, preferably *before* you read the chapter that analyzes it (endings are revealed, so *after* may be less fun).

The writing exercises in this book have all been road-tested in my classrooms. If you take the time to do them, you're likely to reap tangible rewards—be it a sudden insight that opens up a new approach to dealing with your second act or one seemingly small character detail that could set up and pay off one of your script's best gags.

Often in our zeal to get that product—the finished draft—completed, we don't take enough advantage of our writing process. The time that you spend "off the page" (i.e., exploring character backstories, playing with alternative structures, searching for clearer definitions of theme) can prove far more valuable than hours spent agonizing over the perfect dialogue exchange or bit of narrative description. You never know what gold can be mined from digging a little deeper when you work outside the draft itself. *Writing the Romantic Comedy* provides these exercises as an encouragement to go that extra mile.

A NOTE ON WHERE I'M COMING FROM

The various theories and pronouncements found in what follows are based on my having a foothold in a number of relevant camps. As a story analyst for the major studios, I'm a spy in the house of commerce; as part of their vast decision-making process, I'm familiar with the mercurial minds of the executives whose dictates, be they business-sound or bewilderingly whimsical (last year, it was to "set everything in high school") directly affect the marketplace.

As a teacher, I've learned by trial and error which approaches to the material yield the best results (and which opinions are merely that) and which ones have proved useful to aspiring writers. In preparing this book, I've seen and studied hundreds of romantic comedies. The various genre specifications offered here aren't dreamed-up abstractions; here, based on the evidence of many successful "rom-coms," is what consistently seems to work.

And finally, as a working screenwriter in Hollywood, I know, as writer Gene Fowler once said, that "writing is easy: all you have to do is stare at a blank page for an hour until the drops of blood start dripping from your forehead." I know what it's like to grapple with a seemingly insoluble, problematic rewrite under pressure. And I've picked up a few tricks (thank goodness) to make the process bearable.

I've also learned that merely imitating what works isn't quite enough. This is why you won't find this book dictating, as if written in stone, the necessary screenplay page numbers for act breaks. Once you've grasped the rules, sometimes you'll be called upon to bend them—in fact, I hope you can. One of this book's themes is that in addition to keeping the writing real and making it personal, having the courage to take risks can yield the most satisfying professional happy endings.

PART ONE

Getting Started

CHAPTER ONE

Storytelling Fundamentals

I f you're reading this book, you probably have at least some rudimentary knowledge of what constitutes a good screenplay. Chances are, you've heard of the three-act structure and you know that the average script is supposed to be thinner than an L.A. phone book. Many of you may be already itching to skip to the next chapter. But so that all of us can share a common ground of concepts to build on, let's do a quick review of the basics.

A perusal of the field yields, by common consensus, seven essential components of storytelling. Everybody has his or her own variations on these elements, but for our purposes, let's say these are the generally agreed-upon fundamental components that any good screenplay has to have. Put them all to good use, and you're loaded for bear; abandon even one, and your movie will be handicapped.

CHARACTER

Here's an odd instance of what might be called Oscar prescience: I once predicted who would win Best Actor before the movie was shot. That was when a friend slipped me a copy of the Mark Andrus/James L. Brooks script for *As Good as It Gets*, then in preproduction under another title. When I finished the read and dried my tears (besides being moved, I was crying because there was probably no way I'd ever write dialogue as good as Brooks does), I opined that whoever played the part of Melvin was going to win an Academy Award. Told that Jack Nicholson had been cast, I said, "In that case, I'll put money on it."

It was that good a part, that good a character—and every now and then, in a rare moment of honest humility, you'll hear an award-winning actor credit the role for the win. They're no dummies, and any working writer knows that this story component is perhaps the most important of them all. One such scribe nailed it a few thousand years ago (Heraclitus), when he said "Character is destiny." Plot comes from people.

Some say that a story is merely the reaction of characters to crisis and/or conflict. It's certainly true that a story lacking in credible, complex, empathetic people who have strong desires is a story that no amount of sex, violence, or technology can fix. Think of the many memorable movies named after their protagonists—*Forrest Gump, Thelma and Louise, Arthur,* to name a few—and hundreds of actors' careers were virtually created by a seminal role. Where would Harrison Ford be without Han Solo? Stallone without Rocky?

Still, you'd be surprised by how often this absolutely vital storytelling element gets neglected in your average spec screenplay. Haven't these writers ever seen the lack of strong characterizations turn a potential studio blockbuster into a last-resort selection at Blockbuster's? All the star power in the world doesn't make a difference if the characters aren't on the page, which is what MGM found out when Michael Keaton and Geena Davis, both at career peaks, tanked in 1994's *Speechless*. That's why this story component is going to get a lot of serious attention in the pages ahead.

PLOT AND STRUCTURE

Character is only half of the dynamics of a story. A given situation is the other half. Unlike a title such as *Thelma and Louise*, the movie about how one romantic couple came to be isn't called simply *Harry and Sally*, it's called *When Harry Met Sally*. Nice title, because it immediately suggests more than a general story (i.e., everything you need to know about Harry and Sally). It indicates plot—which is, as we've posited, how a particular character deals with a given situation (e.g., when Harry met Sally . . . what happened?). How your characters act (or choose not to act) generally constitutes dramatic development.

A good plot sustains our interest in a story, making us ask "what happens next?" through a canny manipulation of intriguing complications and escalating conflicts. When it comes to plot, there are only three things every one has to have: a beginning, a middle, and an end.

Plot is the specific sequence of events that illuminates your story. *Structure* is your means of organizing that sequence.

Cinematic master Jean Luc Godard once said that every movie needed a beginning, a middle, and an end—but not necessarily in that order. And true, some classics like *Sunset Boulevard* begin with the ending (e.g., the hero found dead in a swimming pool), and some go backward and forward in time simultaneously (e.g., *The English Patient*). But whatever the organizing plan that a story uses, if it's going to satisfy an audience, its plot is generally presented in three viable acts.

Funny thing about threes. Maybe it's hardwired into our DNA, but three seems to be the magic number (as in morning, noon, and night, the Holy Trinity, etc.). You know the feeling when a movie's first act stumbles, when a second act falls apart, or worst of all, when an ending disappoints; the resulting alienation is fatal. Clearly, a well-structured plot is a critical component of good storytelling, and we'll be scrutinizing the ways and means of achieving it.

THEME

If there's one question that gives every screenwriter I know the willies, it's the one that some executives ask—often at the end of a fine-tuned pitch, a model of first-rate storytelling that's just outlined a movie in vivid, you-can-see-it detail. "Sounds great," they say, "but what's the movie *about?*"

Like it or not, that's the question every good storyteller has to answer. If character is the element that tells us *who,* and plot/structure the element that explores *what,* then *theme* is the necessary story component that addresses *why:* Why are you telling us this story? Why these characters in this particular situation? What's the significance—the meaning behind all your digital sound and fury?

Discussing theme, the astute writer and teacher Janet Burroway said (in *Writing Fiction*): "A story speculates on a possible truth." And the test of time shows us that the works which last, on page or screen, do exactly that; they resonate with an idea—an observation, a proposed argument, some concept about the way we live our lives—that gets explored in the course of the story. A movie like *American Beauty* has a purpose, some reason for being, that's palpable; it draws us into its dark depths because it gets at provocative truths. So does a seeming one-joke farce like *Groundhog Day* (the Great American Neglected Classic of the 1990s); both films reward return trips with fresh insights.

Having an idea to be explored is what separates the fluff from the beloved favorites. And it's the secret story-component weapon of the best romantic comedies made to date, as we'll see when we analyze *When Harry Met Sally.*

IMAGERY

Though *Shakespeare in Love* has been justly praised for its wordplay, what many people remember from it isn't a line, but a moment of visual poetry: a luminescent Viola spinning round and round as her poet/playwright lover joyfully unwinds for the first time the cloth that's been binding her femininity. And *There's Something About Mary* is defined in most people's minds by a shot of a smiling Mary, crowned with a uniquely hair-gelled hairdo.

These two wildly disparate romantic comedies from the same year are cited to make a simple point: *imagery* is the very substance of good storytelling, from whichever end of the genre spectrum. Pictorial storytelling has been with us from the dawn of the form (garden, snake, apple), but it's inarguable that a movie without imagery—either imaginative visual metaphors or compelling pictures, period—isn't much of a movie at all.

Think about how much of *Moonstruck's* charm came from that moon, or how a cheap motel room's blanket hung across a clothesline to separate Gable from Colbert has etched *It Happened One Night* in moviegoing history, and you'll have some idea how potent a tool imagery can be. Sadly, great visual storytelling has long been too scarce in romantic comedy, a genre prone to talking-heads scenes. So we'll be paying special attention to imagery as a means of crafting a sit-up-and-take-notice script.

DIALOGUE

If you remember the stellar opening of *Four Weddings and a Funeral*, you'll recall that what engendered instant laughs was the repeated use of a four-letter word. In fact, the only conversation heard in the movie's first few minutes is that single expletive, uttered by the overslept Hugh Grant and his roommate as they rush to attend a good friend's nuptials.

Weddings is also a movie that features one of the best run-on, humiliatingly nonstop confession-of-love monologues ever written (". . . in the words of David Cassidy, in fact, while he was still with the Partridge Family . . ."), so you're *not* being urged to employ only curse words in your script. This is just to note the one story component that's an exception to the rules. You don't *have* to have great *dialogue* to make a great movie (as Keaton and Chaplin's best works amply illustrate). But modern audiences expect the spoken word to be part of their moviegoing experience, and skillful use of it has certainly enlivened our genre. So we'll explore getting the most out of dialogue.

POINT OF VIEW

Which do you prefer as a title for Woody Allen's 1977 breakthrough classic: *Anhedonia* (its working title, which defines a neurotic inability to experience pleasure) or *Annie Hall?* The latter is certainly easier to pronounce and remember, and it makes sense, considering the movie is about Annie. But, wait a second, *is* it about her, or . . . actually, whose story is it?

For writers, this is a central question. Just as *Moby Dick* with Ahab instead of Ishmael as its narrator would be quite a different story, *Annie Hall* recounted by Annie (charming but perhaps incoherent) would yield a different movie. When we speak of *point of view* (POV), we're encompassing both the literal (if the director's choice of camera angle puts us in the physical position of a given character) and the metaphorical (meaning, through whose psychology are we participating in the story's events?). Who are we identifying with, and why are we seeing the story largely through their eyes?

The answer to the *Annie Hall* question is apparent in its first shot, as Alvy Singer, the stand-up comedian and wry narrator, starts us off with a joke (the one about "small portions"), expressing the idea that life is full of misery but over too soon. Despite the title change, it's anhedonic Alvy's movie all the way; his POV is the very backbone of the story, just as *Bridget Jones's Diary's* voice-over narration is the vital vehicle that lets us fully experience the world according to Bridget.

Romantic comedy often offers dual points of view (e.g., the fairly even split in *Shakespeare* and *You've Got Mail*), but the choice and maintainance of a POV is a potent component that all successful screenplays utilize, either subtly (the shifting viewpoints of *Hannah and Her Sisters*) or with in-your-face panache (the narration in *Clueless*); it's the necessary glue that attaches us to the protagonist and gets us involved in the story.

WORLD

The first thing that comes to mind when one thinks of the movie *Fargo* (although some may immediately go to that woodchipper) is most probably a pregnant policewoman in the snow—snow, ice, wind, and more snow. Try to imagine Lawrence without Arabia. And doesn't the archetypical story opening read, "It was a dark and stormy night"?

What's the world of *Breakfast at Tiffany's? Sense and Sensibility?* The fact that these films immediately conjure up their settings demonstrates that place, time, period, weather, atmosphere—in short, those things that compose the *world* of a movie—are vital storytelling components.

The African-American urban scene that permeates *Love Jones,* with its late-night poetry slams, is an integral part of its plot. Eliza Doolittle could only be the heroine of a *Pygmalion/My Fair Lady* world, just as one of her modern-day counterparts, *She's All That*'s Laney is rooted in a contemporary high school milieu. It's not for nothing that a romantic comedy about the dilemma of an imperiled blue-blood high-society wedding is called *The Philadelphia Story.*

A distinctive, vividly realized world can be a key factor in a movie's success, and since many romantic comedy specs fail to take advantage of it, we'll be taking a close look at this story component in the coming chapters.

PUTTING IT TOGETHER

While breaking down a screenplay into its disparate elements is a useful process for clarifying craft issues (and is an especially good approach for rewrites, as we'll see later on), in the best stories all these components are interconnected. A great script is one lively organism where plot and character are inextricable and theme is the lifeblood that courses through every element. That's why even though the upcoming chapter headings make neat separations between those elements, everything's bound to overlap; imagery is as much about theme as world has to do with character.

Which brings us to an eighth, elusive, extra element that bears noting before we go on, and that's *style*—or what the more literary might call "the writer's voice." Certainly every good story expresses its writer's personality. But in the screenwriting world— which is more about creating a workable blueprint for a massive group endeavor than about a lone artiste penning the perfect signature phrase—that meshing of elements into one breathing entity *is* your ultimate self-expression. Your script's voice is the sum total of all the choices you make about every component we've discussed. So if you want to be heard (or seen), you'll want to be sure that your intention and execution on each one of these storytelling fronts is clear, coherent, and creative.

So much for the general stuff.

Now let's get specific.

CHAPTER TWO

The Romantic Comedy
Story Concept

We recognize it the moment we see it.

The meet: A caustic Annette Bening criticizes Michael Douglas's presidency, unaware that he's standing right behind her until he steps forward to introduce himself.

The lose: A frazzled Cher answers Nick Cage's fervent declaration that he's in love with her with a slap across the cheek and the edict: "Snap out of it!"

The get: A rain-drenched Hugh Grant makes radiantly wet Andie MacDowell the oddly backward proposal, "Do you think maybe not being married to me is something you might consider doing for the rest of your life?"

At pretty much any point where we join a romantic comedy, we know we're in one. But why? Does any movie that has a love story and some laughs in it qualify? What *is* a romantic comedy?

11

COMEDY WITH A COUPLE AT THE CORE

Certainly one major difference between comedies and many dramas is that comedies have happy endings, be they satirically bleak or flat-out joyful. And, obviously, a romantic movie contains some kind of a love story. But *Life Is Beautiful* has a happy ending (albeit painfully bittersweet) and a central romance—so why don't we classify it as a romantic comedy?

Let's compare two recent comedies: *Analyze This* and *Shakespeare in Love*. In the first, a psychiatrist's wedding plans are disrupted by his new patient, a Mafia bigwig, but he does get happily married in the end. In the second, a struggling playwright overcomes his writer's block with the help of plucky young actress and gets his best play produced after all.

If something sounded skewed to you in those two "log lines" (one-sentence plot descriptions), you're right. Because isn't *Analyze* mostly about the peculiar bond that develops between a shrink and a gangster? And isn't *Shakespeare* more about how the Bard found his Muse and the love of his life? If you were to remove Billy Crystal's relationship with Lisa Kudrow from *Analyze* and plug in another conflict, you'd still have much the same movie. But excise Gwyneth Paltrow from *Shakespeare in Love*, and you'd really have to change its title to *Shakespeare*.

A romantic comedy is a comedy whose central plot is embodied in a romantic relationship.

Many screenwriters classify the structural components of their tale as A story and B story, or plot and subplot. In a romantic comedy, the A story, or main focus of the movie, is the relationship between its romantic protagonists, and generally the B story's goal won't be obtained without that romance's existence. Every subplot in *Shakespeare in Love* stems from the love affair between Will and Viola. The show goes on only because they go on; their passion fuels every conflict. The couple is at the core of this comedic story—so we call it a romantic comedy.

The classic three-act structure is usually defined in terms of a single protagonist who's trying to obtain a goal.

1. *Conflict:* The hero takes on a problem.
2. *Crisis:* The hero can't solve the problem.
3. *Resolution:* The hero solves the problem.

Thus, in *Analyze This,* the shrink helps the gangster overcome a phobia, but the shrink's romance, while a catalyst for conflict, is ultimately not an essential story element.

In a romantic comedy, the three-act structure is revised as a meet-lose-get formula involving two protagonists.

1. *Meet:* Girl and boy have significant encounters.
2. *Lose:* Girl and boy are separated.
3. *Get:* Girl and boy reunite.

Thus in *Shakespeare in Love,* Will and Viola's involvement leads to his completing a masterpiece that stars her; when they're forced apart, both their happiness and the success of his play are jeopardized, but their onstage reunion, however brief, makes *Romeo and Juliet* a smash and their love immortal.

Rather than asking "will the hero obtain his goal?" *the central question posed by a romantic comedy is: "Will these two individuals become a couple?"* We may be identifying with one protagonist more than the other, and their union may ultimately prove more metaphorical than that found in traditional happy endings (e.g., the close of *Shakespeare in Love*), but our stakes and involvement in the story are focused on the "coupling" problem. Thus, while the resolving of a political crisis makes *The American President* (and presumably his constituents) happy, it's Michael Douglas's reconciliation with Annette Bening that satisfies our story expectations and brings the movie to a close. The all-important legislative bill in *President* is the B plot, while Bening is the A.

THE DYNAMICS OF MEET-LOSE-GET

Given the single most daunting handicap a story could have—the audience knows the ending before it starts—a romantic comedy's major challenge lies in raising a huge doubt in the audience's mind about how the hell these two made-for-each-others are ever going to end up together.

As in most good stories, the strongest romantic comedy plots feature characters with strong desires who come up against formidable obstacles. "A girl hears an interesting guy talking on the radio and, after looking up his phone number, starts dating him" is a pitch that would've killed *Sleepless in Seattle*. But that successful romantic comedy upped its Doubt Quota by utilizing a canny combo of quirky wants and hurdles.

"Wants" come in all the myriad shapes and sizes of human behavior and experience. What immediately raises the interest level in the real *Sleepless* is its creators' employment of a *negative* desire for one protagonist. The character Tom Hanks plays has a strongly stated "antipurpose"; he wants to be alone. He's so convinced that he'll never again find the true love he experienced with his late wife that he doesn't want to be with another woman—doesn't even want to meet one.

The *Sleepless* team doesn't stop there, however; they pile a number of daunting obstacles in the path of the Meg Ryan character's conflicted want (to meet this interesting radio guy, though there's seemingly no future in it). The guy lives thousands of miles away, with name and address unknown; he's got thousands of other women seeking him out—and, by the way, she herself is engaged to be married to another man.

This last little wrinkle is particularly significant. Because if an unattached Meg goes after her man and it looks like she's not going to win him, our sympathy for her goes only so far; "Oh, well," might be our response. But if engaged Meg stands to lose one man in her quest for another . . .

The seed of romantic comedy conflict resides in the "meet." Most romantic comedies start with at least one-half of the potential couple not interested in, or even actively opposed to, finding a mate. But the best romantic comedies blossom when they have an even stronger "lose" embedded in their concept. What have the characters got to lose in losing (or finding) each other?

By midway through *Sleepless,* the audience is convinced that both Tom and Meg are with the wrong significant others. If they don't meet, we're made to feel, they'll lose their one chance of having the great relationship of their lives. For some romantic comedy leads, what's at stake is what the characters stand to lose if they *get* each other. Many romantic comedies create conflict by setting an exterior conflict at odds with the protagonists' personal desire to love and be loved. If the rich man marries the poor girl, he'll lose his inheritance (*Arthur*); if the mobster's girlfriend runs off with another man, they'll both be killed (*Married to the Mob*). This is what raising stakes is about: making that "lose" as vital and extreme as it can be.

But given the genre handicap (that implied and expected happy ending), the savviest romantic comedies don't merely rely on external problems to escalate conflict. They build their conflicts from the inside—from within their leading characters.

INTERNAL AND EXTERNAL CONFLICTS

The romantic comedy genre is often referred to as *character-driven,* meaning that, generally, the people in them are the most powerful story force, rather than, say, a "high concept." In an Arnold Schwarzenegger action-adventure vehicle, you don't need to know anything more about the main character than that he's Arnold Schwarzenegger; the point of the movie is going to be how he kicks his antagonist's butt in extraordinary circumstances. But what creates the penultimate crisis in *Chasing Amy,* for example, is not its boy-meets-lesbian high concept. The boy, Holden, achieves his outer objective—he wins the girl, lesbian Alyssa. Once he's with her, however, his sexual insecurity sabotages him. His conflict is *internal*. Threatened by Alyssa's wild, sexually adventurous past, he ends up so alienating the love of his life that she leaves him.

Romantic comedies, being character-driven, emphasize internal conflicts. Internal (or inner) conflicts are the issues and crises that arise within a character. *External conflict:* Normal man meets abnormal-sized dog who wreaks havoc with his life (*Beethoven*). *Internal conflict:* Screamingly neurotic man meets cute little dog (and pugnacious waitress) who force him to become a more caring human being (*As Good as It Gets*). In the latter, Melvin's psychological transformation is very much the main focus of the story. What is *Annie Hall*, after all, but a feature-length exploration of dueling self-esteem issues?

More often than not, internal conflict is the central motor of a romantic comedy; instead of presenting protagonists at war with antagonists who try to keep them from achieving their goals, the antagonism resides within the protagonist. When it comes to relationships, the hero in *Jerry Maguire* is his own worst enemy; *The Truth About Cats and Dogs'* Cyrano-like heroine Abby creates her own nightmarish trap. *Benny and Joon*'s antagonist is its female lead's mental illness—a more extreme obstacle from within.

If there's any commonality to the kinds of inner issues such characters face, it's this: *romantic comedy protagonists tend to be emotionally incomplete.*

One archetype is the kind of absentminded professor played by Cary Grant in 1938's *Bringing Up Baby*. Dinosaur bone–obsessed David Huxley lives so much in his head that he often misses what's obvious in everyday life. He's so serious, his focus so narrow, that he's not entirely alive—and is unconscious of it. Thus, he's a sitting duck for the aggressive future mate who rocks his musty world: screwball heiress Susan Vance (Katharine Hepburn) is David's wake-up call. She's a whirlwind life force who shows our hapless hero exactly what he's been missing.

Chasing Amy's Holden, *Annie Hall*'s Alvy, *Truth About*'s Abby the veterinarian—all in one way or another lack a certain something that would make them happier, more complete human beings, whether they know it or not. Romantic comedy heroes and heroines are like questions waiting to be answered—because they're starring in stories where love is the ultimate path to fulfillment.

LOVE AS THE KEY TO STORY DEVELOPMENT

Every genre has its subtext. Thrillers are about creating cathartic confrontations with our fears; action adventures are usually enactments of mythic heroism. In romantic comedies, the real subject matter is the power of love.

Love is not merely the catalyst for action in a romantic comedy, it's the shaper of the story arc. Although many romantic comedies seem to initially set up their protagonist's eventual mate as their antagonist, in most cases love itself is the antagonist. It's the force that the story's characters have to reckon with; they either succumb to love's power or reject it. Wrestling with love can force a character to grow or to resist growth, but either way, *love's effect on the central character is what drives the story.*

What pushes *Moonstruck*'s story forward is a kind of spiraling self-awareness on Loretta's part, the direct result of her falling in love with Ronny, the brother of her fiancé Johnny. Once her entanglement with Ronny has awakened her dormant passions, she begins looking at herself and everyone around her through new eyes. The values she's been asked to uphold, she soon realizes, are corrupt: her father, for example, is cheating on her mother. This discovery is partially responsible for sending her back into Ronny's bed. Getting even closer to Ronny enables her to face Johnny's return, the movie's confrontational crisis, with newfound strength.

Such complications in a romantic comedy, a series of stake-raising problems, arise from the characters' internal issues confronting exterior obstacles: being in love encourages taking risks. And the thing that pushes the protagonist from an end-of-second-act crisis into a third-act resolution is generally a recognition or a realization. In a romantic comedy, *crisis provokes the protagonist into comprehending the value of love.*

Thus in *Moonstruck,* Loretta, faced with her fiancé's return, is empowered by being in love; she realizes that she can't deny her own feelings. So even if it's going to throw her family into upheaval, she makes her decision: she's going to tell Johnny about Ronny and break it off. In *Notting Hill,* no sooner has William ended it with Anna than he realizes, "My God, she was trying to tell me that she loves me, and I've blown it." And realizing that Anna's love is more important than his pride, he runs after her to win her back. Something is learned by the romantic comedy protagonist on the way from playing solo to the ultimate duet, and *what a protagonist learns by falling in love determines the outcome of a romantic comedy.*

Love as a transforming power, as an instrument of growth and positive change, is the single most fundamental tenet of the romantic comedy belief system. In *Bringing Up Baby,* David loses everything he's held dear (including his dinosaur skeleton and, nearly, his sanity) but he realizes he's better off. *Baby,* clearly pro-union and anti-isolationist, demonstrates that love (and all the loving tortures that go with it) makes David a better guy to hang out with. It humanizes him.

In a sense, one could restate the paradigm for a three-act structure in a romantic comedy as follows:

1. *Conflict:* Love challenges the characters.

2. *Crisis:* The characters must accept or deny love.

3. *Resolution:* Love transforms the characters.

The most successful romantic comedies utilize this arc to investigate a specific thematic issue. Why has this one couple gone through these particular escalating conflicts to reach this unique moment of crisis? And what values or beliefs are being put to the test by love's transformative power? The best romantic comedies explore such themes, as we'll see in a later chapter on this all-important storytelling component.

SUBGENRES

If our genre's focus on two single people becoming a couple has thus far seemed a bit narrow, you'll be glad to hear that you *can* tweak the basic construct. Historically, three subgenres of our romantic comedy genre have proved particularly durable: *ensemble*, *marital*, and *triangle*. Here's a representative sampling.

Ensemble

Familial

Hannah and Her Sisters (1986)

Mystic Pizza (1988)

Eat Drink Man Woman (1994)

Friends

How to Marry a Millionaire (1953)

Singles (1992)

American Pie (1999)

The paradigm for this form (a central couple's conflicts are echoed, contrasted, or parodied through one or more supporting couples) can be found in Shakespeare's ensemble comedies (*Midsummer Night*, etc.). Romantic comedies with multiple protagonists tend to be organized, when they're good, around thematic conceits. They can cast a wide demographic net, since they often feature couples of disparate age groups. Writers drawn to irky and the anecdotal find fertile opportunities here; the ensemble approach has certainly paid off in prime-time television (e.g., *Friends, Ally McBeal*).

Married

The Awful Truth (1937)

Adam's Rib (1949)

Barefoot in the Park (1967)

War of the Roses (1989)

The Story of Us (1999)

This subgenre's premise is slightly atypical in that girl's already got boy at the top; *staying* together or not is the issue that generally drives these plots. Married romantic comedies naturally serve to explore the vagaries of domesticity and long-term relationships. What sustains love? is often the thematic question, and conflicts tend to center on a couple's survival being put to the test by extramarital antagonists.

Triangle

Design for Living (1933)

The Philadelphia Story (1940)

Cesar and Rosalie (1972)

Broadcast News (1987)

Bridget Jones's Diary (2001)

In a sense, there are two "meets" in a triangle romantic comedy. The instant conflict that a third party brings to any plot has made this strategy eternally popular, and in our genre, those with a penchant for character exploration get to create truly viable alternatives for their protagonists (as opposed to disposable Wrong Guys and Gals). The daunting challenge, if you've done your job well, is fashioning a truly satisfying ending.

WHAT MORE CAN A ROMANTIC COMEDY BE?
THE CROSS-GENRE HYBRID

Despite some structural variation, these subgenre movies do conform, in their broad strokes, to our romantic comedy definition. But now that we've made the distinctions between our kind of movie and all the others, I'd like to introduce a seemingly contradictory idea: many of the most successful romantic comedies have not been romantic comedies, period.

Is *Tootsie* a romantic comedy? No, some argue, it's a high-concept gender-bender. Is *Clueless*? No, it's a teen movie. Is *There's Something About Mary*? No, it's a gross-out comedy.

Actually, all these movies are hybrids: romantic comedy crossed with something else.

Take the Jessica Lange character out of *Tootsie* and you discover that her relationship with Dustin Hoffman's Michael is the linchpin of the entire brilliantly delirious plot. But there's no denying that the man-poses-as-a-woman-to-further-his-career concept remains its co-central concern. *Tootsie* is, in fact, a high-concept gender-bender romantic comedy—just as *Sense and Sensibility* is a period romantic comedy of manners, and sports romantic comedy *Tin Cup* is equal parts putters and puckers.

Though there are many exceptions that prove the rule (e.g., the thoroughly old-fashioned *Pretty Woman*), contemporary mainstream audiences seem amenable to movies that mix it up. And this is true of your buyers (the studios); a romantic comedy that promises crossover potential is more likely to pique their interest than a straight-up traditional one.

Witness the phenomenal success of *Romancing the Stone*, whose huge profit far exceeded the chick-flick and date-crowd numbers that a studio would normally expect from our genre. *Stone*'s canny structure so welds its A and B plots at the hip that they become one central story. For all the uproar over who gets that big emerald, the final clinch between thief Michael Douglas and would-be mark Kathleen Turner is its true resolution. But its adventure-movie aspects pulled in the people who normally wouldn't show up for anything with "romance" in the title.

This strategy—making your script a romantic comedy and then some—is an especially savvy one for the postmillennial market. But it's been going on for years. What follows is a brief overview of a dozen romantic comedy cross-genres, with significant characteristics and a few sample movies cited.

Adventure

Romancing the Stone (1984)

The Princess Bride (1987)

Joe Versus the Volcano (1990)

Seven Days and Seven Nights (1997)

The romantic comedy/adventure movie is distinguished by by exotic locales and elements of high-stakes (i.e., life-and-death) drama. It features action set pieces, and it's a good genre for getting protagonists involved superquickly—thrust together in big jeopardy that forces intimacy upon them.

Crime

Thieves

To Catch a Thief (1955)

How to Steal a Million (1966)

Something Wild (1986)

The Mexican (2001)

Mobsters

Prizzi's Honor (1985)

Married to the Mob (1988)

Honeymoon in Vegas (1992)

The combination of crime and romance capitalizes on the fore-play tension natural to both genres and the exhilaration/fear that follows successful trysts and scams. Violence inevitably enters the picture. Conflicts, especially in the mob-related comedies, tend to center on issues of trust and alliance—not surprising when there are lots of guns being waved around.

Ethnic

She's Got to Have It (1986)

Crossing Delancy (1988)

Women on the Verge of a Nervous Breakdown (1988)

Boomerang (1992)

The Best Man (1999)

While racial issues per se are not necessarily the focus of these movies, the investigation of subcultures and their collision with the mainstream are key. Be they African-American, Jewish, or Hispanic, the protagonists's conflicts often combust over issues of identity and cultural mores, with acceptance and celebration of ethnicity often a tacit theme.

Gay

The Wedding Banquet (1993)

Go Fish (1994)

Jeffrey (1995)

Billy's Hollywood Screen Kiss (1998)

Better than Chocolate (1999)

As in ethnic cross-genre movies, themes of identity and cultural independence play prominently here; the most common obliga-tory scene of such movies is the public revelation (or declaration) of sexual identity. Gay romantic comedies tend to be strong in social commentary and are kindred in spirit to the satire cross-genre.

Gender-Bending

I Was a Male War Bride (1949)

Some Like It Hot (1959)

Tootsie (1982)

Victor/Victoria (1982)

Switch (1991)

In one sense a diametric opposite to the gay cross-genre hybrid, these movies' staunchly heterosexual men don't "enjoy being a girl" (or in *Victoria*'s case, don't enjoy being with a girl who's supposedly a man). Cross-dressing humiliation is a common motif. But empowerment through transcending gender prejudice is also a common theme of a genre that examines sex roles and pokes fun at sexual stereotypes.

Musical

Top Hat (1935)

For Me and My Gal (1942)

Gigi (1958)

My Fair Lady (1964)

Viva Las Vegas (1964)

Although no longer in fashion due largely to the supremacy of music videos (1978's *Grease* being perhaps one of the last major successes in this arena), its obvious strengths (at emotional high points, lovers can burst into song and dance) live on in the animated musical romantic comedy (e.g., 1991's *Beauty and the Beast*). This genre also has a second life in the form of TV musicals, and it could command the big screen again, should, say, a Tom Waits or Bjork decide to take the leap.

Parental

> *Bachelor Mother* (1939)
>
> *Bachelor and the Bobby Soxer* (1947)
>
> *Father Goose* (1964)
>
> *Baby Boom* (1987)
>
> *One Fine Day* (1996)

Also idiosyncratic in structure, these tacit triangle movies usually introduce the antagonist (baby) before protagonist meets mate. Then the prospective mate becomes both a further complication and, ultimately, a solution to the problem that the bundle of joy has created. The basic gag here stems from the inappropriateness of children in a genre that's about courtship; its signifying scene is a nonparent's comedically horrific confrontation with some parenting downside (hold that diaper . . .).

Period

> *A Room with a View* (1986)
>
> *Impromptu* (1990)
>
> *Sense and Sensibility* (1995)
>
> *Shakespeare in Love* (1998)
>
> *Chocolat* (2000)

Great hair, great costumes, cool sets, and a refreshing predilection for the well-chosen phrase are among the pleasures of a hybrid that's recently enjoyed a renaissance. Today, when the introduction of private matters in the public sphere is less than shocking, this genre's ability to make issues of manners and propriety credible is another attraction.

Satire

Social

Nothing Sacred (1937)

It Should Happen to You (1954)

The Graduate (1967)

Modern Romance (1981)

L.A. Story (1991)

Political

State of the Union (1948)

Born Yesterday (1950)

The American President (1995)

Bulworth (1998)

The satirical romantic comedy either skewers a specific social milieu (the cult of celebrity in *Sacred* and *Happen*) or takes on the cultural zeitgeist (1960s alienation in *The Graduate*). The political satire romantic comedy, with its roots in Capra, tends to get "soapboxy," and it is typified by a climactic scene in which a protagonist sentimentally waves the flag before a rapt audience of The People.

Slacker

Trust (1991)

Reality Bites (1994)

Before Sunrise (1995)

Chungking Express (1995)

Chasing Amy (1997)

A kind of antiromantic comedy form that's nonetheless unabashedly romantic, these deliberately quirky stories are peopled by disaffected youths who are determinedly unconventional. Distinguished by scenes in which characters ironically subvert mainstream expectations, either dancing when they're not supposed to (*Bites*) or refusing to dance to anyone's philosophy but their own (*Sunrise*).

Supernatural/Fantasy

Ghosts

Topper (1937)

The Ghost and Mrs. Muir (1947)

Dona Flor and Her Two Husbands (1978)

Truly, Madly, Deeply (1991)

More than Human

I Married a Witch (1942)

Splash (1984)

Earth Girls Are Easy (1989)

Afterlife

Heaven Can Wait (1978)

Chances Are (1989)

Defending Your Life (1991)

This very popular genre hybrid is rich in imaginative conceits: girl meets ghost (*Muir*), boy meets mermaid (*Splash*), girl meets reincarnation (*Chances*). Whereas conflicts revolve around issues typical of the genre norm, climaxes often involve an obligatory "recognition" scene (e.g., the revelation that his date *is* a mermaid provokes *Splash*'s penultimate crisis).

Where the ghostly and unhuman sub-cross-genres are typified by scenes of spooky trickery (how did she/he do *that?*), the afterlife romantic comedy, or populist fantasy, tends to dig a little deeper, generally employing love-is-stronger-than-death themes that lend poignancy to the wildest conceptual contrivances (e.g., *Heaven*).

The secret weapon of this arena, for those of you of a sci-fi/ fantasy bent, is that seemingly impossible happy endings can be achieved by bending reality (e.g., Tom Hanks's sudden ability to breathe underwater at the end of *Splash*).

Teen

Where the Boys Are (1960)

Sixteen Candles (1984)

Say Anything (1989)

Clueless (1995)

She's All That (1999)

Wild parties, major peer pressure, sibling and parental interference, angst-ridden self-examination, and lots of great rock 'n' roll blasting on the soundtrack are the trademark components of this ever-healthy cross-genre, which, along with period romantic comedy, enjoyed a major resurgence toward the century's end. What makes these movies particularly compelling is the deeply, soulfully, over-the-top passions of its teenaged protagonists; these are usually first-love stories—and thus they pack a lot of ready-made, easily empathetic heat.

These are by no means the only romantic comedy cross-genres extant, and, as always, such divisions are more malleable than strict. *American Pie* is as much a sex farce as it is a teen movie— and an ensemble story as well. At any rate, familiarizing yourself with these genres can help you hone the trajectory of your plot and the profiles of your characters.

The next chapter maps out romantic comedy's historical terrain. But before we go there, let's look at your work-in-progress in its embryonic state.

Exercise: Story Concept

1. Make a list of your favorite romantic comedies. Pick one or two you're particularly familiar with and see if you can get across their basic story ideas in a single sentence.

Forget elaborate plot summaries; what you want is the broad strokes. *Pretty Woman,* for example, could be pitched as: "A fun-loving prostitute is hired by an uptight wealthy corporate raider to be his escort for three days, but both their lives irrevocably change when, against all odds, they fall in love."

Do a few of these. Some may be obvious, while others may require more thought.

2. Now answer the question: What is your movie about?

You may have contradictory ideas, some general, some specific: My movie is about what happens when a rocket scientist meets a sexy alien. It's about jealousy. It's about that weird little town my wife and I drove into on our way to Las Vegas. . . .

Spend some time on this. What's the thing that got you interested in writing such a movie? Was it a character? A thematic idea? A plot notion suggested by a news story? A personal experience? Jot down whatever comes to mind.

3. Once you've poked at the idea from a number of angles, see if you can summarize your story in a simple sentence. Again, don't try to cram the whole plot in (you might not *know* the whole plot yet), but lay out at least the basic setup, including the identities of both protagonists, and some sense of the central conflict. Our *Pretty Woman* sentence is really a first-act/second-act sketch, with the third implied, and that's generally the case with these kinds of one-sentence pitches, or premise statements.

As you play with your pitch, many choices may present themselves. Your sentence may be more about plot than character. Use the storytelling components to focus your story concept.

Character: How are you defining your main characters? What's the most important attribute of each? For example, does

(continued)

Exercise: Story Concept   *(continued)*

it matter most that your leading man is a doctor or that he's a habitual womanizer? In romantic comedy, inner conflicts are of paramount importance, so identify your leads by more than their vocation: "*fun-loving* prostitute."

Plot: How would you state the central conflict in your story? Imagine the print ad or *TV Guide* entry for this imaginary movie. What essential information should such copy convey? Be as specific as you can. "Opposites attract and high jinks ensue" says nothing. Look for the active verbs that imply a strong plot development: What's the "lose" beat in your meet-lose-get?

Theme: Given that good movies pose relevant questions, what's the underlying area of exploration in your idea? How can you imply it? Look at our *Pretty Woman* statement and identify a dichotomy embedded in the subtext. What does "fun-loving" versus "uptight" suggest about this movie's theme?

POV: Why do you suppose our model log line begins with the prostitute, not the exec? Thinking about POV (the whose-movie-is-it question) may affect your sentence's construction.

World: Our *Pretty* pitch doesn't seem to involve world, but chances are, that movie isn't set in the outback. Does your sentence read "urban"? "country"? Explore your world.

Imagery and *Dialogue:* Fantasize the trailer for your film: What are the most striking images? Similarly, is there a line of dialogue that "says" what the movie is about?

Finally, think in terms of *Subgenre* and *Cross-genre*. What are your protagonists' ages—teen? married? What's your story's tone—noirish crime? farcical sexy? Defining genre may suggest a specific audience appropriate for your story.

4. Once you've got a sentence you like, try it out. Run the pitch by friends and/or fellow writers. See how the sentence holds up on its own by monitoring their reactions. Are they intrigued? "And then—?" is the ideal response. A good pitch makes its receiver want to know more. If they're confused or not en-

gaged, find out why. For best results, read the sentence to a few people. Collate your responses, and revise accordingly.

Constructing a one-sentence pitch can be a quick way to red-flag potential problem areas. If, for example, your sentence is all about one character, then you need to work on the other half of your romantic equation. If only one protagonist is really needed to fulfill the story concept, you might not even have a romantic comedy on your hands—not, as Seinfeld would say, that there's anything wrong with that; your movie may want to be something else . . . or it may just need this book's help.

Once you have a workable story concept sentence, view it as precisely that: workable. Your pitch is liable to shift as you get deeper into your draft. Think of it as a touchstone-like tool, to keep you on track and in focus. We'll come back to it again as you continue the writing process.

CHAPTER THREE

A Brief History
of Romantic Comedy

Now that we've defined what a romantic comedy is, let's see how it came to be. What follows is a broad-strokes recap on the genre story thus far—mainly the highlights, with a few key films noted to make pertinent points.

ORIGINS AND PRECURSORS

In the Silent Era, there was no such thing as romantic comedy per se; there was only comedy. But by the early 1920s, it was common practice for the male star–dominated comedies to "get a woman in the picture"; both Charlie Chaplin and Buster Keaton routinely wove romantic subplots into their scenarios.

Keaton's 1924 feature, *The Navigator,* gives almost equal time to its female lead, played by actress Kathryn McGuire. In it, millionaire Buster and the pretty socialite neighbor who has rejected his marriage proposal become the sole passengers aboard an abandoned cruise ship that floats out to sea. Although *The Navigator's* real A plot is how-much-fun-can-a-comic-genius-have-with-an-empty-ocean-liner-as-a-prop, the story's main gag revolves around the idea that these two upper-class travelers are the last people in the world who should be left in charge of a ship; between them, they aren't even capable of making a cup of coffee.

At one point, Keaton tackles his sleeping heroine to keep her from falling overboard. Instead of thanking him, the suddenly awakened Kathryn, thinking he's made a pass at her, slaps him. Then, realizing she's perched on the edge of a rolling deck, she jumps into his arms, and Buster, blinded by her octopus-like grip, stumbles precariously round the deck himself. It's definitive romantic comedy conflict: man and woman stuck in the same boat, eternally at cross-purposes. The movie as a whole—including an ending in which the kiss Buster finally wins from Kathryn knocks him into the controls and sends a submarine spinning—looks today like a paradigm for the coming genre.

Keaton and his contemporaries continued making features that used romantic conflict for comedic fodder, but the form as we know it didn't come into its own until after the decade's end, when a couple of things happened that completely altered the shape of popular entertainment: the country went broke, and movies started talking.

While the idea of pairing a male and female star in one feature made good Depression-era box office sense and helped to foster the production of romance-centered stories, the addition of dialogue to the medium's storytelling tool kit was a mixed blessing. As stage hits imported from Broadway put wish-fulfillment fantasies of life among the idle rich on the screen, the restrictions of bulky sound equipment took a lot of the movement out of moviemaking. Where Keaton's freewheeling seaborne *Navigator* looked forward to *Romancing the Stone*, one of 1931's swells-on-screen successes, Noel Coward's *Private Lives*, reeks of stagebound claustrophobia. Robert Montgomery and Norma Shearer, practically embalmed in formal evening wear, face front on a balcony and trade polished pronouncements like "Moonlight can be cruelly deceptive" in between gushes of sentiment and forced brittle laughter. Though *Lives*, dealing with mate swapping among the sophisticates, is a kind of romantic comedy, it's arch and artificial.

But it doesn't take long for this stiff, imported, aristocratic sensibility to breed a homegrown reaction, and in the early 1930s, the alternative emerges embodied in a new kind of woman. One precursor is the down-to-earth, nudge-and-wink Mae West, though her vehicles are more like throwbacks to vaudeville than a step forward. Another is Jean Harlow. Refreshingly irreverent, this wisecracking "Blonde Bombshell" slinks around braless, besting Clark Gable in *Red Dust* (1932) until traditional story conventions put her in her place. With her playful sensuality, Harlow is like the Madonna of her day. Her unabashed sassiness—a contributing factor in conservative Hollywood's alarmed call for a sin-restrictive production code—helps pave the way for the independent, sexually aggressive heroines who really forge the genre form.

THE SCREWBALL ERA

In 1934, Frank Capra's *It Happened One Night*, a low-budget sleeper made on the fly, tells the story of a rebellious rich girl, played by Claudette Colbert, who—mad at her dad, who's trying to prevent her whimsical marriage to a dashing pilot—jumps off the family yacht and takes to the road. After the picture sweeps the Oscars, the "runaway bride" becomes a staple of the genre, as does her inevitable matchup with a simple man of the people. In *Night*, it's Clark Gable, playing a reporter who latches onto Colbert while she's on the lam, trading masculine protection in exchange for her exclusive story.

The movie features some archtypical romantic comedy situations (such as the scene in which Gable and Colbert are forced to share a motel room, their two beds divided by a blanket hung on a clothesline that Gable dubs "the walls of Jericho") and some classic romantic comedy confrontations (the heiress proves herself a better hitchhiker than the common man as she hoists her skirt to adjust the the stocking on one shapely leg and brings the first truck in sight to a screeching halt).

Night's slice of low-rent Americana heralds a lack of pretension that its Depression-era audience happily embraces. And in screenwriter Robert Riskin's hands, the old-fashioned romantic story notion of rich man rescuing poor girl gives way to a more democratic idea: as Colbert gets her feet more firmly on the ground and the cynical Gable falls in love, hero and heroine rescue each other—escaping the constrictions of their respective classes and exposing their true human nature.

Three other key 1934 releases take *Night*'s liberating spirit even further. Their distinguishing characteristic is a strong, unconventional female who dominates her male counterpart. Carole Lombard, barefooted in white silk pajamas, kicks at monstrous egotist John Barrymore's big head in Howard Hawks's *Twentieth Century*. Glamorous, funny, and sexy at the same time, she raises the bar of how wacko a leading lady can be. Feisty Ginger Rogers manages a similar feat in *The Gay Divorcee*, kicking up her heels to more than hold her own with Fred Astaire. And in another genre, Myrna Loy helps put a new spin on the conventional happily married couple: as Nora Charles, she goes highball for highball with her detective husband Nick (William Powell) and helps him solve the murder mystery of *The Thin Man*—a movie, incidentally, whose mixture of crime and romantic comedy elements is a precursor of the cross-genre hybrids to come.

These women, along with rising stars Irene Dunne, Jean Arthur, and Barbara Stanwyck, make good on a basic reversal (an aggressive woman besting a man) that pilots the era's comedies. Some really do fly sky-high—like Gregory La Cava's 1936 farce *My Man Godfrey*. Carole Lombard, a madcap heiress on a scavenger hunt, looking to collect "a forgotten man," finds tramp Godfrey (William Powell) at the city dump, hires him as her butler and falls in love with him. At one point, fed up with her pursuit,

Godfrey dumps his fully clothed mistress in the shower. She flings herself into his arms, exulting in the idea that his anger proves he cares about her. As he threatens to resign, Lombard jumps up and down on the couch like a crazed two-year-old, shrieking "Godfrey loves me! Godfrey loves me!"

The term critics use to describe these off-the-wall antics is *screwball* (of baseball origin, indicating a pitch that breaks in an unexpected direction). The screwball comedy, helmed by the New Woman, with its frenetic slapstick pace and zinger-filled dialogue, becomes increasingly popular.

The genre hits its mature stride with 1937's *The Awful Truth*. In it, Irene Dunne and Cary Grant divorce due to mutual suspicions of infidelity. A court custody battle is waged over their dog, decided when the judge orders the dog to choose which "parent" it prefers, and Dunne wins by cheating with a hidden squeak toy. Separated, neither spouse is happy, and what follows is a study of feuding lovers in denial. In one deftly executed scene at a swank nightclub, Grant and his date Dixie run into Dunne and her obnoxious new beau, played by Ralph Bellamy. With the foursome seated at a table, the estranged couple's glances, physical maneuvers, and verbal innuendos deftly signal just what's wrong with their respective would-be mates, as the awful truth becomes clear: divorced or not, Grant and Dunne belong together. This kind of cinematic miniballet, in which script, director, and performers collaborate to show us the beauty of two people who really are in sync, is one of the joys of the genre.

By the late 1930s, that genre is well defined. Among its highlights are Howard Hawks's *Bringing Up Baby*, featuring the now-ubiquitous Cary Grant paired with Katharine Hepburn, plus Asta, the canine star of *Truth*. *Baby*'s lunatic charm stems from such scenes as one in which Grant and Hepburn try to coax Baby, a runaway leopard, off a neighbor's roof by serenading the beast with its favorite song: "I Can't Give You Anything But Love, Baby." As they harmonize on the lawn below, the dog chimes in barking, with Baby howling happily from the rooftop. This cinematic equivalent of helium inhalation is only a middling success in its time, but later achieves classic status, much beloved by fans of both its director and its two stars.

GOLDEN AGE PEAKS

By the end of the 1930s, screwball comedy is so successful that everybody gets into the act. Ernst Lubitsch's 1939 *Ninotchka* is advertised with the slogan "Garbo laughs!" though movie lore says that her laugh had to be dubbed in. Whereas 1939 is considered the peak of Hollywood's Golden Age (the year when *Gone With the Wind* and *The Wizard of Oz* were finished practically simultaneously by the same director, Victor Fleming), the peak period for romantic comedy is 1940 to 1941.

In *The Shop Around the Corner*, Lubitsch pairs Jimmy Stewart and Margaret Sullavan in the definitive "correspondence comedy"—she doesn't realize that the secret pen pal she's been romancing through the mail is the very guy she works with at the store every day and thinks she can't stand (you may recognize this plot as the basis for 1998's pale remake, *You've Got Mail*). And 1940 is also the year that Howard Hawks remakes Ben Hecht and Charles MacArthur's *The Front Page* with a woman in the role of male reporter Hildy Johnson. At the time considered the fastest-talking movie ever made, *His Girl Friday* may still hold the title, with Cary Grant and Rosalind Russell sparring at lightning speed. In 1940, under the urbane direction of George Cukor, Katharine Hepburn turns her sleek Broadway stage vehicle *The Philadelphia Story* into the biggest hit of her career. In it, jilted at the altar, Kate has to choose between Cary Grant and Jimmy Stewart as her substitute hub: a real only-in-Hollywood dilemma (and a good example of the triangle subgenre).

The year 1941 delivers writer/director/producer Preston Sturges's classic, *The Lady Eve*. Henry Fonda is the Pike's ale millionaire who's been up the Amazon studying snakes and is now the most-sought-after bachelor aboard a luxury liner; Barbara Stanwyck is the cardsharp con-man's daughter who sizes him up for slaughter. And in their battle of the sexes, the genre attains a height of both formal sophistication and comedic invention that has rarely been surpassed.

Romantic comedy peaks, then never quite regains its purity as the 1940s continue. Want to hazard a guess as to why?

THE WAR AND ITS AFTERMATH

The immediate effect of a world war on our genre is that light-hearted high jinks become more difficult to sustain—especially when one-half of the equation gets taken off the playing field and shipped overseas. But World War II's effect on the national psyche is even more pronounced by its bitter end. There's psychological fallout from the war's horrors, the A-bomb, and the Holocaust that makes the screwball ethic impossible to sustain. America suffers a real loss of innocence. As Pauline Kael once put it, "The self-critical comic spirit of the '30s was the comedy of a country that didn't yet hate itself."

Another pervasive effect of the war is a changed perception of women, who've been forced to enter formerly all-male arenas and hold their own. Thus screwball's New Woman, becomes less a figure of fanciful fun and more a reality—even a threat. In the world of film noir, such aggressive females now get cast as truly dangerous women—witness Barbara Stanwyck as a literal man killer in *Double Indemnity*. As James Harvey points out in his invaluable book, *Romantic Comedy*, in post-war comedies, the independent woman is brought to ground by the conservative, complacent male.

At the same time, the major studios, enjoying postwar prosperity, consolidate their power—and become more conservative. What they produce, in the wake of wacky courtship comedy, with more women out of the house and into the business world, are comedies that mine the humor that comes from the collision between work and domesticity.

Thus what today looks like the best in late 1940s' romantic comedy are the marital romantic comedies made by the most successful team of the time: Katharine Hepburn and Spencer Tracy. In *Adam's Rib*, as a pair of feuding attorneys, with pithy dialogue penned by the husband-wife team of Garson Kanin and Ruth Gordon, their relationship makes memorably quirky music. Both Hepburn's pre–women's lib soapboxing and the steam that seems to rise from Tracy's ears have beautifully worn the test of time. (We've seen the same techniques put to good use in such contemporary domestic TV sitcoms as *Mad About You*.)

Along with the genre's loss of innocence comes an expansion. The audience begins to enjoy and even expect a mixture of standard romantic comedy elements with attributes of other genres. Hawks's *I Was a Male War Bride* mixes the gender-bending cross-genre of romantic comedy with war comedy: Cary Grant plays a soldier who poses as a woman so that he can consummate his marriage to WAC Ann Sheridan. And years before *Bewitched* (and today's *Sabrina the Teenage Witch*), our genre invents the original model: Veronica Lake romancing Fredric March in Rene Clair's mix of romantic comedy and the supernatural, *I Married a Witch*.

This genre mixing is a trend that breaks wide open in later years. But what the next, uncertain, romantic comedy decade produces is much of the same old thing.

THE TRANSITIONAL 1950S

That the 1950s yield few memorable romantic comedies is due to the genre's very existense being under siege at the time. The big threat? Lucy and Ricky Ricardo, Ralph and Alice Kramden, and . . . the whole plethora of comedic couples who are suddenly taking up America's attention—on the small screen. In the late 1950s, television absorbs a lot of the audience that has historically supported romantic comedy. Many of the early half-hour situation comedies take their cues from late 1940s marital romantic comedy features; Lucille Ball's *I Love Lucy* is, in a sense, the serialized adventures of a married screwball heroine.

The movies of this era that stand out today do so by making canny use of mythic archetypes, such as the Oscar-winning musical *Gigi*, a "Pygmalion in Paris" fable. In Cukor and Kanin's *Born Yesterday*, journalist William Holden is hired by crooked lobbyist Broderick Crawford to give his mistress Judy Holliday a little education and class, and in true fairy-tale form, prince Holden's kiss wakes up the sleeping Holliday: she starts wearing glasses and ditches Crawford. In Billy Wilder's glossy Cinderella story, chauffeur's daughter Sabrina (Audrey Hepburn in the title role) wants to dance at the ball with . . . William Holden again, the reigning romantic comedy lead. David's older brother, played by Humphrey Bogart, knows Sabrina's prince is a heartless playboy—and soon double-courted Sabrina is in a *Philadelphia Story*–style triangle dilemma. But it's the mythic motor that makes these movies work, as it still does today.

In the 1950s, writer-director Billy Wilder hits his comedic peak, mixing crime genre and gender-bending elements in a tale of two musicians on the lam from mobsters, who are forced to leave town as women in an all-girl band. In *Some Like It Hot*, makeshift femmes Tony Curtis and Jack Lemmon find their charade no easy task to pull off, and Lemmon is understandably awed when he gets a look at the real thing: Marilyn Monroe. As he tells Curtis after watching her sashay past them, "She must have some sort of built-in motor. I tell you, it's a whole different sex!"

The 1950s also yields a cross-genre precursor of contemporary hybrids. Alfred Hitchcock had worked a titillating blend of thriller and tongue-in-cheek romance throughout his career (1935's *The 39 Steps* had a memorably erotic couple on the run in handcuffs), but in 1955 he puts the romantic comedy front and center. Thrill-seeking heiress Grace Kelly plays cat and mouse with a suspected jewel thief, the ubiquitous Cary Grant, in *To Catch a Thief*, and the mixture of criminal thrills and sexual heat proves extremely successful . . . as it continues to be in our current market.

A NEW SOPHISTICATION

For romantic comedies, the so-called Swinging Sixties gets off to a very conservative start with a series of sniggering sex comedies that make their prime subject the de-virginization of a repressed businesswoman. Doris Day: feminist warrior or fossil? You be the judge. At any rate, her trademark fuming and fussing (usually with Rock Hudson) make *Pillow Talk* and *Lover Come Back* hits that spawn a number of formulaic variations on the theme.

If TV and conservatism dealt our genre a blow in the 1950s, the loosening of sexual mores and a concurrently spiraling divorce rate make formulaic romantic comedy ever harder to pull off. Where's the tension when sex doesn't have to mean marriage, and happily ever after lasts until the lawyers get called? But a new sophistication soon starts to freshen up the genre.

In Blake Edwards's adaptation of Truman Capote's novella *Breakfast at Tiffany's*, an aspiring novelist moves into socialite Holly Golightly's building and becomes fascinated with this free spirit who's actually a debt-ridden gold digger. What makes their story a bracingly modern one are the seamy realities that underscore their conflicted courtship: the guy (George Peppard) is a kept man sleeping with an older woman (Patricia Neal), while the girl (the incandescent Audrey Hepburn) is tacitly an escort girl in her pursuit of eligible bachelors. Instead of Gable and Colbert's famous "wall of Jericho," we now see Hepburn, cocktail in hand at 4 A.M., casually slip into half-naked Peppard's bed to share a cigarette as "just friends" before they both nod off.

How cool, how sophisticated . . . how sixties. The film includes, amid such casual aren't-we-adult glamour, some wild bohemian parties, but beneath the wackiness is a whiff of bittersweet cynicism. It pervades the decade, as societal mores shift. A hybrid like Stanley Donen's *Two for the Road* is both romantic comedy and dark, character-driven divorce drama. This 1967 movie, scripted by Frederic Raphael, also exhibits the influence of contemporary British films. Chic stylization imported from swinging London is one thing, but the late 1960s brings a slew of new sophisticated ideas and filmic innovations into the genre, as European auteurs like Fellini and Truffaut gain international prominence. In 1969, you can see the heady effect of both the New Wave and L.A.'s homegrown hippiedom in such romantic/social comedies as Paul Mazursky's *Bob & Carol & Ted & Alice.* But the most significant result of this wind from the East is the major effect it has on a certain American auteur—who even buys into the subtitles.

THE MODERN ERA

In *Annie Hall,* a bespectacled short guy and a rather oddly dressed woman share a nervous, getting-to-know-you bottle of white wine on the terrace of a Manhattan apartment. It's hard to say who's more self-conscious, but we get an insight into their respective inner states as their conversation gets visually underscored by printed titles that reveal what they're really thinking:

> ANNIE
> Well, I would—I would like to take a
> serious photography course soon.
> (TITLE: He probably thinks I'm a yo-yo.)
>
> ALVY
> Photography's interesting, 'cause, you
> know, it's—a new art form, and a, uh, a set
> of asethetic criteria have not emerged yet.
> (TITLE: I wonder what she looks like naked?)

Woody Allen entering his prime is an artist inspired: by Bergman, Fellini, the French, and his own comically neurotic relationships. And his landmark movie almost single-handedly sets the tone for grown-up romantic comedy in the 1970s.

With assists from a first-rate team—Ralph Rosenblum's inventive editing, the gorgeous cinematography of Gordon Willis, the help of his witty cowriter Marshall Brickman—Allen's little movie nails the zeitgeist of its time and sweeps the major Academy Awards, winning Oscars for Best Picture, Actress, Direction, and Screenplay. Its poignant mixture of comedy and commentary on relationships, loneliness, death, and the one cultural advantage of Los Angeles sets a modern tone for our genre that lingers to this day. Allen moves on from what's primarily a romantic comedy to complex cross-genre ensemble pieces that are more like morality plays, like the masterful *Manhattan,* with its dialogue moving from Kierkegaard to school yard as its angst-ridden male protagonists debate the meaning of existence in one moment, then argue over who saw a woman first in another.

This willingness to take on issues in a romantic comedy context is equally influential on filmmakers to follow. But the 1970s is also typified by the glossy, middle-of-the-road, theatrical-rooted comedies of Neil Simon (e.g., Marsha Mason versus Oscar-winning Richard Dreyfuss in Simon's *The Goodbye Girl*).

Another genre that infuses new life into romantic comedy in the 1970s is the populist fantasy—think *It's a Wonderful Life* or any movie that brings fate or a fantastical element (magic, a wish come true) into an everyman or everywoman character's life. One of the savviest mixes of this genre with romantic comedy is Buck Henry and Warren Beatty's *Heaven Can Wait.* Warren plays a football player who's wrongly snatched into Heaven by inept angel Buck. Julie Christie is the factor that makes Warren pick the body of a nearly murdered millionaire; after he's won her (and a football season), he loses her—only to win her again when he's died and been reincarnated at the movie's end. The appeal of this kind of romantic fantasy is its affirmation that true love can transcend mere mortality.

1980S: CROSS-GENRE RENAISSANCE

He's rich, he's lovable, he's drunk: the late, great writer-director Steve Gordon's *Arthur* makes a full-fledged alcoholic the oddball hero of one of the best romantic comedies of the 1980s. In a way, he's a quintessential lead for a decade that enjoys a new conspicuous consumption in real life and the most glamorous high life on screen since the screwball's heyday. As played to perfection by Dudley Moore, this spoiled rich boy won't grow up until he's reformed through the love of both a good woman (Liza Minnelli) and that of his unlikely buddy, the incomparable butler Hobson (John Gielgud).

Arthur is a prime example of the genre hybrids we see with increasing frequency from this decade onward. It's a coming-of-age comedy (alcoholic rich boy-man sobers up . . .), but its romantic relationship propels the plot (. . . and grows up when he falls in love); much as *Arthur* is about Arthur, its romance is the story's primary motor. Both themes (relationship and growth) are inextricably linked from start to finish.

This sort of combo-platter construction, coupled with the good-times prosperity of the Young Professional decade, rejuvenates the romantic comedy form. In fact, one of the most successful comedies of all time uses the "combo" gambit: the 1982 classic *Tootsie,* directed by Sydney Pollack and starring Dustin Hoffman. *Tootsie* is piloted by a brilliant screenplay that half the writers in Hollywood claimed to have worked on (with Murray Schisgal, Larry Gelbart, and an uncredited Elaine May the trio of record). In addition to being the ne plus ultra of heterosexual drag movies, *Tootsie* is a comedy about acting, a meditation on the nature of friendship, a delicious satire of soap operas, and a famously funny exploration of the female versus male point of view. Its "I was a better man with you—as a woman—than I ever was as a man" line is one of the few themes-stated-in-dialogue lines that most movie lovers can quote.

A strong theme is the backbone of one of the 1980s' most enduring hits, *When Harry Met Sally.* Rob Reiner's helming of Nora

Ephron's script is a success largely due to its relentless plucking at the same string—the question, a cultural hot point, of whether men and women *can* be friends and whether a romance can be founded on friendship. Its thematic material elevates *Harry* from being—with its postcard shots of Manhattan, tinkly old music on the soundtrack, and upscale Jewish humor—just another Woody Allen–influenced conventional romantic comedy.

The eighties is a decade particularly rich in great romantic comedies, including one of the few (ten to date) to garner an Oscar for Best Original Screenplay: John Patrick Shanley's *Moonstruck*. This much-beloved paean to Italian-American culture is a good example of another of our genre's subgenres: the ensemble film. Since Shanley's area of thematic exploration has to do with family, Cage and Cher's romance is paralleled by story lines involving each parent, and his canvas is filled out with richly realized supporting roles.

The melding of genres is what most distinguishes this fertile romantic comedy decade. There's romantic comedy supernatural (*Splash*), sports (*Bull Durham*), teen (*Sixteen Candles*), mob (*Prizzi's Honor*), and, significant in terms of things to come, a fascinating cross-genre piece that doesn't quite work: Jonathan Demme's *Something Wild*.

In it, Jeff Daniels and Melanie Griffith are an archetypical odd couple. Daniels, as a staid businessman, runs into sexy downtown free-spirit Lulu (Griffith), who lures him into a motel room for some kinky midday sex and quickly embroils him in her outlaw life. The film starts out a classic screwball, with the dominating female and her bemused, pursued man getting deeper into convention-busting predicaments. But the film takes a serious left turn when Lulu's psychotic ex-husband (Ray Liotta) shows up. The handcuffs Lulu had used to playfully manacle him to their motel bed now imprison Daniels in the kitchen while Liotta attacks Griffith in a homicidal rage. Although the story ends in a slightly improbable happy ending, audiences at the time don't know what to make of *Something Wild*'s genre mix of screwball-gone-noir. But today we see it as the precursor to one of the next decade's favorite genres: the crime comedy.

PUSHING THE ENVELOPE IN THE 1990S

It's one of the oldest story ideas: a guy has to take out the boss's wife, entertain her, and bring her home happy, her virtue unsullied . . . and invariably, problems ensue. But when the guy's a heroin-shooting hit man, and the problem that arises is her near-fatal drug overdose—we must be in the 1990s.

Is *Pulp Fiction* a romantic comedy? Of course not, but the first third of it absolutely is: the John Travolta/Uma Thurman date-that-goes-south story. Quentin Tarantino's hugely influential 1994 hit is one of the defining movies of our past century's last decade, and we cite it here to take note of a parallel genre trend. As America's values mature (or some would say, become hopelessly corrupted), so does our perception of what's sexy and what's funny. Much as the romantic comedy has drawn upon other genres to stay alive and kicking, in the 1990s the crime and action genres get a new lease on life by adding a strong romantic comedy element to their mix. Thus, in Tony Scott's splashy version of another Tarantino script, *True Romance*, Christian Slater plays a low-life punk who murders his prostitute girlfriend's pimp and returns to tell her (Rosanna Arquette) about it. "I think what you did is so romantic," she coos, and then, noticing a cut on his face, cries, "Oh baby, you're bleeding!" The latter could be the warm-and-fuzzy catchphrase for the kind of action/crime-parody/romance-parody/who-knows-what-genre-we're-in movies that fill out the decade, from *True Lies* ("I married a spy") to the plethora of funny-criminals-in-love flicks (*Out of Sight*, etc.).

Meanwhile, in our genre proper, the 1990s starts off with a bang, with the most successful romantic comedy, box office gross–wise, in film history: *Pretty Woman*. In it, millionaire busi-

nessman Richard Gere picks up Hollywood Boulevard hooker Julia
Roberts and likes her so much that he hires her to spend the week
with him. A Cinderella story, complete with a hotel manager fairy
godfather and a prince in a white limo bearing flowers at the end,
Pretty Woman is actually the last totally 1980s movie: it's really
about the joy of credit cards. Gere's plastic transforms prostitute
into princess; she gets the good life; and her prince gets reformed
from corporate takeover shark to nice guy (he decides not to wipe
out the elderly Ralph Bellamy, in a late-life genre return). With
Garry Marshall's sunny revamping of a famously dark spec script
(originally featuring a black prostitute who's abandoned at the
end), this guilty-pleasure movie tells us: we're all whores, but given
enough money, we can afford to be whores with hearts of gold.

But *Pretty Woman* is, in a sense, the formulaic exception to
the rule. It's actually the *un*formulaic romantic comedies of the
1990s, the ones that truly stretch out and genuinely tweak the
genre, that prove the most interesting and successful. For example, there's the one where boy doesn't meet girl until the last
minutes of the movie. Tom Hanks tells a radio shrink about missing his late wife, a fascinated Meg Ryan listens, and *Sleepless in
Seattle,* as the DJ nicknames Hanks, becomes the idealized object
of romantic Ryan's affections. A number of far-fetched contrivances ultimately bring these two star-crossed soul mates together, but *Sleepless* becomes one of the Top 100 high-grossing
movies to date.

Then there's an underrated sleeper where the lovers don't
meet until after they're both dead: Albert Brooks melds populist
fantasy with romantic comedy in *Defending Your Life,* where his
courtship with Meryl Streep plays out in a shrewdly amusing
afterlife theme park. The decade also yields another one-of-a-
kind movie, now building a reputation as a cult classic, where
boy meets girl, boy meets girl, and boy keeps on meeting girl until
he figures out how to get it right: Harold Ramis's adaptation of a
brilliantly constructed screenplay by Danny Rubin, *Groundhog
Day.* Cynical newscaster Bill Murray gets stuck in a bizarre time

warp where he's forced to repeat the same terrible February 2, ad infinitum, until sweet and pure producer Andie MacDowell becomes the means to his salvation. MacDowell is also the desired object in a film rife with verbal brilliance: the witty Richard Curtis script directed by Mike Newell, *Four Weddings and a Funeral.* As the title indicates, this romantic comedy's distinction lies in its unconventional structure: boy meets (and continually loses) girl in and around a number of weddings—including, finally, his own.

What this latter quartet of films have in common is their unique, high-concept hooks; they take the old meet-lose-get formula and push it in fresh, unexpected directions.

This is true of some other noteworthy 1990s' entrees, such as the boy-meets-girl-in-alternate-realities movie *Sliding Doors,* and the two-boys-meet-lesbian triangle movie, *Chasing Amy.* While *Doors* is perhaps a reflection of our eroding belief in the myth that there's only one love out there for each of us, *Amy,* a slacker romance, is related to a cross-genre that gets a lot of exposure in the century's end: the teen romantic comedy. Its blossoming (*Clueless,* *She's All That,* etc.) is simultaneous with the renaissance of another hybrid: the period romantic comedy. Rampant with Austen adaptations and their ilk, the decade's last peak is Mark Norman and Tom Stoppard's costumed tour de farce *Shakespeare in Love.* Thus, with both the adult and teen ends of the romance spectrum covered (and the demographic-busting *There's Something About Mary* in the middle), twentieth century romantic comedy comes to a healthy, still-expansive close.

In the postmillennial present, with the lines between genres increasingly blurred, the basic romantic comedy elements still thrive. But with today's audience all too aware (after a few decades of focus on dysfunction) just how difficult it is to make a successful match, all bets are truly off. The next phase of this durable genre's development is very much up to you.

Exercise: Exploring the Genre

Pick a romantic comedy, either from within the preceding chapter or from the "100 Notable Films" listed in the appendix, which seems to have at least one significant element in common with your project. Watch the movie. After viewing it, consider the following questions:

> Can you sum up its story concept in a sentence?
>
> Can you identify its three acts?
>
> What are the protagonists' inner conflicts?
>
> What, if anything, do the central characters learn over the course of their romantic adventure?
>
> Does the movie belong to a subgenre? Cross-genre?
>
> What do you suppose made this movie popular (or unpopular) in its day?
>
> What has dated the movie? What still seems timely?
>
> Who might be currently cast in a faithful remake of it? What adjustments to setting and tone might be made?
>
> Given this movie's premise as a starting point, what would you do differently today in terms of plot development? Characterizations?
>
> Can you define an essential difference between this movie's sensibility and your own? Or, if you felt mostly in sync with it, can you define the reason why?

PART TWO

Into the Thick of It

CHAPTER FOUR

Character Chemistry

If you start from an interesting character, and build on why he is who he is, and what he wants, you can build a fascinating plot, whether it's simple or complex.

SCOTT FRANK

You tell the story from inside the character. That's probably the most important thing in writing, and the thing that least happens in Hollywood.

BRUCE JOEL RUBIN

Harry and Sally, Annie Hall and Alvy, Shakespeare and Viola, Michael Dorsey and Julie, Loretta Castorini and Ronny Cammareri—all of these memorable romantic comedy twosomes have at least one important thing in common: we care about them.

How come?

Creating lead characters that an audience will care about is the primary job of a romantic comedy screenwriter. No amount of gags, sexiness, or wacky story notions can make up for the two gaping holes left in a script if its protagonists aren't made of vividly engaging, three-dimensional flesh and blood.

Many novice screenwriters who neglect characterization assume that casting is going to do their job for them. When asked to describe their female lead, they may say, "She's Meg Ryan." Well, besides the fact that Meg herself wasn't enough to lure audiences to *Addicted to Love* or *Joe Versus the Volcano*, this kind of thinking is ass-backwards. What do you suppose Meg Ryan is looking for as her next role? A clone of herself who barely exists on the page? No, she's looking for a part that's so juicy and exciting, so wonderfully written, that she'll want to snatch it off the market before any other actress in town gets a chance to read the script.

Though a fresh story idea is certainly a great draw, romantic comedies are all the more dependent on compelling protagonists to attract talent, buyers, and audiences. So what are the basic ingredients one uses in building a good character?

FOUR KEYS TO CHARACTERIZATION: PURPOSE, EMPATHY, COMPLEXITY, AND CREDIBILITY

If there's any one thing that the most popular movie heroes and heroines have in common, it's their overriding want, their burning desire—for love, for justice, for success. The first and most important building block of character is *purpose*. What a character wants is the first thing you need to know about your creation, because that desire is the thing the audience is going to latch onto, the throughline that's going to take them all the way through your story. And for a want to be truly effective, it has to be understandable. Is it enough for characters to want to be happy? No, that's far too general; if they want to be successful, we need to know in what way. The strongest characters have a purpose that's specific.

Take *Tootsie*'s Michael Dorsey. What does he want? He wants to be a working actor so desperately that he'll pretend to be a woman if that'll get him the gig. This kind of crazy intensity can make a character lovable—romantic, actually. But note that the job he wants is extremely well defined. He has work, after all; he's an acting teacher. But that doesn't satisfy him. He's consumed with an overpowering purpose, and it's a specific one: he wants a job in his chosen profession.

Good. But is this want, in and of itself, enough to make us care about Michael? You probably know aspiring actors or artists who are driven to succeed, and though you may not have the heart to tell them, you have an idea about why they never seem to make it: they're just not very good. But look at Michael Dorsey in the opening of *Tootsie:* he reads different parts at myriad auditions convincingly; we see him in rehearsal for a legitimate Broadway play; and his acting students hang on his every word. On this basis, we believe that Michael is what he purports to be—a good actor. This character has *credibility*.

In this regard, the detail work in *Tootsie*'s opening does a masterful job. The film's first shots show Michael applying stage glue to his upper lip and afixing a mustache—then flexing his mouth to be sure it won't easily fall off (i.e., he's well acquainted with such props). Scenes in various theaters have all the greasepaint smell and echoing acoustics we associate with such places. And then there's the final image of Michael at work: of course he's a waiter. Isn't waiting on tables the grudgingly chosen day job of every other actor in New York City?

All right, then: Michael Dorsey has an understandable purpose, and he's believable. Do we love him yet? Not as much as we could, because a talented actor who can't get a job raises a logical question: why not?

The opening sequence gives us one clear answer—look at what he's up against. Voices from unseen powers that be torment Michael at one audition after another: he's too short, he's too tall, he's too young, he's too old. The nightmare that is show business for a struggling actor gets vividly portrayed, and the payoff—since we believe Michael is a good actor and we're impressed by his fervent passion to achieve his goal—is that we have *empathy* for the guy. We've all been in Michael's position at least once in our lives—wanting something desperately, being qualified to get it, and yet being denied it. We identify with the character because in some essential way, he's like us.

An important distinction needs to be made here between *empathy* (experiencing someone else's feelings as one's own) and *sympathy* (sharing the feelings or interests of someone else). When it comes to characterization, the difference isn't moot. Sympathy is about sharing somebody else's feelings; you can imagine what being sad feels like for them, but *you're* not sad. To experience someone else's feelings as your own, to completely identify with that person, to have the feelings they're having, simultaneously—that's empathy.

There's a common misconception that characters need to be sympathetic. Not necessarily. Godfather Don Corleone is a monster. We don't sympathize with his methods and his murderous morality. But we're fascinated by his power and passion, and we identify with his devotion to his family. We feel his love for Michael and his other sons as palpably as the love we feel for our own loved ones. Similarly, as Michael Dorsey struggles against unfair odds, we feel it in our guts.

So, our Tootsie-to-be has a purpose, he's credible, and he's empathetic. I'd buy him a drink at this point, but what's going to keep me inextricably involved with him for over two hours of screen time? I know lots of talented actors who are up against The Biz and just don't get The Break. So what is it about Michael in particular that makes him so unique?

The answer again lies in *Tootsie*'s opening montage (a worthy case study in itself for skillful exposition). We see Michael when he's *got* a part, and a good one—he's playing Count Tolstoy, the lead in a Tolstoy biographical drama. The play's British director interrupts Michael midway through a rehearsal of his death scene with a request that he move to the middle of the stage; the left side of the house can't see him. But this doesn't sit well with the actor.

> MICHAEL
> You want me to . . . stand up and walk
> while I'm dying?

> DIRECTOR
> I know it's awkward but we'll just have to
> do it.
>
> MICHAEL
> Why?
>
> DIRECTOR
> I just told you. Now do it.
>
> MICHAEL
> Not with me as Tolstoy!
>
> Michael drops his script and cane and exits.

Now I know what Michael's real problem is. It's him!

And this is instantly more interesting. Because a character who's getting in his own way is a character who has more than one side to him. He's got an inner conflict that's fueling his outer conflicts. He's got, in a word, *complexity.*

In the old silent movies, a character who came out of a saloon and petted the dog on the steps was the hero; the guy who came out and kicked the dog was clearly the villain. These days, we're more intrigued by the man who cold-bloodedly shoots down three guys . . . then comes out of the saloon and pets the dog. We're fascinated by characters who surprise us—who reveal formerly unseen aspects of their personality as we get to know them. Complex characters who have contradictions and quirks keep us interested as long as they're credible. In this, Michael certainly measures up. We see that as a teacher and a pro with integrity, he wants to do things his own way. So it makes ironic but perfect sense that he'd refuse to take directions he doesn't agree with—and shoot himself in the foot.

Purpose, credibility, empathy, and *complexity* are the four keys to building a solid character. Neglect any one element at your own peril. But once you've got them all in place, the second part of the process comes into play: how do you get these character qualities onto the page?

FIVE WAYS OF BRINGING YOUR CHARACTER TO LIFE

You've just seen *Annie Hall.* Someone who's never seen it asks you, "What's Annie like?" One scene that may come to mind is after the tennis game where Annie first meets Alvy. She says a shy goodbye, she's on her way out the door, and he stops her with a "You play very well." Diane Keaton—wearing that famous but still incongruous oversized tie-and-vest combo—turns back, a deer caught in the Woodman's horn-rimmed high beams.

> ANNIE
>
> Oh, yeah? So do you. Oh, God, whatta—
> *(Making sounds and laughing)*
> Whatta dumb thing to say, right? I mean,
> you say it, "You play well," and right
> away . . . I have to say well. Oh,
> Oh . . . God, Annie.
> *(She gestures with her hand)*
> Well . . . oh, well . . . La-dee-da, la-dee-da,
> la-la . . .

Ruefully shaking her head, she turns to leave, but he doesn't want her to go. She's too delicious. So let's break it down. What's the methodology Allen employs to make neurotic insecurity so endearing in *Annie Hall?*

Speech: Once you've seen the movie, chances are you could identify Annie blindfolded, purely on the basis of her voice. Not just its tenor and tone, but its *rhythm*—the cubist stutter of her conversation is instantly identifiable. Her *grammar,* with its plethora of contractions ("y'know," "whatta," "gonna"), her *expressions* (those musical "la-dee-da's," the many "oh, well's"), her *vocabulary* ("Grammy" for grandmother, "jerk" as the pejorative epithet of choice), even her accent (three parts WASP to one part ethnicized New Yorker), add up to a truly unique vocal style.

Appearance: You may remember the *face* (that crinkled smile, the squint in her luminous eyes when they're not hiding behind little round sunglasses) and the *body* (gangly on the tennis court, sexy in an unconscious, loose-limbed way). There's her slightly stooped *posture,* which straightens as she starts liking herself better. The hands flapping around her face are one *gesture* among many, along with the way she leans in with her chin, nuzzling the air between her and Alvy in moments of affection. The big tie and man's vest are just one facet of her *clothing and accessories;* Annie's a walking flea market of hats, antique choker pins, and so on. The sum total is an *attitude,* a *state of being*—her eclectic appearance says "work in progress," and she backs into many scenes so self-effacingly it's as if her very presence were an apologetic afterthought.

Action: Do you remember what happens after Alvy and Annie work out that she's going to give him a lift uptown? Alvy gets very afraid—because Annie Hall drives like a maniac. The most obvious throughline in her *behavior* is that it's marvelously unpredictable. But over the course of the movie, certain consistencies begin to surface. In that sweet, funny scene where the dinner lobsters get loose, Annie's *reaction*—to grab a camera and start snapping—tells us that she has the instincts of a creative artist. Her *discovery* that someone she respects (singer Tony Lacey) thinks she's talented leads to a *decision* to go to California, and this development—a contrast between what she didn't do before (take big risks) and what she does do now—tells us that she's growing, changing, becoming more secure.

Thought: One of the most artful aspects of *Annie Hall* is its ability to get inside of a character's inner thought process. We can literally read Annie's (and Alvy's) mind in that subtitled scene on her terrace, where the contrast between what she says and what she thinks is truly illuminating. But we also hear her *inner voice* in the scene where a phantom Annie climbs out of bed and considers doing some drawing while her body remains in the bed with Alvy; we later hear her voice-over on the soundtrack while she and Alvy fly back to New York together. Her *memories* are vividly enacted, such as the moment in which she, Alvy, and friend Rob literally step into a scene from Annie's hippie days; older Annie watches younger Annie let a pretentious experimental actor fondle her foot.

Interpretation: Finally, we learn a bit more about Annie Hall through another character—we get *indirect information* when Alvy tells us about Annie in the opening monologue ("a year ago, we were in love") and in his voice-overs and asides to the audience (as when he turns to us, midargument with Annie, and says about her Freudian slip, "You heard that because you were there, so I'm not crazy"). In fiction, this technique would be termed *authorial interpretation,* and in an auteurist work like this writer-director's, Alvy is clearly a stand-in for Allen, inferring meanings from his character's behavior and telling us things that Annie herself may not necessarily know.

A savvy screenwriter uses all these methods of portraying character, and often character complexity is achieved by contradicting one method of presentation with another. "I hate him," your leading lady says, and we notice that she's still absently fondling the bracelet he gave her.

Now that we've established the basic keys to building character and the means of conveying it, let's look at the specific characterization requirements of our genre.

THE LEADING MAN: NOT IN IT FOR THE SEX

For nearly four decades, Cary Grant was to the romantic comedy what John Wayne was to the Western—the embodiment of the genre. Books have been written about Grant's distinctive appeal, a unique combination of qualities adding up to a romantic comedy lead ideal: never too sophisticated to get slapstick silly, he was as calculatedly smart as he was capable of spontaneous lunacy; no matter how feminized he was forced to be, he remained fundamentally, admirably male to the core; and as involved as he may have gotten in the action, he maintained a certain ironic detachment, a cool self-awareness that made him an ideal audience surrogate.

These days everybody's got their own idea of a dream date: Brad Pitt, Leonardo, and women and men alike respond to Harrison Ford. But if good looks and a great butt are the only requirements for an ideal leading man, how do we explain Billy Crystal? Ben Stiller, Robin Williams, and even Adam Sandler have been successful as romantic leads. Tom Hanks doesn't necessarily exude smoldering sexuality, but he seems to be doing just fine as a national love object, thanks.

Clearly, we accept a broad range of physical appearances in our romantic comedy leading men. An informal survey of the genre yields just as much diversity in basic personality—from Hugh Grant's diffident persona to Joe Fiennes's Shakespearian fire and poetry. When I asked my students what works for them in a male lead, I got a litany of unsurprising "attractive" attributes: Mr. Right is smart, caring, funny . . .

Funny? This bears examination. Some romantic comedy writers think that their leading man has to literally be funny: whip out the one-liners and play deft physical pranks. But that's not always the case. Although Dudley Moore's first twenty minutes in *Arthur* are as good as any stand-up's act before or since, Henry Fonda is nothing if not serious in *The Lady Eve*. No, the kind of funny my students meant ("he's got a good sense of humor") indicates a specific attribute—not just the ability to cleverly comment on a situation, which implies that your character is awake to the moment, but an ability to laugh at himself, which implies an attractive self-awareness.

Just as a laugh at your own expense bridges the gap between you and other people (i.e., we're all only human), leading men who can laugh at themselves earn the trust of leading ladies and audiences alike, since the humility implied speaks to an innate decency. It also speaks to a basic romantic comedy principle: the power of positive intimacy. The man is publicly exposing some private stuff and inviting the woman to follow suit. Ideally, intimacy fosters more of the same.

Though the same humility-flavored humor is also a great quality in a female lead, this kind of self-awareness is particularly attractive in a male protagonist because, as any woman will tell you, men hate to be wrong. Being wrong suggests weakness, and men, as any man will tell you, are supposed to be strong. "Strong" is another attribute that cropped up in discussion—again, covering a multitude of variations. Though John Cusack in *Say Anything* isn't a physical dynamo, we do perceive him to be strong in purpose. But what's stronger (i.e., more secure) than a man who's man enough to admit he's wrong? Our ideal romantic comedy male lead, then, is strong but sensitive—able to leap tall problems in a single bound and, should he stumble, be merry about it.

In other words, he's Cary Grant.

But seriously, given all the many mixes of these good qualities we've seen on the screen, the only absolute rule regarding your romantic comedy male lead has to be expressed in the negative. There is one no-no, a cultural bias so powerful that it remains unbroken in our genre: *he can't be in it only for the sex.*

Romance is about love, remember? We tend to view a man who's romantic for only as long as it takes to make a conquest as a cad—a hero to envious men, perhaps, if he's good enough to consistently get away with it, but not a proper romantic hero. And though all sex in a cinematic romance is great sex (don't you love that about the movies?), we don't think much of a groom who says he's getting married only because his bride is great in bed.

Wait a second, some may cry, what about all those romantic comedy womanizers and playboys, like *Pretty Woman*'s Richard Gere? He was just out for sex when he first hooked up with Julia Roberts. Well, first of all, as the screenplay neatly contrived it, he *wasn't* looking for sex when he met her, he was looking for directions. But more important, he wasn't in it just for the sex once things got serious. That's the point: whether a male lead in our genre has been a sexaholic or a serial monogamist, once he meets his match (i.e., the female protagonist), love wins out over lust. The womanizer stops notching his bedpost, and Mr. Uncommittable commits. The leading man can be a thief (*To Catch a Thief*), even a murderer (*True Romance*), but love—true love—is what he's ultimately after.

THE FEMALE LEAD: NOT IN IT FOR THE MONEY

What goes for genre men in terms of physical appeal is equally true of the opposite sex. For every Julia Roberts, there's a Janeane Garofalo exception to prove the rule, as demonstrated in *The Truth About Cats and Dogs*, wherein Janeane got the guy—and Uma Thurman didn't. Sandra Bullock doesn't live up to supermodel physical ideals, but even her weakest romantic comedy vehicles make money.

Similarly, the various personalities of romantic comedy leading ladies run the gamut, from extroverts like Annie Hall, who can't help but reveal her feelings, to introverted or hidden personalities like that cool cookie of a cabaret singer Suzie Diamond (Michelle Pfeiffer) in *The Fabulous Baker Boys*.

Suzie comes on tough, tight-lipped, and world-weary, her clothing calculatedly revealing, her makeup masklike. She slinks in to audition for the openly dubious piano-playing team of Jeff and Beau Bridges and, after admitting that her only prior "showbiz" experience was working for an escort service, takes command of the room by singing so soulfully that by the number's end, she's not only got the job, she's got them (and us) wondering, "Who *is* this woman?"

Suzie is definitely strong, but the kind of strength she exhibits is not stereotypically female. In this, she's typical of romantic comedy heroines from the earliest days of the genre—which was piloted, if you remember, by unconventionally powerful females who turned the usual romantic dynamic around: they were women who dominated, or at least held their own with, men whom they pursued.

Just as the romantic comedy male lead is made more compelling by going against the clichéd male grain (in his sense of humor/self-awareness, he reveals a vulnerability that's not usually associated with the hero in most other genres), the romantic comedy female protagonist still tends to be, like her screwball ancestors, an aggressive, active, on-top-of-it kind of woman. Where some degree of vulnerability is expected of most heroines, it's her unexpected resistance to this norm that makes our heroine attractive. We expect her to be, if not a feminist, inherently modern in her sensibility.

We like 'em feisty, not feeble, so even if they start out more wallflower than warrior, they're not going to let their gender get in the way of what they want. Our ideal romantic comedy heroine is sensitive but strong; she's able to bond and nurture, understand her own feelings and those of others, but, if misunderstood and rejected, able to take it like a man.

In other words, she's Meg Ryan.

But seriously, given all the variations on this theme that our diverse genre permits, the only written-in-stone rule that applies to female protagonists can again be defined in the negative (a corollary to the male one): *she can't be in it only for the money.*

We resist the woman who pursues romance because she's clearly just looking for the Good Provider package: a high-salaried husband who can come up with the house, two-car garage, and college education for the kids. Though some women may admire the girl who lands an alpha-male mogul, our cultural bias, in terms of romantic comedy heroines, is against the gold digger. Though no romantic comedy heroes, however low on the economic totem pole, turn out to be genuine losers (don't you love that about the movies?), we don't think much of the bride who says she's getting married only for security.

The seeming exceptions are directly analogous to our male "womanizing playboy" premise. Sugar, as played by Marilyn Monroe in *Some Like It Hot,* is a self-declared gold digger—but she's always falling for musicians, who are archetypically out-ofpocket, and in the end, learning that saxophonist Tony Curtis is no millionaire, she takes it happily in stride. Just as the disavowal of pure sexual pleasure is often the symbol of character growth for romantic comedy men, the woman who's willing to sacrifice a prospective mate who's loaded for one who's not (i.e., risk security for love) is the one who wins our support. The leading lady can be a whore (*Pretty Woman*), suicidal (*The Apartment*), even a murderess (Almodovar's *Matador*) as long as true love—not a trust fund—is what she's ultimately after.

THE BELLAMY: MS. OR MR. WRONG

There are a few supporting characters who traditionally fulfill specific functions in romantic comedy scenarios. While you may not need or want such conventional personages inhabiting your story, it's helpful to have a working knowledge of what they can do for you.

One such hardy perennial is the Other Man or Woman, the Wrong Guy or Girl. In the screwball era, Ralph Bellamy was the prime rejected suitor of choice, playing the earnest, stodgy fellow who didn't get the joke or the girl. Presentable enough in terms of social status, he was neither deep in temperment nor desirable in appearance, and he was usually saddled with a profession that screamed boredom (e.g., selling insurance, in *His Girl Friday*) or a problem that red-flagged trouble (e.g., his too-beloved mother in *The Awful Truth* and *Friday*). Given the presence of such wild-card heroines as Rosalind Russell and Irene Dunne, what then, we might ask, is he even doing in the picture?

Solid and dependable, Bellamy represents the qualities his heroines have been unable to secure in their desired heroes—in both cases, played by a charmingly tricky and unreliable Cary Grant. But at the same time, Bellamy's personality is no match for his female lead's. When it comes to repartee and chemistry, he's clueless; one dead giveaway is his inappropriate and obnoxiously braying laugh. What becomes obvious, when we see Dunne or Russell with Bellamy, is how much more with-it they are than he is, and their riskier, less-conventional qualities are highlighted in contrast.

The Bellamy (so named to give the man who patented this archetype his due) has a dual function: while presenting a conceivable alternative to the romantic antagonist (and thus becoming an obstacle to the central romance), this supporting character helps define who the protagonist is and isn't.

Thus, in *Sleepless in Seattle*, Bill Pullman (who, at least until he turned presidential in *Independence Day*, cornered the Bellamy market in the 1990s) seems a viable mate for Meg Ryan. But the clues are in place, exhibited at an engagement dinner with Meg's family: his many allergies, which limit the wedding reception menu, his slightly off sense of humor (no one gets his *Pride of the Yankees*' Lou Gehrig impersonation), and his fairly spineless capitulation to whatever his father-in-law wants. This gets topped off, should we have any doubts, by a brief shot of Bill and Meg in bed, showing her awakened by his allergetic, wheezing snore. He may be a nice guy, and Meg may even love him, but in his very decent-but-dull ordinariness, he's a Bellamy for sure—an unhappy romantic compromise, the epitome of "settling."

The female Bellamy serves the same function. She may be nice, as Tom Hanks's new girlfriend is in *Sleepless*, but she lacks that special joie de vivre we expect from a romantic comedy Ms. Right. This one, in fact, is given an obnoxious braying laugh, which works just as well in 1993 as it did in 1937 as a tacit-romance deal breaker. Her inability to relate to Tom's son, and vice versa, nails the coffin shut.

The "merely nice" kiss of death is by no means the only way to go. *Arthur* features a frightening female Bellamy, played by Jill Eikenberry as a kind of blue-blood Fiancée from Hell, resembling more a dominatrix schoolmarm than a prospective mate. "I'm much stronger than you are," she informs a dazed Dudley Moore, who's in love with poor Liza, but has to marry rich Jill to keep from being disowned. "I know how alone you are. I hate how alone you are. I've cried because you're so alone. But don't be afraid, Arthur," she continues ominously. "You're never going to be alone again." Arthur's response—and we don't blame him—is to hail the waiter for another drink.

The male or female Bellamy is a great opportunity for an alert screenwriter. They can be used to better the case for your lead couple as a meant-for-each-other match and to spotlight a particular character quality in either protagonist. As the *Arthur* example suggests, the most effective Bellamy is one who poses a genuine threat to your central romance.

THE BUDDY: MORE THAN MERELY A PAL

Just as the Bellamy becomes a good barometer of your protagonists' personalities by way of contrast, the romantic comedy *Buddy* serves a similar function by being like-minded. The best friend of your leading man and/or woman acts as a kind of characterization mirror.

Thus both the Rob Reiner and Rosie O'Donnell characters in *Sleepless* serve as confidants who reflect their chums' respective concerns and issues, defining and assessing them. When Tom Hanks needs his butt appraised, Rob's his man; when Meg tries to deny that she's infatuated, Rosie's there to meaningfully raise her eyebrows. But both supports, were this their only job, would be liable to end up on the cutting room floor. What else is keeping them on screen?

Well, they're exposition helpers. From Rob we get some necessary detail work about how much time has passed since Tom last dated, and Rosie clues us in to Meg's weakness for *An Affair to Remember*. But a closer examination of their roles yields a more important function. What's the real reason for that Rob-tells-Tom-about-tiramisu routine? If you were looking at the writer's outline or an index card, the beat of the scene would probably be stated as: "Rob convinces Tom to ask someone out."

Buddies move the story forward. After registering the necessary knee-jerk objections, Rosie in *Sleepless* actively helps her
friend in finding Mr. Sleepless. Conversely, a Buddy looking out
for his friend's best interests can seriously gum up the works, as
we'll see when we look at *The Lady Eve*. But whether they're for
or against their best friend's object of affection, the Buddy should
have a specific role in the plot's development.

The danger in Buddy-writing lies in familiarity. We're so used
to this character by now that we often need a fresh angle to in-
crease our interest. One successful Buddy tweak is employed in
When Harry Met Sally. Harry and Sally try to fix each other up
with their respective best friends—only to have the characters
played by Carrie Fisher and Bruno Kirby end up going home with
each other instead. This event further underlines Harry and
Sally's affinity for each other (and leaves them both still unattached). Carrie and Bruno then become a "Buddy couple," acting
as a counterpoint/support system for the movie's duration.

Malcolm Lee's *The Best Man* employs a kind of "Buddy cir-
cle," with each of the Taye Diggs character's friends nudging
him toward his moment of self-awareness. My favorite Buddy
tweak is Hobson the butler, played by John Gielgud in *Arthur*.
The idea of an irreverent servant as best friend, though by now a
stereotype (mainly due to scads of screenwriters trying to remake Hobson), was fresher in 1981, but it's the subtext that
makes this Buddy so memorable. Hobson is clearly Arthur's surrogate father, and he not only enacts an exterior conflict beat
(i.e., bringing the lovers together at a crucial juncture), but he
helps play out Arthur's inner conflict. When Hobson becomes
fatally ill, Arthur is finally forced to grow up; child becomes father to the man.

This combo (servant as unlikely pal and surrogate dad) makes
for an unusually rich characterization (it won Gielgud an Oscar).
Doubling up on roles and functions is always a good way to
deepen your characters. Look, for example, at what Richard
Curtis did, in *Four Weddings and a Funeral*, as Charles (Hugh

Grant), watching his unattainable lover (Andie MacDowell) dance with her new husband, is joined by his chum Fiona (Kristin Scott Thomas).

> FIONA
> You like this girl, don't you?

> CHARLES
> Yes, yes—it's a strange thing when at last it happens.

That was a sentence spoken without irony to a true friend.

> CHARLES (cont'd)
> What about you, Fifi—identified a future partner for life?

> FIONA
> No need, really. The deed is done. I've been in love with the same bloke for ages.

> CHARLES
> Who's that?

> FIONA
> (After a pause, very casually)
> You, Charlie. It's always been you, since we first met, oh so many years ago.

This sudden transformation from Buddy into sympathetic, unintended Bellamy adds a new level of depth and poignancy to the back end of *Four Weddings*—though it doesn't directly affect the plot, since it soon becomes clear that Fiona and Charles can never be a couple. For an even more complex and intriguing character evolution, we turn to James Brooks's *Broadcast News*.

News is a romantic comedy/drama with a smart, sneaky approach to its central conflict: We don't fully realize we're in a triangle story until shortly before its protagonists do. For the movie's first half, Aaron, the reporter-with-integrity played by

Albert Brooks, plays Buddy to news producer Jane (Holly Hunter), more or less staying out of her romantic way until it becomes apparent that she's about to get seriously involved with charming-but-superficial fledgling anchorman Tom (William Hurt). The scene where Aaron finally steps forward and tries to stop her from sleeping with Tom is capped by a memorable impassioned plea:

> AARON
>
> I know you care about him. I've never seen
> you like this with anybody. So don't get me
> wrong when I tell you that Tom, while
> being a very nice guy . . . is the Devil.

Jane rises, angrily moving away.

> JANE
>
> This isn't friendship. You're crazy, you know
> that?

> AARON
>
> Whaddya think the Devil's gonna look like,
> if he's around?

> JANE
>
> God . . . !

> AARON
>
> Come on, nobody's gonna be taken in by a
> guy with a long red pointy tail! What's he
> gonna sound like?
> *(Hissing, raking the air)*
> No. I'm semiserious here!

> JANE
>
> You're serious?

> AARON
>
> He will be attractive, he'll be nice and
> helpful, he'll get a job where he influences

a great, God-fearing nation. . . . He'll never
do an evil thing, he'll never deliberately
hurt a living thing—he'll just bit by little
bit lower our standards where they're
important. Just a tiny little bit! Just coax
along flash over substance, just a tiny little
bit. And he'll talk about all of us "really
being salesman!"

Jane turns her back on him and stalks off toward the
door.

AARON (cont'd)
And he'll get all the great women.

In this marvelously crafted moment, Aaron is Buddy,
Bellamy, serious romantic rival, and antagonist in one; in fact,
while passionately articulating one of his writer-director's key
thematic ideas, he transcends all such categories—he's a fully realized human being. This is, of course, what we're all striving to
achieve in our drafts: flesh-and-blood, three-dimensional characters. So if you're employing one of these supports, bear in mind
that they must be more than merely functional. A Bellamy who's
clearly a write-off and a Buddy who's just there to say "you go,
girl!" don't have enough reason to live and can lead to a lifeless
screenplay. The best kind of supporting character is one who surprises us. The tension that drives the plot of *Forces of Nature*
comes from a subversion of expectations, because the leading
lady played by Sandra Bullock turns out to be a Bellamy, while
the seeming-Bellamy played by Maura Tierney ends up getting
the guy.

To put our plot-comes-from-people thesis to the test, let's
look at a movie that's rich in both lead and supporting roles. Our
first Case Study provides ample demonstration of how, given a
strong concept, the right cast of characters can provide all the
story conflict a writer needs.

CASE STUDY

Tootsie

Screenplay: Murray Schisgal and Larry Gelbart; story
by Larry Gelbart and Don McGuire
Director: Sydney Pollack
Leads: Dustin Hoffman and Jessica Lange
Released by Columbia Pictures in 1982 (110 min.)

Log line: An out of work actor poses as a woman to
win a role on a soap opera, but finds keeping his
secret—and his job—difficult as he falls in love with
an actress on the show.

Synopsis

Actor Michael Dorsey (Dustin Hoffman), though very talented and well
loved by his acting students, is considered difficult to work with and is
unable to get a job. He wants to raise money for a play, written by his
roommate Jeff (Bill Murray), that he can perform in with longtime friend
and student Sandy (Teri Garr). When, despite Michael's coaching, Sandy
is dismissed from an audition for the part of a hospital administrator on a
long-running daytime TV soap opera, and he learns from his agent
George (Sydney Pollack) that another actor has gotten a part he's cov-
eted, Michael resolves to prove he's hirable. He dresses and makes himself up as a woman to audition for the part Sandy didn't get—and gets it.

As Michael (now "Dorothy Michaels") begins work on the soap, he
becomes friendly with beautiful actress Julie (Jessica Lange), while fending
off advances from lecherous actor Van Horn (George Gaynes) and trying
to accept direction from the show's pompous director Ron (Dabney
Coleman), Julie's womanizing boyfriend. Before long, Michael falls hard
for Julie—and, when he's vacationing with her and her baby Amy at her
dad Les's farm, Les himself (Charles Durning) falls in love with "Dorothy."

As Dorothy's popularity on the show increases due to Michael's
rewriting his lines to make Dorothy a stronger character, Michael franti-
cally juggles his dual identities, both of which are getting impossible to

maintain. He can't appease a resentful Sandy (whom he's slept with once and neglected), fend off Van Horn, or keep Les (who's ready to marry him) at bay. And when he can't resist trying to kiss Julie, she thinks he's a lesbian and flees, ending their friendship.

Desperate to get out of his ironclad contract, Michael is finally forced to publicly unmask himself during a live telecast. Though Julie is at first enraged, Michael ultimately manages to earn her (and her father's) forgiveness.

* *

The "big reveal" scene in *Tootsie*, in which an actress descends a staircase on the set of TV's *Southwest General* to whip off her wig and reveal that she (Dorothy Michaels) is a he (Michael Dorsey), has justly become one of the most well-loved comedy climaxes in movie history. And one of the things that makes it so memorable is that although Michael seems to be flying solo here—making up his lines as he goes along—he's actually anything but alone. No, in addition to the millions of viewers riveted to this live telecast, there's Michael's potential soul mate Julie, his best friend Jeff, his rejected friend and lover Sandy, his two male suitors, his agent, plus his director, producer, and entire crew—a multitude of people, each with something at stake, hang on Michael's every word. Their reactions, seen in cutaways as Michael's shocking revelation occurs, are priceless.

And therein lies the tale.

Our emotional involvement in Michael's dilemma mirrors the involvement of at least seven intriguing characters, and this, I submit, is one-half the secret of *Tootsie*'s success. The other half obviously lies in Tootsie him/herself, because everything that happens in this story stems from Michael Dorsey's personal problem and his peculiar attempt to solve it.

Tootsie is a genre hybrid (gender-bender farce and romantic comedy), and its genesis was a high-concept script (unemployed male actor gets job playing a woman on a soap opera) by Don McGuire and Bob Kaufman. But some three, four, or more writers down the road, it developed into a story that hinges on the resolution of a romantic relationship and conforms to the romantic comedy characteristics we've cited, especially in its choice of emotionally incomplete protagonist Michael Dorsey.

What *is* Michael's problem? Well, he needs to get a job—that's his exterior conflict. But his inner conflict is what makes things interesting. We've noted that his tendency to be "too much to handle" sabotages his job opportunities. But as we see more of him in the first act setup, we realize that psychologically there's a provocative "what's missing?" in Michael's personality. Much as we admire his dedication to his work and his energy, he's a jerk when it comes to women—chasing after them at his surprise party while barely remembering who they are. And, as good a friend as he seems to be, there's something inherently selfish about Michael's behavior. He wants to get Jeff's play done so *he* can direct and act in it. When Sandy doesn't get her audition, he takes it personally (after all his great coaching!). Her disappointment then gets completely subsumed by Michael's outrage when another actor gets a part he believes should have been his.

Michael is a classic testosterone-blinded male: in it for himself, above all else, and seriously lacking in "feminine nature." Confronted with a baby at that same party, for example, he literally doesn't see it. He can be a giving person, we sense, only when there's something in it for him. Thus, there's an irony—rich in story development potential—when he pulls an outrageous stunt to get what he wants by posing as Dorothy Michaels at the soap audition. Michael isn't looking beyond his own immediate desire, but in the best be-careful-what-you-wish-for tradition, he's about to discover that no man, even when he's wearing a skirt, is an island.

Hindsight is all too easy once the hard work is done, and with *Tootsie*, it's particularly dicey to praise "the writer," given its many contributors. But one way or another, Pollack, Hoffman, and their team kept an eye on one thematic ball (the "armature of the story," as Pollack calls it in Susan Dworkin's fascinating on-the-set study, *Making Tootsie*): "A man dresses up as a woman and thereby learns to be a better man."

So okay, given such a theme and story concept, let's see how it could develop into a feature-length screenplay. A man gets a job on a soap opera as a woman, and high jinks ensue. Given Michael Dorsey to start with, what would you do?

Well, do we want Michael married? Seems unlikely. But a single guy living on his own doesn't suggest complications, so . . . how about a Buddy roommate, someone who can try to help Michael pull off his charade or get fed up with it? Add Jeff.

If Michael is single, let's give him a love interest. To maximize the problems falling in love could cause, let's make it someone who knows him as Dorothy. Add Julie.

But hey, if we really want to put him in hot water, how about a secondary love interest, some kind of a girlfriend in his regular, "real" life? Add Sandy.

How about the professional side of his life? Someone's got to deal with the logistics of his new career. Add George.

We've established that Michael is difficult to work with, so certainly complications could arise on the set from his director (add Ron) and maybe his producer (add Rita).

And if Michael is successfully passing as a woman, let's have some men interested in him . . . somebody on the set (add John Van Horn) and somebody off the set (add Les).

Think we've got enough potential conflicts on tap? Here's how it shapes up:

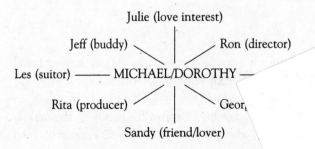

Julie (love interest)

Jeff (buddy)   Ron (director)

Les (suitor) ——— MICHAEL/DOROTHY —

Rita (producer)   Geor

Sandy (friend/lover)

Any need for adultery, murder, a tornado? Of course not. Given their story concept, the writers knew that by shrewdly adding the right mix of people to Michael's basic dilemma, they had plot aplenty. What's interesting about the half-dozen subplots in *Tootsie* is that they all stem from character choices, choices that probably came from asking questions like, "What sort of person should Michael's director be?" and "Who's his potential mate, and why does she press his buttons?" The answers show that the supporting characters are all in some ways reflections of Michael and thus force him to confront his issues.

Julie

Function: In getting his job, Michael fulfills his exterior goal. So Julie's primary function in the story is as a catalyst for change in Michael. When he falls for Julie, the underpinnings of his inner goal (self-fulfillment) surface: he wants to love and be loved. Because he's got to have her, inner wins over outer—he's willing to sacrifice his job to get Julie.

Reflection: Why does Michael love Julie? Sure, she's beautiful and sexy. But she's also a single mom with an infant and a female friend of the first order: vulnerable, honest, warm. For a guy who needs some softening up, Julie represents the ultimate female, a giving nurturer who encourages sharing deep levels of intimacy. Julie reflects what's missing in Michael.

Sandy

Function: Sandy is a crucial story catalyst (1) in that her failed audition is what leads Michael to pose as Dorothy and (2) in that her critique of Dorothy is what leads, ironically, to Michael truly *becoming* Dorothy. It's Sandy, in the middle of the movie, who goads Michael into making up his own dialogue for Dorothy—which leads to him becoming a national phenomenon and the object of Les's affection.

Reflection: Sandy is also the movie's Bellamy. Why is Sandy the wrong woman for Michael? Because she's self-destructively insecure and passive. As an actress, she's the quintessence of self-pity, easily defeated by the industry. She's the enemy, and thus a kind of anti-Michael: she reflects everything that Michael is fighting against.

Les

Function: By pursuing Michael-as-Dorothy, Les creates the most perverse kind of romantic triangle: he's the love interest's dad. What could be more problematic?

Reflection: In his characterization, he's everything Michael isn't in another sense: stable, secure, workingman Les epitomizes good old-fashioned American values. He's a guy's guy, a dad's dad; he was clearly a loving, monogamous husband, and in his corny chivalrous way, he demonstrates the classic male courtship stance. Les is a reflection of the values Michael has rejected up till now . . . but could embrace should he marry Julie.

Van Horn

Function: The soap's comically pathetic "Dr. Brewster" clearly functions as a work complication for Michael, and his dirty-old-man antics culminate in an attack on Michael at home that nearly blows his cover.

Reflection: What about him speaks to an inner Michael issue? Well, his behavior in that loft attack is amusingly familiar. When Dorothy tries to fend him off, saying she doesn't want to get emotionally involved, Van Horn says, "Then I'll take straight sex." "I don't want to hurt you," Dorothy protests, and he says, "I don't mind!" These gags are reminiscent of Michael at his birthday party, collecting phone numbers from any woman in sight. Van Horn in his desperation reflects a nightmare vision of who Michael—without his "Tootsie" transformation—could be in thirty years' time: a bachelor has-been.

Ron

Function: Ron clearly functions as Michael's nemesis, his director-antagonist on the set, and, as Julie's lover, Michael's off-the-set rival.

Reflection: If there's anyone in our hall of mirrors who most strongly resembles Michael, it's this selfish, controlling, dishonest manipulator. On one level, he's the successful Michael Dorsey of the soap opera world, the "best in the business," who gets his way with everybody on the set. But on a deeper level, he's what Joseph Campbell fans would term a "shadow" character—a distorted mirror who shows a protagonist his own darker side.

When Jeff asks Michael how he can treat Sandy so poorly, lying to her, Michael rationalizes: "I never told Sandy I wouldn't see other women. If I did tell her, it would only hurt her feelings." Some ten movie minutes later, Dorothy confronts Ron, who explains *his* unfaithful behavior with Julie: "I never said I wouldn't see other women. It's just that I know she doesn't want me to see other women, so I lie to keep from hurting her." We see Michael-as-Dorothy take this in, and later he tells Ron, "I understand you a lot better than you think I do." Ron is a catalyst for Michael's realization that he treats women badly, and he reflects what Michael shouldn't be, to be successful.

Jeff and George

Functions: Roommate and agent share plot catalyst functions: Jeff's unproduced play and George's claim that Michael will never find the money to finance it ("No one will hire you!") are what propel Michael into "Tootsie-dom."

Reflections: They both also act as Michael's conscience and credibility testers. Jeff, the classic Buddy sidekick, serves (despite his flakiness) as a voice of reason, reflecting the untenable absurdity of Michael's situation ("You know, when you were playing Cyrano and stuck the saber underneath my armpit through the couch, I didn't say anything . . . but I don't see any reason why I should pretend I don't live here just because you're not 'that kind of a girl.' ") George is a one-man audience surrogate, Michael's ultimate straight man who asks *why* at each outrageous development ("Les thinks you're a lesbian?") while simultaneously monitoring its believability. "There's no way out," he informs Michael when he's desperate to break his contract, "We're talking major fraud here."

Both confidants keep shining a light at Michael's blind spot, reminding him that he's not alone in this self-created madness and that his actions have consequences.

Rita

Function: Producer Rita Marshall's plot function, clear and simple, is to hire Michael-as-Dorothy. But she's also the cleverest "hidden Michael" of them all.

Reflection: A woman in a suit, with not-so-great but attractive looks, in a man's position of power, independent, her own boss, controlling even Ron through skillful manipulation . . . Rita *is* Tootsie! She could be Michael's role model for womanhood; she's everything Michael-as-Dorothy aspires to be.

While all the supporting character choices in *Tootsie* are logically suggested by Michael's strange situation (outer conflict, man dresses as woman), their specific psychologies and personalities engage and confront his inner conflict (to become a better man). And the plethora of subplots work in tandem to speak to the movie's theme. What ultimately marks Michael's growth is a new selflessness, born of his love for Julie, and his inextricable, deeper involvement in the lives of everyone around him. George articulates this shortly before that climactic staircase unveiling. "Something's weird about you," he tells Michael. "Since when do you care so much about what other people feel?"

It's worth noting that the film's one major contrivance—an accident that forces the soap opera to be broadcast live—is no arbitrary act of God. This catalyst for Michael's "big reveal" is set up early on, when we hear about (and briefly see) a tape editor sitting in the tape room with his ever present bottle of celery tonic. The later must-go-live beat occurs because "our future ex-editor" spilled his drink on the show's second reel. Even this crucial "accident," in the famously patchwork collaborative miracle that is *Tootsie*, comes from character: it's the fault of that stupid guy who lost his job over a soda.

....

COUPLE CHEMISTRY

Though people often talk of the on-screen chemistry between certain costars, not many acknowledge that this quality of unique, physical/spiritual connection has to exist first on the screenplay page. That special kind of romantic "sympatico" doesn't come out of mere body heat and thin air. Your job as a writer is to forge such a bond by digging as deep as you can into your protagonists' characterizations. What you're looking for is the subtext hidden inside the old cliché, "opposites attract." Two people who seem to be opposites are not automatically magnetic. But they may well have interlocking needs.

Consider Jack Sprat and his wife, or any couple you may know who seem to do a good job of combining their disparate strengths and weaknesses. Just as Michael-the-harsh and Julie-the-soft make such a good match in *Tootsie*, or Loretta-lacking-passion and Ronny-the-passionate so logically combust in *Moonstruck*, the best romantic comedy couples represent a triumph of good teamwork. *Jerry Maguire*'s signature line, "You complete me," gets to the heart of this idea. You're looking for leads with dovetailing needs in search of fulfillment.

Thus, while compatibility between prospective mates often comes from like-mindedness (*Pretty Woman*'s prostitute and corporate raider share an appreciation for all that money can buy), what lies beneath the obvious affinities is often a dynamic stoked by dueling "incompletes." Beneath Edward's powerful, straitlaced veneer in *Pretty Woman*, we learn, is a little boy still hurting from the lack of his late father's unqualified love. He recognizes Vivian's bruised self-esteem and appreciates her innocent side, her delightfully childlike propensity for fun. The repressed little kid in him responds: "I wish I could come out and play with her" . . . while the nurturing, feminine side of Vivian offers him the unconditional love he lacks. At the same time, Vivian sees in Edward the security and status she's never had, along with a refreshing absence of judgmental class prejudice—and a glint of mischief in his eye that lets her know he *could* be fun if she got him loosened up enough.

Sure, Richard Gere and Julia Roberts make a great-looking couple. But what the characters of Edward and Vivian supply, in J. F. Lawton's script, is a psychological connection to support the pheromones. We understand that each character has something specific that the other one needs, whether they're aware of this or not. Would a good-time girl like Vivian push the necessary buttons for a wired Michael Dorsey or an operatic Ronny Cammareri? Can't see it. Your protagonists should come equipped—like interlocking puzzle pieces—with just the right-shaped edges to match each other's profile.

Often, romantic comedy leads who spark and combust also share an innate unconventionality—witness *Romancing the Stone*'s reclusive romance writer and misanthropic mercenary. At odds with society as individuals, they bond in a kind of benign anarchy once they're together. Misfits who fit only each other, they now find strength to take the risks that others might avoid. Aligned in their unbridled embrace of the irrational (love), these heroes and heroines share a belief that their private world takes precedence over mundane reality. They demonstrate a corollary to the genre's thematic bias: individual freedoms and happiness win out over societal conformity. In the romantic comedy universe, being free to be "us" comes first. And those too uptight to support such behavior (the Bellamys and other figures of authority) become the butt of the jokes.

Create two incompletes who complete each other, seeming opposites who unite in a belief that love comes first—that's the key to crafting a chemical equation that'll set off sparks.

SUMMARY

To construct compelling characters, make sure they have an understandable purpose, that they're believable (credible), that they inspire empathy, and that they're complex enough to sustain interest. One dependable method of developing complexity is to give your character a recognizable inner conflict. Characterization is best conveyed through speech, action, appearance, thought, and indirect information (interpretation).

Romantic comedy leading men exemplify the desirable qualities generally found in heroes, with one proviso: they're not in the central relationship only for sex. Romantic comedy leading ladies are like heroines in most genres, but our cultural bias dictates that they can't be in it only for the money.

Two supporting roles that are common to our genre are the *Bellamy* (the wrong mate) and the *Buddy*. The Bellamy is an obstacle to the central romance and helps define the nature of the protagonists by way of contrast; the Buddy helps move the story forward while acting as a kind of protagonist characterization mirror. But the most compelling supports are those who transcend their functions, such as a friend who becomes a romantic rival; you should strive to create three-dimensional characters who can't be "typed" at all.

So-called chemistry between romantic comedy leads comes from delving deep into their characterizations and coming up with inner conflicts for each that in some way correspond. Just as all the characters in a well-crafted movie speak in some way to their central character's issues, your protagonist should have specific inner needs that only their prospective mate can fulfill. And both should share a belief that love and happiness are more important than observing societal conventions.

Exercise: Exploring Character

One method of investigating your characters is a time-honored one well known to actors. An actor given a character to play often interrogates this imaginary personage on matters both pragmatic and private. By improvising answers, the actor can come up with all kinds of insights that prove useful in portraying the given role.

Similarly, a writer can submit a character to the same kind of question-and-answer session. The answers your own unconscious sometimes supplies will surprise you and open up deeper regions to explore, sometimes even within characters who don't seem to have a complicated inner life.

The most seemingly extraneous details may pay off in the subtext or text of your script. *Pretty Woman*'s Edward, for example, has a fear of heights—which makes his ascent up Vivian's fire escape at the climax all the more significant. This interesting idiosyncrasy is just the kind of psychological nugget that a sodium Pentothal session with your character may unearth.

(continued)

Exercise: Exploring Character *(continued)*

Character Q & A

Here are some questions to ask your characters. Imagine—as their deepest, closest friend and confidant—that they won't need to hold anything back from you and will tell you as much as they're able to tell. Most important, *write down their answers in their own, first-person voice* (e.g., "I'm in decent shape, but I'd like to lose some weight"). To really get inside your character, speak only as they might, using their vocabulary, attitudes, emotions and point of view.

> Describe yourself physically (are you attractive? in what way? what kind of clothes do you wear?):
>
> Where are you coming from (ethnicity, religion, social class, neighborhood—rural, suburban, urban geography)
>
> What's your educational background?
>
> What's your philosophy (attitude toward life, belief system)?
>
> Talk about your familial relationships (with mom, dad, grandparents, children, siblings):
>
> How do you respond emotionally to crisis?
>
> Are you generally passive or aggressive? an outsider or an insider? heroic or antiheroic?
>
> What are your quirks and contradictions?
>
> Do you have special talents?
>
> What do you want?
>
> What do you need?
>
> What do you fear most?
>
> Do you have a blind spot or flaw?
>
> What's good for you? What's bad for you?
>
> What decision do you need to make?

What's the most significant action you can take?

What do you need to learn?

Character Issues Specific to Romantic Comedy

Romantic Status

Is this your character's first love? Is he or she
> single?
> promiscuous?
> lovelorn?
> looking for commitment?
> married? (happily? adulterous? divorced?)

Age

Is your character's movie a
> coming-of-age romance (*Belle Epoque*)?
> teen romance (*Clueless*)?
> adult (*When Harry Met Sally*)?
> middle-aged (*Ten*)?

Occupation

Do they even have a job?
> No, because they're rich (*Holiday, Arthur*).
> Yes, because they're poor (*Working Girl, Pretty Woman*).

Is it one that their prospective mate finds adversarial (*Adam's
Rib, Prizzi's Honor*)? Or does the job bring them together
(*Broadcast News, Tootsie*)?

Romantic History

Previously they've
> lost a great love (*Sleepless*).
> never had a great love (*Four Weddings*).
> been bad at relationships (*Annie Hall*).
> broken up with the antagonist (*His Girl Friday*).

(continued)

Exercise: Exploring Character   *(continued)*

They relate to the opposite sex as

the answer (*Sleepless, Truly, Madly, Deeply*).

the enemy (*When Harry, Truth About Cats*).

Sexuality

Passive (Sam, in *Addicted to Love*)?

Aggressive (Maggie, in *Addicted to Love*)?

Repressed (*Romancing the Stone*)?

Deviant (*Something Wild*)?

CHAPTER FIVE

Developing Theme

*You've got to know what you think you're writing about. I
mean what the damn thing is about, first of all. In some cases
you never quite decide and then you get into trouble.*
                                                    BUCK HENRY

*Themes that I like to explore have to do with questions and
problems I have about myself.*
                                        RICHARD LAGRAVENESE

What do you want to know, in the writing of it?
                                              DEENA METZGER

A former student recently came to me for consultation on a
romantic comedy she'd written that wasn't getting a good
response. Here was her pitch: Joe, an American, orders
himself a foreign bride via an Internet service. For both Joe and
his prospective wife Jan, the marriage isn't about love, it's about
practicalities, with both of them hoping to satisfy pragmatic
needs. But when Jan arrives to marry Joe, she finds that he's mis-
represented his appearance and his circumstances, and they don't
get along at all. So Jan angrily demands that Joe now find her a legitimate mate.

As Joe helps Jan, "they fall in love and end up together," I
supplied. The writer resignedly agreed that yes, of course, that's
how the story went, and this seemed to be her problem: no matter
how she tried to twist and tweak it, her romantic comedy always
seemed to end up on a pat and predictable course. Since by now

87

she herself seemed fairly unenthusiastic about the story, my logical question was, "What got you interested in the idea in the first place?"

Well, this guy Joe, she allowed; she knew such men existed, and she was fascinated to know: What kind of a person would *do* a thing like that—enter into such a clinically arranged marriage? Good question. Some of the feedback she'd gotten made her wonder if such a man could really be the hero of a romantic comedy. Depends on his motivations for making such a seemingly unromantic choice, I conjectured, and the specifics of his life situation. Did the writer know anyone who was like this guy? How about within the marriages she saw around her?

Instead of trying to solve plot problems, we began a freewheeling discussion of marriage in general, and the writer's marriage in specific. Although she at first resisted delving into "personal stuff," the more we talked, the more interesting the talk became. Because it turned out the writer had strong opinions on the subject. It turned out she wasn't sure if she believed that a successful marriage was predicated on a storybook romance. Her own marriage hadn't been wildly romantic in origin, but had lasted twenty years and was still going strong, while she'd seen a lot of brides and grooms who'd started out madly in love quickly crash and burn. So the question we found ourselves pursuing was, "What *is* the vital ingredient that makes a marriage work?" Is it honesty? teamwork? a trust fund?

Whatever the real answer was, the question challenged us. Once we got onto this track, we were both more enthusiastic about her material, and we were able to start thinking about her characters in fresher, more intriguing ways. Maybe Joe thought *x* was the key and Jan thought it was *y*. Maybe they both had to discover that the secret marital ingredient was actually *z*.

Within the hour, the writer had a more well-defined protagonist, an antiromantic antihero with real issues to resolve. And suddenly the whole trajectory of her story was anything but predictable. The writer left our discussion no longer knowing if Joe and

Jan would end up together, but she knew something much more vital: she knew the reason she was telling this story. She'd connected with what was important about it for her, and in doing so, she'd gotten me hooked. As a newly married man, I was genuinely curious to see where a story that tackled this issue would lead.

A screenwriter's resistance to getting into "personal stuff" is absurd. It's *got* to be personal, if anyone's going to care about your story, and *theme* is the arena where your personal experience, attitudes, and insights come into play. Experienced writers understand that what's universal comes out of what's most personal—out of a fiercely personal, passionate point of view. Just as we relate to characters who have strong wants, we relate to writing that's strongly felt.

A good romantic comedy doesn't only show us how a couple gets together, it explores what their getting together means. What is it about this couple's conflict that has something to do with *us*? Answering that question has proven to be one of the most important ingredients in making a contemporary romantic comedy work. Theme, premise, point—whatever you call it, this slippery extra-special something has got to be there.

What's it about?

Describing your plot doesn't necessarily answer the question. When people in the business pose it, they really want to know why the plot goes the way it goes—and why you think your story needs to be told. What's an audience going to relate to in it? What will they take away from it after the lights come on? What'll make them come back to it for another viewing?

What's it about?

Do you really know, so clearly and so fully you don't even have to think about it? If you do, bless you, but you might want to read this chapter anyway, even if it's just so you can pat yourself on the back afterward and say I told you so. Because the theme issue in screenwriting is probably the trickiest one of all. Many a potentially great romantic comedy has fallen on this particular sword and died without ever feeling or seeing the fatal wound.

When a movie fails, it's hardly ever blamed on the lack of a theme—yet no A-list writers in Hollywood ever go into a draft unless they're armed with one that works.

One that works for *them* is what bears emphasizing. A theme isn't some outside-in element, a message that needs to be pasted onto a story to make it more meaningful for the world at large. It's a personal idea that becomes a powerful storytelling tool. Once the writer of "Joe and Jan" knew she was trying to define the secret of a successful marriage, she was able to shape her characters and plot accordingly. The writer had something to learn, and her characters were going to help her learn it.

Something to learn. A point of view. A meaning. These are all pretty general notions. So let's begin with a definition.

WHAT IS THEME?

Here are two helpful approaches to defining theme that come from writers of fiction. The first is Stephen Minot's: "Theme comments on the human condition." Though not every screenwriter writes about people exclusively, writers are human and can't help writing about even aliens from a human point of view. Minot's statement implies universality: a writer who has something to say about being human is speaking to all of us.

The second approach comes from Janet Burroway: "Theme speculates on a possible truth." This has more active phrasing, implying exploration and discovery. It's an attractive idea, borne out by the many enduring movies that came from writers who were writing to learn something.

Both statements are good for starters, but practically speaking, how do you put a "comment" to work inside a draft? What does "speculation" actually look like on the page?

The tool I suggest using, when working with theme, is an *axiom*. A dictionary's definition of an axiom is particularly apt for working screenwriters. To paraphrase Webster, *an axiom is a statement, accepted as true, that's used as the basis for an argument.*

"A statement, accepted as true" echoes Burroway's "possible truth." Let's say that after some exploration, a screenwriter decides that the vital ingredient in a successful marriage is trust. She then makes this her "basis for argument," her guideline for the development of story lines. Given this possibly true idea about trust, the screenwriter sees how each of her characters embodies or disproves it. How about an unfaithful husband who abuses the trust in his marriage to keep it going? A couple of acrobats who feud all day and have to catch each other in midair at night? The writer's plot will put her axiom to the test.

The derivation of the word *axiom* makes it especially appropriate. It comes from the Latin and Greek, meaning "something worthy." This speaks to the nature of your truth and your plot. Is it truly interesting? intriguing? worth exploring? An audience coming to a romantic comedy is prepared to laugh, perhaps cry, and to have an experience that's meaningful to them. Whatever truth and argument you're choosing to explore should have real relevance and resonance to the culture you're in. What you're talking about when you talk about love is, hopefully, part of a conversation that your contemporaries are already having.

But where does theme enter a piece, and how? The thrust of your axiom may not be clear to you at the outset. We should never underestimate the importance of our unconscious in the writing process, and sometimes the underlying meaning of a story is discovered as a writer blindly follows her characters. How far in advance do you need to have your theme defined?

CLOSED THEME AND OPEN THEME

One of the past century's most influential screenwriting books is not about movies at all. *The Art of Dramatic Writing* by Lejos Egri is a book on playwriting, but its principles, applicable to movies, have been picked up on by many screenwriting gurus and scribes. This may be partially due to Egri's devotion to the three-act structure and his dogged insistence on observing classic (Aristotelian) rules of dramatization—a novel approach to try in a business that isn't exactly up on rules or classics. (I once heard a junior executive call something "a classic, like *Ace Ventura*.")

Egri's word of choice in the theme arena is *premise*. He insists that a writer can't begin a play, let alone sustain it, without a premise, a clearly defined statement of purpose—an axiom, of sorts. But Egri demands that an axiomatic statement be an active one, made up of three parts. If you want to explore dishonesty, Egri says, it's not enough to say your play is "about dishonesty." What's the problem with dishonesty? Why is it the wrong way to go? Well, for one thing, the truth is bound to come out sooner or later. Fine, then, state your premise as "Dishonesty leads to exposure."

What's implied in this premise is a protagonist, embodying dishonesty, who gets his comeuppance. And each part of such a statement suggests part of a logical three-act structure. "Dishonesty" is your first act (setup), "leads to" is your second act (conflict and crisis), and "exposure" is your third (resolution). Voilà! Theme and structure, wedded in four words. You can see why such a concept has proved enticing to writers struggling to whip unruly drafts into shape. Having such a premise can certainly keep your major story beats on track.

Many a screenwriter has gone this tried-and-true route. It works. But personally, I don't agree with Egri. What bothers me about applying an Egri premise to a work in progress is that it aces out discovery. Having your thematic material decided so definitively at the outset effectively sabotages exploration. If all of your conclusions are foregone as you begin telling your story, you risk telling a story that's too pat and familiar. You've closed off your options, which is why I think of this approach as working with a "closed" theme.

Let's say that what intrigues me about dishonesty is how often it *doesn't* lead to exposure. Maybe I want to write about a character—not so hard to find in today's ruthless working world—who's routinely dishonest but has nonetheless become hugely successful. I'm interested in exploring the effects of chronic dishonesty on a person's psyche. Is there really such a thing as karma? How do people who are forced to be dishonest (in top secret government employ, for example) deal with truth in their personal lives? How do they make distinctions? Is honesty always the best policy, absolutely? What about an honesty that destroys someone's life? What, then, are the ethics of honesty?

If in writing my screenplay I'm really trying to learn something about dishonesty, then I don't want to start out with a premise that leads to a neat, predetermined resolution. I want an axiom that's open-ended—an "open" theme. What I've found—evidenced in interview after interview—is that the best screenwriters most often start their spec scripts because they're trying to answer a question that's important to them. And the answers are discovered in the process of writing their drafts.

Having an axiom expressed in the form of a question is an effective method of defining your thematic turf. "Is selective dishonesty a necessary component of a successful romantic relationship?" or "How honest does a mate have to be?" would be perfectly valid axiomatic questions for the Joe-and-Jan writer to use to begin a first draft. Another contemporary notion of working with an open theme is to take a core idea and put it through variations, much in the manner that a symphony states a musical theme and then develops it. "How is love sustained—through honesty or dishonesty?" Such an exploratory axiom might yield complex, even contradictory conclusions. Woody Allen's *Crimes and Misdemeanors* is a masterful example of this kind of theme work, which leaves disturbingly ambiguous questions unanswered at its close.

The latter approach may come under the don't-try-this-at-home heading for a novice screenwriter; if structure and basic story sense is still your weak area, then employing "an Egri" as you start out might prove far more helpful for your draft. But remaining open to discovery (i.e., allowing the writing to open up your closed premise once you've completed a first pass) is another viable way to go.

This brings up an oft-debated issue concerning theme. Somewhere between "Don't start without an axiom you can write on the wall" and E. M. Forster's famous "How do I know what I think until I see what I say?" is an interesting gray (or rainbow-colored) area. As we've noted, many writers go in with only a question or a character issue to explore. A general rule of thumb would be to have at least an area of interest identified. Richard Curtis has noted that the genesis of *Four Weddings* came out of his observation that for some years, the only time he was able to get together with a particular group of friends was when he ran into them at weddings. He then became intrigued by the idea of telling the story of this group, using the weddings as a structure. We can say that the intersection of "group of friends" and "weddings" was an *area of interest* that led him down other thematic paths—the question of what might keep the group's most eligible bachelor from getting married, for example.

Some writers, who have the time and dedication to let their process be truly organic, follow Forster's lead and write a whole draft with no conscious notion of axiom or theme whatsoever. Then they look at the story they've told to see what comment or question their unconscious has raised within it. Sometimes the repetition of an idiosyncratic action or image is the unconscious waving a flag. What are you telling yourself thematically, for example, if you've written about a free spirit who always finds himself caught in confined spaces?

But ultimately, at some juncture—be it the end of extensive outlining or the completion of a first draft—the conscious has to join forces with the unconscious and start to shape the material. If your material is going to resonate meaningfully, conveying your personal point of view and speaking to a larger audience, some kind of axiomatic truth has to be expressed.

HOW IS THEME EXPRESSED?

"Why are you leaving me?" Joe beseeches Jan. "I was only telling you the truth." Jan pauses on the threshold. "Well, honesty isn't always the best policy!" she retorts, and the door slams. All that's missing is the subtitle: *Get It?*

The first and foremost, most obvious rule of working with theme is that it can't be artificially imposed on the material—or artificially expressed. Writers have to avoid what's been dubbed the "Fortune Cookie Fallacy," meaning, if one of your characters verbalizes your axiom as banally as it's expressed in one of Hung Fat's fortunes, your theme may be just as disposable.

Actually, if you're working with a viable theme in your screenplay, it's already being expressed without such on-the-nose soapbox pronouncements. Your characters are embodiments of thematic concerns; they're the ones arguing the sides of your possible truth. And who wins the argument is crucial. A writer's attitude, belief system, and/or point of view gets expressed in three places: in the growth of the main character, in the resolution of the story, and in the storylines of its subplots.

Theme in character growth: A quote from yet another fiction writer, Robert Penn Warren, is pinned to my writing room wall: "The secret subject of any story is what we learn, or fail to learn, over time."

As we've noted, the transformative power of love is an underlying, long-abiding romantic comedy idea; it's the *über*theme of the genre itself. In the most involving romantic comedies, how the main character is affected by love, what the main character chooses to do when love enters his/her life, or whether the character is changed by love is often the point of the story. What has your character learned by meeting, losing, getting? Answer that question and you enter the realm of theme.

Theme in story resolution: It Happened One Night ends with its upper-class heroine (Claudette Colbert) running out on her society wedding to be happily reunited with the working-class good guy played by Clark Gable. This bride's flight signifies her embrace of better values. Contrast the climax of *Runaway Bride*: when Julia Roberts leaves Richard Gere at the altar, it means she hasn't gotten over her neurosis; when she later suggests they have another kind of wedding, it signifies that she's worked through (rather patly and off-camera) her self-actualization issues. Two different thematic takes, but a common testing ground: where your protagonists end up is the clearest indication of the point you're trying to make.

Theme in subplots: Similarly, the subplots of a romantic comedy are another arena where theme is played out. *Moonstruck*'s concerns about "settling or not settling"—central to the romance between Ronny and Loretta—are acted out in the secondary story lines featuring Loretta's parents. *Tootsie*'s preoccupation with the meaning of friendship, slipped deftly but clearly into the final scene between Michael and Julie ("We've done the hard part," he tells her, "we're already good friends"), is echoed throughout the movie in its various subplots (e.g., an angry Sandy telling Michael, "I'd take [your lying] from a lover, Michael—I don't take it from my friends!").

Note that a vital corollary to all this is *thematic consistency*. If our "Joe and Jan" writer reaches the conclusion that trust is the essential foundation of a successful marriage, then we'd better see a resolution that illustrates the triumph of trust—not an ending that emphasizes, say, great sexual chemistry or the amassing of wealth. In fact, any storytelling component that doesn't conform to a screenplay's theme confuses and diffuses a movie; an audience intuitively feels the wrong turn taken. One of your jobs as a writer is to test every character arc, image, and story line in your script against your axiom. If the same theme is being expressed in some way throughout, your story will have the integrity it needs.

To see how theme is developed through characters, plot resolution and subplot, let's turn to a case study.

CASE STUDY

When Harry Met Sally

Screenplay: Nora Ephron
Director: Rob Reiner
Leads: Billy Crystal and Meg Ryan
Released by Castle Rock in 1989 (96 min.)

Log line: Over many years, two seeming opposites
forge a male-female friendship—which nearly ends
disastrously when they become lovers.

Synopsis

Harry Burns and Sally Albright meet in the late 1970s when they share a drive from their Chicago University campus to New York City after graduation. Cynical Harry doesn't believe that men and women can be friends because sexual attraction always gets in the way, and bright-eyed optimist Sally is appalled when Harry makes a pass at her, since he's supposedly in love with her good friend Amanda. They part when they arrive in Manhattan.

Five years later they briefly meet again on an airplane. Sally's surprised to hear that Harry's getting married, but his determinedly male point of view alienates her once more. Five years after this, they run into each other in a New York City bookstore; Sally's just broken up with her longtime boyfriend Joe, and Harry's being divorced by his wife Helen. Both have matured, and they become friends. This is a new experience for Harry, but he warms to it; they support each other through a difficult period of single life. Still, their unspoken attraction is a subliminal threat, especially after Sally exhibits her sexuality in an argument, proving to Harry that women can successfully fake orgasms.

Harry's best friend Jess and Sally's best friend Marie fall in love, move in together, and are preparing to marry. Sally, devastated to learn that Joe's getting married, turns to Harry for consolation . . . and the two end up making love. Harry, scared by this turn, alienates Sally with his in-denial behavior. After a big blowout, she refuses to see him anymore. Harry slowly but surely comes to the realization that he's in love with Sally, and he runs to find her at a New Year's party, where his fervent love declaration and tacit marriage proposal win her back. The friends become mates for life.

· ·

When Harry Met Sally, a huge success upon its release, seems to be one of the few romantic comedies that men wholeheartedly embrace. This is probably because it unashamedly expresses a quintessentially male, antiromantic point of view. Nora Ephron's script gets away with this by having Harry's dark sentiments instantly countered by sunny Sally's more expected and accepted female point of view and, of course, by having Harry ultimately embrace that POV in a love-conquers-all finale.

What most people remember about the movie, besides its justly celebrated orgasm-in-a-deli centerpiece, is its ostensible subject matter: the question of whether a man and a woman can sustain a friendship without sex. While the script itself is a model of economy and clarity that belongs on any romantic comedy writer's shelf, in the published edition of the screenplay, Nora Ephron has provided us with an uncommonly honest, informative, and useful analysis of the creation of a movie from a screenwriter's POV. And interestingly, her introduction reveals that—according to its author, at least—the gender-friendship question is *not* what *Harry* is about.

The genesis of the movie stems from an idea that Rob Reiner brought to Ephron (and we should all be so lucky):

> He wanted to make a movie about a man and a woman who become friends, as opposed to lovers; they make a deliberate decision not to have sex because sex ruins everything; and then they have sex and it ruins everything. And I said, let's do it.

In the course of discussing the story, Ephron sits with Reiner and his producing partner Andrew Scheinman and learns about how men perceive and deal with the opposite sex. She's appalled ("sort of my wildest nightmares of what men thought"), but soon puts the news to good use, as she realizes ("long before I had any idea of what was actually going to happen in the movie itself") that she can model her male protagonist on Rob Reiner.

> So I began with Harry, based on Rob. And because Harry was bleak and depressed, it followed absolutely that Sally would be cheerful and chirpy and relentlessly, pointlessly, unrealistically, idiotically optimistic. Which is, it turns out, very much like me.

Note that Ephron starts with character, not plot. And what she assumes, in developing her story concept ("it followed absolutely"), is not only good romantic comedy conflict (she's making her leads as dynamically opposed as possible), it's an example of what we've identified as a means of expressing theme: her two main characters are going to represent two sides of the argument she's beginning to explore. Finally, note her comment that Sally is much like herself. Will this script get personal for the writer? It already has. Ephron goes on to say that as she began her first draft, she did have a subject in mind,

> . . . which was not, by the way, whether men and women could be friends. The movie instead was a way for me to write about being single—about the difficult, frustrating, awful, funny search for happiness in an American city where the primary emotion is unrequited love.

And there we have it, from the writer's mouth. Given the concept suggested by Reiner and Scheinman, and characters based on Reiner and herself, Ephron began to use the story as a means to express her experience, insights, and point of view about being single. The beauty part, in terms of seeding conflict, is that she had an ally. While she explored the single life from a woman's POV, she had Reiner on board to express the man's.

> Movies generally start out belonging to the writer and
> end up belonging to the director . . . what made this
> movie different was that Rob had a character who could
> say whatever he believed, and if I disagreed, I had Sally to
> say so for me.

This is the dialectic that's been largely responsible for the movie's universal appeal. *Harry* couldn't have ended up being a chick flick with Reiner at the helm—who was, remember, the man who seeded the idea in the first place. Following Reiner's lead, Ephron worked out a story in which Harry and Sally become lovers after being friends and then decide to go their separate ways; what they've learned has prepared them both for the next important romance in their lives:

> I wrote a first draft about two people who get each other
> from the breakup of the first big relationship in their lives
> to the beginning of the second. Rob went off and made
> *Stand By Me*. We met again and decided that Harry and
> Sally belonged together.

Note here an important factor in working with theme and story: flexibility. While such changes in intent don't erase Ephron's original thematic area of interest (i.e., urban single life), we can read between the lines; evidently Ephron and Reiner realized that with two such lovable not-quite lovers on their hands, a happier ending would be more satisfying. This decision has significant repercussions for the finished film's ultimate meaning, as we'll see, but for now, observe Ephron's admirable willingness to keep shaping and redefining her story arc. She goes on to describe writing an additional half-dozen drafts.

Ephron is unusually gracious in crediting her creative team and the actors. Late in the process it was Meg Ryan, for example, who suggested actually faking the orgasm in the deli, and comedian Billy Crystal came up with the scene's topper (given to an older customer played by Rob's mother, Estelle Reiner): "I'll have what she's having." Again, we should all have such an ideal collaborative process in our work.

Ephron goes on to describe how the finished film reflects everyone's input, and her conclusions show how much her own conception of the movie's theme has shifted over four years of rewriting (plus the shooting of the actual picture):

> Rob believes that men and women can't be friends . . . I disagree . . . and both of us are right. Which brings me to what *When Harry Met Sally* is really about—not, as I said, whether men and women can be friends, but about how different men and women are.

Aha. Somewhere between "the single life" and "the male-female friendship issue," we've landed on a third thematic throughline: gender difference. So what do you think? Is *Harry* true to Ephron's original area of interest? Reiner's axiomatic question? Ephron's hindsight conclusion? I believe that the movie has all three things embedded in it and that, cumulatively, these thematic strains add up to something else again.

While Reiner's contribution forms the backbone of the central story line (remaining true to his original concept in everything but the ending), Ephron's thematic subject is evidenced in the dialogue throughout and in some nonverbal montages—it fills out the canvas of the movie. Every time Harry and Sally aren't debating or enacting the difficulties of forging a friendship with someone of the opposite sex, the "funny, awful" aspects of single life pick up the slack. Thus, in between what we'll call for the moment "Reiner's stuff"—the scene of Harry and Sally's second meeting (airplane) and their third (bookstore)—we have "Ephron's stuff": a scene where Sally and her female friends discuss the travails of singledom in the context of Sally's recent breakup (Marie, reacting in horror, "But you guys were a couple. You had someone to go places with. You had a date on national holidays!").

The third thematic strain, "differences between men and women," surfaces wherever Reiner's focus and Ephron's focus intersect. A scene in which Harry and Jess discuss Harry's meaning-less sexual encounter of the previous night has Harry marveling that he and Sally can openly discuss such a date, while Jess remains fixated on Harry's conquest: "You made a woman meow?!" This cuts to Sally and Harry at the deli and Sally's incredulous/disgusted interrogation of Harry on what *she* finds significant: How did he manage his quick exit from the date?

Man impressed, woman appalled; the catalyst for Sally's orgasm demonstration comes out of this collision of differences. When Harry smugly insists that no woman has ever faked an orgasm with him, Sally notes bitterly: "Oh right, I forgot. You're a man." And she proceeds to prove him wrong.

Alrighty, then—single life, men-women friendships, gender differences . . . but does this stew of thematic ideas ever cohere? What, after all, is the *theme* of *When Harry Met Sally?*

Let's test our theories. We said that character growth is one area in which theme is expressed. So what does Harry learn over the course of the story? It's laid out for us in the penultimate scene, when Harry rushes to Sally's side and declares his love, only to be initially rejected. "You can't just show up here," she informs him, "tell me you love me, and expect to make everything all right. It doesn't work that way." Harry rallies:

> How about this way? I love how you get cold when it's seventy-one degrees out. I love that it takes you an hour and a half to order a sandwich. I love that you get a little crinkle right there when you're looking at me like I'm nuts. I love that after I spend the day with you, I can still smell your perfume on my clothes. And I love that you're the last person I want to talk to before I go to sleep at night . . .

Harry goes on to say he wants to spend the rest of his life with Sally, but what's most important about his wonderfully specific enumeration of what makes her lovable is this subtext: the very things that used to rankle Harry about Sally have turned into her

most endearing attributes. Harry used to couch all his pronouncements about gender differences in negative, hostile terms. But
falling in love with her has created a shift. *Harry now accepts and
appreciates the differences between them.*

Now check the story resolution. When Ephron and Reiner
decided they wanted Harry and Sally to end up together, they
were pointing their disparate thematic materials in one direction.
To have let these two lovers drift apart would have been to embrace the tyranny of difference. You see, the movie would've said,
men and women *are* deeply incompatible, they can't be friends because they're too damn different. Instead, the joyful defeat in the
finished product tells us, *vive la différence,* or, to put it more
soberly: accept the inevitable compromise.

Here's a hypothetical "Egri" for it: Embracing gender differences leads to romantic happiness. An axiomatic question could've
been: How can two such different genders achieve compatibility?
As a last spot check, consider the subplot: the mirror personalities
of the two protagonists, Jess and Marie, do in fact quickly hurtle
past their gender differences and achieve domestic harmony by
dealing with them equitably. The one low-key fight between them
that we're witness to shows Marie, in time-honored gender role tradition, correcting Jess's bad taste by ridding their home of his
wagon-wheel coffee table. His capitulation after her show of good
faith (she's suffered with the table thus far and will continue to suffer should he insist) indicates that they'll still live happily ever after.

Right after the movie's ominous second-act climax (Harry
and Sally make love), Ephron neatly underlines this point with a
deft recapitulation of her favored thematic strain, as Jess and
Marie, cocooned in their premarital bed, end their respective
phone calls from the traumatized postcoital Harry and Sally. "Tell
me I'll never have to be out there again," Marie says. "You'll never
have to be out there again," Jess says, and they kiss. Thus, with a
shudder in the direction of that "awful, funny" single life, the
movie subtly nudges us in the direction of its conclusion: Getting
past those differences is worth it.

I specifically chose *Harry* for this case study because—in spite of variants on its "man versus woman" issue being sounded in the dialogue, images and beats of nearly every scene—its theme remains in some respects entertainingly elastic. There are many other romantic comedies built on more straight-up, textbook axioms, but *Harry* (and Ephron's discourse) demonstrates how a good theme is a flexible, ever growing entity and, unlike fortune cookie slogans, is so much an organic part of the whole that it can't be patly extracted. When a writer is working theme into every element, the movie itself is what best expresses it.

One interesting thing about the unconscious aspect of theme work is that a movie may mean different things to its creators—and to its audiences. But the point is its presence, which unifies character and story development and adds to the substance and power of a romantic comedy. Though what I'm positing as *Harry*'s theme was never articulated as such by its creators, its ultimately positive spin on the singles/gender-friendship/difference issues can be palpably felt in the finished film. And whether or not you agree with my specific take on the axiomatic truth at its heart, there's no denying that the presence of *When Harry Met Sally*'s theme is what made it one of the most distinctive romantic comedies of the modern era.

SUMMARY

Theme is the arena in which our personal passions get expressed. The most compelling stories come out of a writer's personal exploration of human experience, and this is especially true in our character-driven genre.

A good tool to use in working with theme is an axiom—a possible truth that's going to be argued or explored in the working out of your story. Some writers like to work with a predetermined (closed) premise, a statement that lays out the entire trajectory of a story in thematic terms. It's often more rewarding for a writer to approach material with a question that the writer would like to explore; this kind of open thematic approach allows more room for discovery.

Whether one begins with an axiom or arrives at one after an exploratory first draft, a romantic comedy's theme is generally expressed through the growth of its central character, the resolution of the story, and the nature of the subplots employed. It's important that the same theme be consistently expressed throughout. Working with universally resonant material elevates the movie's significance and accessibility, whether or not the ultimate message its audience comes away with is exactly the one originally intended.

Exercise: Developing Theme

1. *Making it personal* (intended for those beginning a first draft): Think of one of the most painful, humiliating, embarrassing things that ever happened to you with someone of the opposite sex.

Now take a deep breath, and see if by writing a brief paragraph or two about the experience you can find the humor in retrospect.

Once you've done this, identify a question or two that the experience raised. Can you fashion your question into an axiomatic theme?

Now do a more freely fictionalized rewrite on your true-life incident, making it more clearly illustrate that theme.

This is the screenplay theme process in microcosm. You might want to try it with your lead character. Is there an incident in your outlined story that lends itself to such exploration? Something in the character's backstory?

(continued)

Exercise: Developing Theme *(continued)*

2. *Listening to your draft* (intended for those who have a completed draft and are approaching a rewrite): Analyze the arc of your protagonist(s) over the course of the story. Does your lead character learn something and/or grow in some way, however incremental? Define that lesson or growth in a simple sentence.

Similarly, what does the resolution of your story express in thematic terms? Write the sentence.

Address your subplot(s). How does your subplot echo, contrast, or play out the issues evinced in your "character growth" and "resolution" sentences? Write the sentence.

Now combine the essence of all three sentences into one axiomatic statement or question that speaks to the heart of your your thematic intent. If that proves difficult, pay close attention to where any one of the three statements diverges. Play what-if to see how a character, story ending, and/or subplot could be altered so that it better expresses your master sentence, or working axiom.

3*a*. *Theme in imagery* (for all writers still in search of a viable axiom): Identify an area of interest for your piece. Free-associate around it (e.g., from the word *weddings,* what do you see in your mind's eye?). Now jot down whatever images and phrases come to mind. Do any of these speak to theme?

3*b*. Set your working title aside and brainstorm a short list that addresses theme (my favorite is *Enemies: A Love Story*).

3*c*. Look through your piece and see if there are any recurring motifs—in story beat, dialogue, and imagery. Are people always on the run? Stuck in the same place? What is a movie short on physical contact but full of recording devices, phones, and TVs (e.g., *sex, lies and videotape*) trying to say?

CHAPTER SIX

Structuring Conflict

Ultimately, what you are trying to do is to find what the story's going to be: the ultimate, basic thread that you can hang everything else on. Once I have the spine of the piece, and everything that can be threaded to hang off that spine, that is it. And if I can use it, super. If I can't use it, no matter how good the material is, it has to go.

WILLIAM GOLDMAN

D o you have a viable romantic comedy story concept? Does it feature compelling characters who have strong conflicts? And do these conflicts speak to some thematic area that's of personal interest to you? Then you're ready to get down to the real grunt work of screenwriting: structuring your story.

Screenwriters are obsessed with structure. Working in a medium where getting the butts in the seats and keeping them there is the seeming be-all and end-all, writers agonize over the proper act breaks and plot points. Screenwriting textbooks relentlessly analyze such distinctions, developing elaborate systems that sometimes include the page numbers where each necessary "pinch" is supposed to appear. Most of them deem structure so crucial that they advocate having every scene and sequence carefully mapped out in advance; it seems that to write otherwise is sheer folly, an exercise in futility.

But this screenwriter's blueprinting approach to story leaves many writers of fiction bemused. How do you make discoveries? they ask. Where's the room for exploration, for flights of fancy? How do you develop a story with any depth if you know exactly where you're going each step of the way? And meanwhile, the complaint one hears from moviegoers, screenwriters, and even the makers of movies themselves is that mainstream movies are too formulaic. They're all the same, everyone snipes. We could predict almost every plot point in the last three movies we saw; can't anybody do something a little different?

Given all of this, it's with some trepidation that I introduce the idea of a "formula" for plotting the romantic comedy. The word *formula* is a bit of a misnomer, with pejorative associations. Yet it's undeniable that in one successful romantic comedy after another, a certain plot pattern is consistently utilized in traversing some one-and-a-half to two hours of screen time. Here's the bad news: putting such a ready-made paradigm to work will not magically solve all of your story problems. The good news? Those of you who have a more freewheeling, risk-chasing, indie bent will still find it to be a helpful tool. Because what we're talking about here when we talk about *formula* is simply a workable construct—a means of organizing the broad strokes of romantic comedy conflict that has proven viable over some eighty years of moviemaking.

A perusal of those eight decades yields seven particular *beats*, or plot points, which romantic comedy screenwriters have employed time and time again with effective results. They're really just variations on the logical major beats that all screenwriters gravitate to within a three-act structure. They're organic to that form, which, more often than not, is the one that most romantic comedies naturally employ. They're also organic to the archetypal story of two people who start out single and end up coupled.

The course of true love, no matter how mysterious or magical it may be in its particulars, has some predictable way stations. Usually there's a significant early encounter, eventually followed by a moment in which the potential mates realize they may be at the start of a longer story. Further into the courtship there's an involving event, be it physical or emotional (hopefully both), where the hook goes in and the stakes get higher. And generally the new love is tested before a commitment gets made. The lovers have to rise to the occasion, meet the challenge—and even then, the decision to finally commit looms as a last hurdle before their ultimate clinch. The traditional construct of romantic comedy story development follows the intuitive logic of a credible courtship tale, so it stands to reason that writers and audiences embrace it.

Obviously, the path to developing and structuring a persuasive story for your romantic comedy lies somewhere between the poles—having a road map with fixed directions on the one hand and having the room to follow inspiration wherever it takes you on the other. The traditional formula supplies a writer with effective goalposts, which serve to support a story's structure and keep its intentions on track. But you'll find there's still a lot of untrod story ground to cover between them, with plenty of room for your imagination to get a workout.

SEVEN BASIC ROMANTIC COMEDY BEATS

There is general agreement, across all genre borders, that many successful movies are constructed in three acts, and romantic comedies most often follow that form, with the third act usually the shortest, the second the longest, and the first averaging out to somewhere around a half hour's worth of screen time.

Here's a graph of such a structure—sometimes referred to as *the bridge* due to its all-important linchpin beats at the ends of acts one and two—with our seven beats sketched in at their approximate story-line locations. (We'll discuss each beat in turn.)

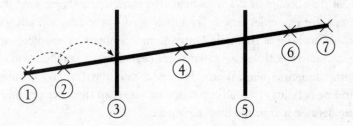

1. The Chemical Equation: Setup

A scene or sequence identifying the exterior and/or interior conflict (i.e., unfulfilled desire), the "what's wrong with this picture" implied in the protagonist's (and/or the antagonist's) current status quo.

Although in a sense most first acts are *all* setup, the romantic comedy requires a more specific introduction to its primary-point-of-view character. Very early on (often in the opening scene), there's a defining moment, akin to that hero-pets-the-dog cliché we mentioned earlier, that tells us this is what our lead is like . . . and this is what he/she is lacking.

For example, *Sleepless in Seattle* begins with a sequence that establishes the death of Sam's wife, his assuming the mantle of single fatherhood, and the misery of his mourning. The defining moment, which ends this pre-credit sequence, is when Sam, at the airport en route to his new home, stops his well-meaning friend's pitch about finding love again with the pronouncement, "It doesn't happen twice." We now know essentially all we need to know about Sam and his problem.

Generally, the secondary lead (i.e., the prospective mate) gets a similar setup moment, which follows soon after. Thus, in *Sleepless,* a sequence follows that introduces Annie and her situation, which includes an imminent marriage to a Bellamy named Walter. The defining moment occurs when she's trying on her wedding dress in the attic with her mom. On the heels of a nagging realization that her relationship lacks magic, the dress tears—a bad omen. We now know what's up with Annie.

Sometimes the setup for the secondary lead is saved for a reveal that occurs in the next beat (the cute meet). *Romancing the Stone,* for example, sets up its female lead in the first act, but we know nothing of the male until she meets him. Occasionally, we get to know both leads as they meet each other, a combination of setup and cute meet. *When Harry Met Sally* starts as Harry, Sally, and we set out on a road trip together, and both their personalities are defined within the first sequence.

The subtext for this first setup beat is that what we perceive as missing in our primary protagonist's situation and/or psychology will very likely be fulfilled by the potential mate. The setup doesn't speak only to exterior conflict (Sam, a widower, is relocating) but to interior (Sam doesn't believe he'll ever fall in love again). It speaks to why this particular character *should* meet our secondary lead. Sam doesn't think lightning can strike twice, and Annie has just realized that she's looking for lightning—thus the term *chemical equation*. This person plus that person, the setup implies, will equal something new—something that makes sense.

2. Cute Meet: Catalyst

The inciting incident that brings man and woman together and into conflict; an inventive but credible contrivance, often amusing, which in some way sets the tone for the action to come.

The first meeting between a romantic comedy's two leads is usually unusual. It's somehow charged with significance, which, if you think about it, makes perfect sense. When you meet a couple in real life who've obviously got something good going on, how they met is an inevitable question, and more often than not there's an interesting answer. The meeting, after all, is something that has irrevocably changed their lives. Screen life, given all the schematic designs that good writers can employ, takes this basic truism one step further. A good romantic comedy makes the meeting genuinely meaningful. It resonates.

Screwball approaches to this moment can be misleading in that their quirkiness often obscures a primary function: the successful cute meet is not arbitrary, but in some microcosmic, thematic, and plot-significant way is the beginning of a throughline for the relationship, suggesting a kind of signature gesture for the couple's dynamic.

For example, in *Bringing Up Baby*, serious David's first encounter with anything-but-serious Susan sets the tone for all that follows. He's trying to retrieve his golf ball so he can return to his task, pitching a business proposition to his opponent, while she, airily misinterpreting everything he says, is determined to play her own game with his ball, play with him, and have fun, period. His all-work demeanor gets continually disrupted by her pure-play attitude (their chemical equation) every time they meet thereafter.

A necessary clarification of this catalystic moment is that neither *cute* nor *meet* should be taken too literally. Often, a future romantic comedy couple has met (meaning they know each other) before the beat occurs. So the significant encounter and catalyst for the plot is a meeting in the metaphorical sense; it's when they "really meet." Sometimes the future couple's meeting is not cute in the sense of amusingly odd or quirky—but it is special, and it has a memorable, distinctive quality.

For example, in *As Good as It Gets*, hyperneurotic Melvin and stressed-out waitress Carol have already established a professional relationship before the movie begins. But the first time we see them together, with Carol serving Melvin at her restaurant, Melvin makes a huge mistake that turns things personal. He makes a nastily nihilistic remark about Carol's ailing son, and Carol, with lacerating emotional intensity, forces an apology from him. This crucial encounter, while technically no "cute meet," is the catalyst for all that follows.

3. A Sexy Complication: Turning Point

Traditionally occurring at the end of Act 1, a new development that raises story stakes and clearly defines the protagonist's goal; most successful when it sets man and woman at cross-purposes and/or their inner emotions at odds with the goal.

Reams of screenwriting text have been written about the all-important first-act break. It's the critical moment in just about any movie, when the story's central conflict is crystallized in no uncertain terms. A problem is defined that forces the central character to act or react; now we know what the story is about, and we have a pretty good idea (generally better than the characters do) about where we're headed next.

In romantic comedy, as we noted in our discussion of story concepts, internal conflicts often drive the action and determine the outcome of an exterior conflict. The turning point is the juncture where such inner and outer arcs collide and combust. There are two common approaches to this crucial turn:

1. Given a romantic attraction that's strong and unconflicted, an exterior story conflict creates the problem, setting man and woman at odds. For example, *Arthur* at the end of Act 1 is clearly falling in love with Linda, but he's told he'll be disinherited if he doesn't marry Susan.

2. Given no exterior story conflict that presents an immediate obstacle or problem, then the romantic attraction is conflicted by one or both characters having an internal issue that short-circuits consummation. For example, in *The Truth About Cats and Dogs,* single talk-radio veterinarian Abby (Janeane Garofalo) has successfully won the attentions of available bachelor Brian (Ben Chaplin) by helping him train a dog over the phone. Brian calls back to ask her out. But when he asks her what she looks like (how will he recognize her?), her low-self-esteem issue surfaces; convinced he'll be disappointed by her physical appearance, she describes instead her knockout model acquaintance, Noelle (Uma Thurman) . . . and stands him up.

4. The Hook: Midpoint

A situation that irrevocably binds the protagonist with the antagonist (often while tweaking sexual tensions) and has further implications for the outcome of the relationship.

Given the length of an average second act, it only stands to reason that most screenplays need a significant event or emotional boost of some kind, smack dab in the middle, that will rev up the motor of the story. The hook, or midpoint, is basically a higher-stakes variation on the problem created by the first turning point. In romantic comedy, it specifically speaks to the level of emotional involvement. At Act 1's end, either or both of the protagonists have an out: they could scotch the romance and chalk it up as a road not taken. But some event hooks them, at the story's middle, closing off such an exit. From here on out, these two are in it together.

An example of a traditional midpoint occurs at the mathematical middle (forty-six minutes into a ninety-two-minute movie) of *His Girl Friday*. Having finally overcome all the snaky efforts of her former husband, editor Walter, to keep her from leaving the newspaper and marrying a Bellamy, reporter Hildy happily announces to all her cronies in the newsroom that she's walking out the door for good. Then shots ring out from the street below and the room erupts in chaos; the very man Hildy's just interviewed for a front-page story has broken out of jail. Hildy's on the phone to Walter and back on the job in an instant, wedding forgotten—and her connection with Walter reestablished.

The most effective midpoints, in addition to being functional, tend to be metaphorical; while cinching the central story conflict, they recapitulate the movie's theme. For example, when *Bringing Up Baby*'s leopard gets loose, Susan gets David to finally let loose in the wilds of Connecticut.

In some contemporary romantic comedies, the hook moment is more a metaphor than a plot development. The famous Sally-fakes-an-orgasm-in-the-deli scene from *Harry Met Sally* begins that film's midpoint. How does it function? Well, it's the first time that Sally wins an argument with Harry, uncontested, making a point about women that puts them on equal footing. More important, Sally's performance confronts Harry with her sexuality; he sees her as a woman in a more intimate way than he ever has before. The midpoint section closes with the suddenly awkward kiss between Harry and Sally on New Year's Eve. This hook subtly drives the theme of the movie forward, effectively setting up . . .

5. Swivel: Second Turning Point

Traditionally occurring at the end of Act 2, stakes reach their highest point as the romantic relationship's importance jeopardizes the
protagonist's chance to succeed at his stated goal—or vice versa—
and his goal shifts.

This is the point in the story where the characters have caught
up with the audience (we already know they're meant to be together). The awful truths can no longer be avoided, and the next action taken will determine the romance's outcome. This "turning
point of no return" is termed a *swivel* because the protagonist in a romantic comedy is forced to turn one way or another: he either
chooses love over his original goal or sacrifices love to get that goal.

When Harry has sex with Sally, the central thesis of his identity
is tested. This man who can't be friends with lovers has just turned
his best friend into a lover. Will he now be true to his school (i.e.,
end the friendship), or will he change his way of living?

Tootsie, due to its myriad subplots, has a chain of crises as its
turning point: when Michael-as-Dorothy tries to kiss Julie, Julie
thinks Dorothy is a lesbian; Les proposes to Dorothy; Van Horn
makes a pass at Dorothy; Sandy makes Michael admit he's in love
with someone else; George tells Michael he can't get out of his
contract; and Julie tells Dorothy they can no longer be friends.
The cumulative effect is the same: Michael must choose between
his original goal (the job) and Julie.

6. The Dark Moment: Crisis Climax

Wherein the consequences of the swivel decision yield disaster;
generally, the humiliating scene where private motivations are revealed, and either the relationship and/or the protagonist's goal is
seemingly lost forever.

If the central activity of the romantic comedy is foreplay, then
this beat is a cold shower–like interruption, where the protagonist

stands naked and vulnerable and, true to nightmare tradition, often has his most horrible secret exposed in the most public manner possible. It seems that all is lost and the two leads can't possibly live happily ever after.

Tootsie, as we've seen, is marvelously true to form: knowing that he risks losing Julie in telling the truth, Michael reveals to the world that Dorothy is really a man. Julie promptly punches Michael in the stomach and walks out of his life.

More often than not, the dark-moment beat leads swiftly to the seventh and final beat.

7. Joyful Defeat: Resolution

A reconciliation that reaffirms the primal importance of the relationship; usually a happy ending that implies marriage or a serious commitment, often at the cost of some personal sacrifice to the protagonist.

The old-fashioned screwball, with its aggressive woman pursuing a more passive man, has a subtext evinced in its happy endings: the man's apprehensions about being successfully snared. Boy has got girl, but he also is "got"; having done the crime, he'll now have to do the time.

Today, a similarly bittersweet ambivalence often permeates the so-called happy ending. Consider, for example, former lifetime bachelor Hugh Grant's oh-so-carefully worded not-really-a-proposal to Andie MacDowell in *Four Weddings'* closing scene. This contemporary tone reflects our current awareness of just how fragile and beleaguered the institution of marriage has become. Even in the world of romantic fantasy, we're not easily convinced that a couple can have it all. We've come to expect that a successful resolution will require some sacrifice, either practical (i.e., they won't have millions, but they'll have each other) or philosophical (i.e., they're together . . . for now).

In fact, resolution no longer means that the featured couple will literally remain together. As *Annie Hall* demonstrated, a boy and girl's story can resolve in their being more happy apart than together. More recently, *Shakespeare in Love* ended with a skillfully crafted, emotionally resonant compromise. In Viola's playing Juliet opposite Will's Romeo during the play's premiere, they enact the symbolic peak and pinnacle of their relationship. This resolution gives way to a poignant parting, suggesting a metaphorical "ever after": from here to eternity Will and his muse will be united as she lives on in the heroines of his subsequent plays. It's a sad victory—a joyful defeat.

Using these seven beats as structural supports is a practice that has long served screenwriters in sustaining romantic comedy conflicts. While they're no written-in-stone necessity for every plot, their progression has an organic logic that often prevents undue contrivance.

To see how this traditional construct organizes conflict in a story, here's a recent successful romantic comedy, broken down in beats. It's the one where boy meets movie star:

Notting Hill

1. *Setup (the chemical equation).* The opening montage establishes that Anna Scott is one of the most famous actresses in the world. Directly following, William Thacker establishes (in voice-over and montage) that he's an absolute nobody, divorced, in a dead-end job, living with a peculiar flatmate, and totally romance/glamour-free. *Anna seems to have everything William doesn't have.*

2. *Catalyst (the cute meet).* Anna wanders into William's shop and buys a book; he's charming and doesn't blow her civilian cover. Moments later, he bumps into her on the street and spills orange juice over both of them. He offers her his apartment to clean up in and change, and he is rewarded by a surprisingly heated kiss. Anna leaves. *The star has set and commanded the scene; William is ripe for conquest.*

3. *First turning point (a sexy complication).* William has crossed off the encounter as an odd, memorable little moment . . . but discovering that Anna has called him, goes to see her at her hotel—only to be mistaken for a journalist covering her latest movie junket. *Just as the gulf between them seems impossibly wide, Anna asks William out on a date.*

4. *Midpoint (the hook).* Anna asks William to spend the night with her, but when William joins her in her hotel, her movie star boyfriend has shown up, and he boorishly dismisses William, who's posing as a waiter so as not to cause trouble for Anna. *Leaving, William is disturbed to realize that he's more than merely disappointed—he's in love.*

5. *Second turning point (the swivel).* William and Anna have consummated their attraction at Will's flat, and all is glorious—until the clandestine lovers open his front door to find all of Britain's media snapping photos of them. Anna panics and lashes out at William: *I'll always regret this, Anna says, and, choosing career over love, exits.*

6. *Climax (the dark moment).* Some time later, Anna seeks William out, apologizes, and requests a second chance, asking William to love her. But William, now gun-shy (some more misunderstandings have transpired), turns her down. Miserable, he seeks the consolation of his friends—*only to realize, from their reactions, that he's done the wrong thing.*

7. *Resolution (joyful defeat).* After a madcap chase to reach Anna before she leaves the country, William pushes his way into the midst of a press conference. *He abjectly apologizes, begging Anna to have him after all—and she happily agrees.* A coda shows William as the cowed companion to Anna's movie royalty, but a final shot implies domestic bliss.

You'll note some clever tweaking of the paradigm in Curtis's execution. The catalyst, for example, is actually made up of two "cute meets," though the sequence as a whole amounts to the same thing;

Anna's control of the situation and William's charmingly awkward rising to the occasion sets up their dynamic for the movie's duration. The midpoint is supposed to bring the lovers closer together—but in this case, the beat is interrupted by the boyfriend. Nonetheless, the midpoint is still very much a hook because the essence of the beat is that William realizes he's in love with Anna, and from there on out, suffers accordingly.

Notting is an example of the formula in its pure state (i.e., with virtually no subplot complicating the romantic story). Romantic comedies that have more on their plate tend to be a bit more un-orthodox. A hybrid like *Tootsie,* for example, starts its romance a lot later in the movie than the norm because the gender-bender story line requires a longer setup. But once Michael and Julie "meet cute" (on the set of the soap opera), the arc of their relationship follows form.

When you break a successful romantic comedy down to its seven beats, watch the way inner and outer conflicts dovetail and combust within this framework. *Shakespeare in Love*'s midpoint, a montage sequence following Will and Viola's first lovemaking, melds exterior action and inner emotions in a seamless blend of life and art, as Will and Viola's love fuels the creation of *Romeo and Juliet.* From the unbinding of Viola in her bedroom to the dual nurses (real nurse and actor nurse) calling the lovers from both bed and stage at the sequence's end, it's the essence of the movie in microcosm. *Notting*'s second turning point is truly a swivel-like turn: Anna Scott shifts from glowing lover to glowering enemy as she chooses her career (outer conflict) over William's love (inner) in no uncertain terms. And, hurting for William, we wait to see this wrong made right.

There's a world of imaginative difference between the way these disparate romantic comedies employ their basic story moves. To further illustrate just how versatile the formula can be, let's sub-mit a movie to the test that is 180 degrees to the left of *Notting Hill*'s slick, studio commerciality.

Chasing Amy

1. *Setup (the chemical equation).* Holden and his partner Banky are the cocreators of a comic book that has given them rising credibility in their field, evidenced by fan interest at a comic book convention. *Holden and Banky are extremely tight best friends and partners.*

2. *Catalyst (the cute meet).* Holden and Banky participate in a put-on stunt enacted by their gay black friend Hooper, who introduces them to fellow graphic artist Alyssa. She's familiar with Holden's work and seems interested in him; the foursome heads out for drinks. *Holden and Alyssa seem to have like-minded sensibilities.*

3. *First turning point (a sexy complication).* Holden and Alyssa hit it off, discover they come from the same small Jersey suburb, and seem headed for romance—despite Banky's protective jealousy—until Holden learns that Alyssa is a lesbian. *Holden finds Alyssa frustratingly unattainable.*

4. *Midpoint (the hook).* Holden tries to be just friends with Alyssa, but falls in love, in spite of Banky's incredulity. Holden eventually declares his love to Alyssa, even though he may lose her. To his relief, she (though initially angered by the difficult choice he's forced on her) reciprocates. *Holden and Alyssa become lovers.*

5. *Second turning point (the swivel).* Banky, attempting to regain control over his errant friend, digs up dirt on Alyssa from her high school days, when she reportedly had a sexual tryst with two men. A disturbed Holden confronts Alyssa. *Hurt and maddened by his mistrust (and his siding with Banky), Alyssa walks out on Holden.*

6. *Climax (the dark moment).* In a misguided attempt to assuage his own insecurities and win Alyssa back, Holden suggests that she and Banky join in three-way sex with him. Though

Banky (not surprisingly) is game, *realizing Holden is wrong for her, Alyssa leaves him for good.*

7. *Resolution (joyful defeat).* Some time later, after he's pro-duced a comic book tribute to show her he understands how wrong he was, Holden, who's parted ways with Banky, meets Alyssa briefly at another convention. But their moment has also irrevocably passed. *Holden, Banky, and Alyssa, having learned from their experience, are moving on.*

Indie (literally, independent) generally suggests a movie that's strong on anything *but* conventional structure and plot, but Kevin Smith's triangle story not only fulfills the standard formulaic beats, it does so by the book, with each beat clocking in at its expected time (the midpoint at the mathematical mid-dle, etc.). Each progressive development is organic, as, with the inexorable logic of a nightmare, the lovers fight to make a go of it and fail.

An old screenwriting adage states: "Tell simple stories with complicated emotions." *Amy* represents the quintessence of that principle. It *is* a simple story, but Holden, Alyssa, and Banky aren't simple people. Their complicated feelings, behavior, and re-sponses are what fill up the nice fat spaces that such a solid arma-ture allows. Given this skeleton, Smith has plenty of room to let his characters riff, duel, and parry. There's time for freewheeling tangents like a radical-politic analysis of *Star Wars* and a compari-son of sexual body scars. While off-the-wall routines give the ap-pearance of a loose, loopy structure, Smith has constructed a tightly wound time bomb of a story, which is part of its sneaky, subversive charm.

An audience responds intuitively to structure, but usually in a wholly subliminal way—if a movie's working well, no one stands up at a second-act turning point to derisively cry, "Not that old beat again!" Some of the most original romantic comedies are that way precisely because they cleverly disguise their formulaic beats within an inventive design. *Four Weddings and a Funeral* is just this sort of shell game; it feels, as we watch it, like a five-parter (as each section is announced with a new wedding invite). But it actually employs the same seven beats. *Groundhog Day* and *Sliding Doors* have formulaic structures, yet seem anything but. The cute meet in *Sleepless* occurs over the radio, with boy and girl thousands of miles apart.

The flesh and blood you choose to fashion over this story skeleton can be as unique as one human being is from another. And once you're familiar with the form, you'll see that there's fun to be had in stretching its limits and in subverting expected conventional approaches to these beats. There is such a thing as a two-act movie (e.g., *Full Metal Jacket*), and a few more complex romantic comedy hybrids defy conventional seven-beat analysis (*Shakespeare in Love,* for example, hits some beats right on the nose, while doubling up and reconfiguring others). But certainly, at the beginning of a first draft or a rewrite, you'll find that having such a traditional structure to play with, no matter how familiar, will help organize and inspire your most creative impulses.

SUMMARY

The romantic comedy generally breaks the traditional three-act structure into seven essential beats: the *setup* (a chemical equation), the *catalyst* (cute meet), the *first turning point,* or first-act break (a sexy complication), the *midpoint* (hook), the *second turning point,* or second-act break (the swivel), the *climax* (dark moment), and *resolution* (joyful defeat).

This organic way of structuring a story is built on an interplay between exterior conflict and inner conflict. It's an armature that works. Master it first, and you may soon be able to tweak it, as the best romantic comedies do.

Exercise: Finding Your Seven Beats

1. Watching one of your favorite romantic comedies, see if you can recognize the beats as they arrive. Or, before viewing a movie that you're familiar with, chart out the beats according to your memory of the story. Then see how accurate you've been.

Some movies that lend themselves to such analysis in a fairly straightforward fashion are *His Girl Friday, Arthur, When Harry Met Sally, Splash, Working Girl, Pretty Woman,* and *Sense and Sensibility.*

2a. If you're embarking on a first draft:

Use your pitch as a starting point for an expanded, seven-beat version of your story. If a beat proves problematic, slug a general idea in its place (though "something bad happens" is a dangerously vague end-of-second-act idea, it's reasonable to say "John does something that makes Mary mistrust him, and she leaves" if that's as much as you presently know). But sketch out at least one viable seven-beat outline of your story, using no more than a sentence or two for each beat.

Test each beat for inner/outer conflicts. Does each story development in some way speak to both?

2b. If you're beginning a rewrite:

Don't look at that draft or refer to any earlier outlines. Off the top of your head, sketch out what you believe to be the seven beats of your story.

Now go back to your draft and see if they're really there on the page. Major deviations may prove subject for further research (e.g., *is* this a romantic comedy?). Minor adjustments concerning placement (e.g., a cute meet that comes in the second act, a midpoint that's not really near the middle) should cue you about possible revisions in pace and tension. Use your idealized or your realistically readjusted seven-beat outline as a rewrite map. These are your most important beats. Are you really hitting them? Do they each speak in some way to both inner and outer conflicts?

(continued)

Exercise: Finding Your Seven Beats   *(continued)*

3. For both first drafters and rewriters:

Setting aside your current seven-beat outline, start over again with the same two protagonists—either keeping the same setup and/or ending or beginning from scratch. Explore a completely different arc for your plot—an alternative version of your two characters' dynamic.

Stay open to possibilities. You may find an oh-they'd-never-do-*that* beat that turns out to be a keeper. Plug it into your first seven-beat outline and see what happens.

CHAPTER SEVEN

Keeping It Credible

It's like building a house. You have to have a base where the house is going to stand. Writing a movie is a mixture of architecture and, forgive me the pompous word, the poetry, or storytelling. It has to have a solid base so the second act follows the first and it's strong enough to keep the audience in its seats for the third.

BILLY WILDER

According to one of his biographers, the legendary writer-director Billy Wilder's highest accolade of praise for an actor or technician's work was "realistic." This from a man whose far-fetched screenplay premises included a full-grown woman passing herself off as a twelve-year-old (*The Major and the Minor*) and two men fleeing gangsters who pose as female musicians in an all-girl band (*Some Like It Hot*). But Wilder's praise actually makes a lot of sense; he of all writers knew just how much hard work it took to make an audience believe in the impossible.

That particular trick is a romantic comedy writer's toughest hurdle. The hidden challenge of every romantic comedy lies in getting its audience to believe that these two people absolutely *must* end up together. And at the same time, we have to contrive dire circumstances so convincing that the audience will believe— at least for a dark moment or two—that our lovers *won't* reach that happy end. All of this (speaking of impossible) takes place in a realm, supposedly the world we live in, where true love is obtainable and overcomes every obstacle.

You've got to establish *credibility*. In a genre that's often close to fairy-tale fantasy—yet has to appear grounded in reality to win audience involvement—issues of logic and plausibility are particularly significant.

CREATING A PLAUSIBLE WORLD

Wilder's quote about building a house also applies to plot structure, but it serves as a good metaphor for the function of credibility. Your romantic comedy has to be grounded on a solid base to support its flights of fancy. And the story component that gets the biggest workout in building such a base is *world*—an amalgam of elements that help create your story's reality: its setting or location, time period, season, atmosphere, cultural/sociopolitical context, and tone.

The world of any movie can be as fantastical or as realistic as it wants to be. But it has to be constructed carefully, following general precepts of commonsense logic. Oscar-winning *Shakespeare in Love* is certainly proof that viewers will happily buy into the most incredible of contrivances. I, for one, never believed for a moment that Gwyneth Paltrow was actually passing for a guy with that fake mustache plastered on her puss—but it didn't hamper my enjoyment of the story for a moment. That's because *Shakespeare*'s writers used extensive *research* and evoked a specific *sensibility* to create a world where Viola's mustache made sense.

Research

Marc Norman, the original writer on *Shakespeare in Love*, started out with the idea of showing Will in his "upstart crow" days, just as he was getting his foothold in the world of Elizabethan theater. Even before eventual cowriter Tom Stoppard (a Brit steeped in theatrical lore) signed on, American Norman did his homework and found the very linchpin of his plot, born of a simple historical fact: women were not allowed on the stage in 1585; it was the law. With male actors routinely impersonating women on stage, it's easy to see why women posing as men was a common plot device of the time.

Norman shrewdly capitalized on this phenomenon in working out his story line. In a world where no woman would ever be expected to be seen on a stage, the script reasons, why couldn't a woman actor (with breasts bound, men's clothing, mustache glued in place) impersonate a man? We accept the contrivance on screen (grudgingly or happily) because the setting, time period, and sociopolitical context are firmly established. We see through Viola's disguise, but we're not wholly incredulous when none of her contemporaries do.

Norman's research also yielded other crucial plot elements. He found that theatrical contractual obligations were as byzantine and binding as they are today, that theater companies were cutthroat rivals, and that theaters were routinely shut down due to vagaries of nature (e.g., plague) and royal whim. All of this is made clear to us early on, through Norman and Stoppard's expert exposition. In a world where theatrical laws are a matter of life and death, the movie tells us, the stakes surrounding Viola's impersonation become exceedingly high. Thus we accept dramatic developments which might seem truly odd in the context of our own world.

Research is just as important and helpful in plot construction when you're writing contemporary. *Notting Hill* makes sure that nothing about the physical and psychological distance between lowly William and exalted Anna pops the balloon of that movie's world. The business about movie star Anna's employing the names of comic book characters as her "cover" at various hotels has the ring of truth, despite its quirkiness. Having known one celebrity who changed her phone number every few months and always formed real or nonsense words out of the digits ("Castkey," she'd say, and you'd write this down as her new number), I'd wager that Richard Curtis was familiar with such ploys from a real-life star. And this simple fact yields a crucial running gag, which even features in the movie's climax.

A romantic comedy writer's research is especially important regarding character credibility. The choice of a telling detail can make all the difference. If your leading lady is a stockbroker, we expect to hear her talking of offerings and buyouts. Similarly, the settings and atmosphere surrounding a given romantic encounter can add a lot of ballast to an otherwise imaginary event. The beautiful private park at night that is enjoyed by Grant and Roberts in *Notting Hill* doesn't arise from nowhere but from the specifics of that geographical area.

Sensibility

The first flashback in *Annie Hall* takes place in a doctor's office, circa the early 1940s. Research has evidently gone into its set design and costuming—the dress Alvy Singer's mom is wearing is vintage perfection. But there's one telling detail that Allen wrote into the scene which nudges factual research into another area: he's got his doctor puffing away on a cigarette. This is historically accurate (a pre–World War II doctor wouldn't be half as cancer-conscious as his contemporary equivalent), but it's also funny. This visual joke speaks to the specific humor of the scene. The doctor cavalierly assures young death-phobic Alvy that he has nothing to fear from the universe ending in the far-off future— while he himself is smugly smoking a cancerstick. But the joke is also in keeping with an overall comedic sensibility that suffuses *Annie Hall:* many of the characters in its world are walking contradictions, embracing the very things that may be bad for them or drive them crazy. The movie ends, if you remember, with

Woody Allen's joke about a family continuing to live with a certifiably crazy son who thinks he's a chicken—because they need the eggs.

Anytime you evoke a world by manipulating setting, atmosphere, etc., you are making *tonal choices*. Your world reflects an implicit point of view, and this sensibility, hand in hand with the products of your research, grounds your story and makes it credible. The *Annie Hall* flashback didn't need the doctor's cigarette to establish credibility, but this humorous touch adds to the movie's pervasive consistency of tone.

In its opening scene, *Shakespeare in Love* immediately establishes that it's a farce by playing a situation that involves real, physical pain for laughs. Theater owner Henslowe is having his feet burned by an annoyed backer, Fennyman, but Henslowe's pathetic, crazed wheeling and dealing, as well as Fennyman's malicious indifference, takes the emphasis off the scene's pain and peril—as does the very fast turnaround that occurs when Henslowe saves his hide by bartering Will Shakespeare's new comedy. "Romeo and Ethel the Pirate's Daughter," he offers. "Good title," says Fennyman, and Henslowe is released. As an introduction to what follows, a certain kind of sensibility is defined: there will be jeopardy, and it will be real, but we can expect that quick wits and whimsical quirks of fate and personality will overcome it.

Similarly, *There's Something About Mary* puts its hapless lead through excruciating torments, but its anything-goes gross-out comedic sensibility takes the edge off—so much so that late in the movie, Ben Stiller emerges from a horrific encounter with a fishhook seemingly unscathed. We accept this, because we're in a tonal world that has consistently shown us people bouncing back from serious physical mishaps.

Consistency, you may notice, is a word that keeps cropping up in this discussion. What research yields and sensibility evokes is only believable if it's grounded in recognizable laws of logic that don't get bent or broken.

PLAYING BY THE RULES

Entering a darkened movie theater, you know that you're leaving so-called reality and entering the realm of imagination, but you don't usually check your brain at the door. You bring what you know of real life to bear on what you're about to see. This is why writers speak of *suspension of disbelief* as a basic tenet of credibility building. It's not that you come in ready to believe anything, it's that you're willing to suspend your disbelief to enjoy a specific story—that is, if the writer and his/her team have done their job.

Say you want to fashion a romantic comedy around the device of a flying pig. Now, we know damn well that pigs don't fly. So you have to show us one that does, convincingly, based on research (how big do its wings need to be to support all that fat?) and sensibility (if we're in a world where trees talk, no problem, but if we're in a more realistic world, then the range of people's reactions to this miracle will cue us about whether we're in deadpan black comedy or goofy farce).

The key moment at which an audience is asked to suspend its disbelief is generally dealt with in one time-honored manner: dead-on. If your romantic comedy hero says he can read minds, than your heroine acts as audience surrogate, saying "No way!" As hero convinces heroine that he can, in fact, tell what she is thinking, we (if the scene's execution is deft and amusing) buy into the unbelievable premise along with her. *Tootsie*, you may recall, had two such credibility monitors, in George and Jeff.

Occasionally, your story takes place in a world that's inherently incredible, so your hero/heroine isn't going to be the one who can act as convincing naysayer. What you utilize then is your audience's own real-life experience. Your leading lady steps outside one morning with her coffee, has a brief conversation with her favorite eucalyptus (the tree says it's nursing a cold), then climbs aboard her winged pig (whose neck rig includes a coffee-cup holder). Problem is, the pig won't start; she can't get it off the ground. "Damn, Elma," says our heroine, "How many of those pies did you eat?" By this time, given such reality parallels, your audience hopefully has bought into this make-believe world, since it exhibits enough recognizable, logical human behavior.

The one rule of thumb regarding suspension of disbelief is that there must be rules. Your story has to have well-defined rules and regulations, and once you've set them up, you'd better adhere to them. Hell hath no fury like an audience which recognizes it's been unfairly tricked. If your mind-reading hero reads the mind of a Japanese businessman to overcome some crucial plot obstacle, the alert audience member will cry foul. Since when did our hero learn how to translate Japanese?

A corollary to this is the one-time-only principle. Given skill-ful writing, we'll accept that mind reader. But don't expect us to believe it if he suddenly walks on water in the third act. Your story's suspension-of-disbelief moment usually occurs early on; this willful fantasizing is asked of us only once. If you keep propos-ing leaps of logic after the first successful vault, your audience won't want to go there with you.

When, despite the popularity of its star Sarah Michelle Gellar, 1999's *Simply Irresistible* tanked with barely a ripple, re-view after review cited (along with this American romantic comedy's "borrowings" from Spain's *Like Water for Chocolate*) the basic implausibility of its premise: a magic crab suddenly in-vesting inept restaurateur Gellar with supernatural cooking powers. Yet magic has been a viable catalyst for many a smash success (remember *Big*?), and "angel falls in love with human" proved to be the attractive story hook for the previous year's successful romance, *City of Angels*. Evidently things unreal are not, of themselves, a barrier to audience acceptance.

What's crucial is clarity. The problem with *Simply*'s magic crab was a basic fuzziness about the whole concept. It wasn't clear why Gellar became the lucky recipient of the crab and exactly what this mystical creature's specific powers were. As more and more seemingly unrelated magical events transpired, the only consistency in the device lay in its consistent confusion. The rules of your particular game have to be laid out in no uncertain terms—and as soon as they possibly can be. In matters of credibility, a well-managed setup is a vital factor.

THE CREDIBLE STORY: SETUP AND PAYOFF

We have Chekhov to thank for one of the most famous observations regarding the setup and payoff of a given device. He suggested, regarding the playwriting of his turn-of-the-century era, that if one introduced a gun onstage in the first act, it had better go off by the end of the third. This basic principle is equally important when applied in reverse: if you've got a gun going off in the third act, we'd better have seen it somewhere on the premises in the first.

Screenwriters routinely employ what are known as *plants* in the openings and first acts of their movies. Within the setup of a given story, the writer plants various seeds—be they props (e.g., a gun), bits of dialogue (e.g., "he hasn't seen *her* in years"), or an element of characterization (e.g., Johnny's whistling always precedes his entrance). These seeds are sown to yield full-blown flowers at the back end of the story. Thus, if we see Johnny's gun on the hall side table and know that she-who-he-hasn't-seen-in-years is in Johnny's bed with his best friend, then the unexpected sound of familiar whistling in the hall makes for a particularly resonant payoff.

A well-crafted setup, in addition to taking care of exposition and creating credibility for later developments, has the added attraction of creating a special kind of audience involvement. We're a smart crowd, and we can usually recognize a plant when we see one, even subliminally. So we wait, feeling even smarter, to see how the setup will pay off.

Sometimes setups and payoffs are separated by enough screen time to take the unduly contrived sting out of them. A romantic comedy heroine who takes out an insurance policy on her philandering husband Monday morning and discovers that he's dropped dead Monday afternoon can look suspicious not only to the movie's detective, but to us.

A good setup creates anticipation and simultaneously solves credibility problems. A masterful example of this can be found in Billy Wilder and I. A. L. Diamond's *Some Like It Hot*. The early scenes of this classic romantic/drag comedy introduce us to the jazz musicians Jerry and Joe (Jack Lemmon and Tony Curtis) and credibly paint their Roaring Twenties world. It's one in which appearances are deceiving, as evidenced by a funeral parlor that's actually the cover for a speakeasy, with coffins that arrive bearing, not corpses, but bottles of illegal booze. A raid on the speakeasy puts Joe and Jerry out of work, and they approach the office of a showbiz agent. The agent's secretary, getting even with Joe for his having jilted her, tells the guys there may be a job—but we learn, as Wilder cuts to inside the agent's office, that what the man is desperately looking for is two *women* musicians to replace dropouts from an all-girl band headed to a gig at a resort in Florida. Curtis and Lemmon soon realize they've been set up . . . but within minutes, so are we.

JERRY

Wait a minute, Joe. Let's talk this over.
    (*To Poliakoff*)
Why *couldn't* we do it? Last year, when we
played in that gypsy tearoom, we wore gold
earrings. And you remember when you
booked us with that Hawaiian band?
    (*Pantomiming*)
Grass skirts!

POLIAKOFF

    (*To Joe*)
What's with him—he drinks?

> JOE
>
> No. And he ain't been eating so good,
> either. He's got an empty stomach and it's
> gone to his head.

> JERRY
>
> But, Joe—three weeks in Florida! We could
> borrow some clothes from the girls in the
> chorus—

> JOE
>
> You've flipped your wig!

> JERRY
>
> Now you're talking! We pick up a couple of
> secondhand wigs—a little padding here
> and there—call ourselves Josephine and
> Geraldine—

> JOE
>
> Josephine and Geraldine!
> *(Disgusted)*
> Come on!

He drags Jerry toward the door.

Poliakoff does have a gig for them, it turns out, at a Saint Valentine's dance. This seemingly arbitrary detail is a plant that later yields major significance: retrieving their car from a garage to get to the dance, Jerry and Joe get caught witnessing the infamous Saint Valentine's Day Massacre. Gangsters shoot a couple of holes in Jerry's bass, but they escape, now running for their life, with "every hood in Chicago" looking for them. Jerry's confused when Joe stops to make a phone call:

> JERRY
>
> We got to get out of town. Maybe we ought
> to grow beards.

JOE

We *are* going out of town. But we're going to shave.

JERRY

Shave? At a time like this? Those guys got machine guns—they're going to blast our heads off—and you want to shave?

JOE

Shave our *legs,* stupid.

Joe reaches Poliakoff, speaking in a tremulous soprano as he volunteers for the all-girl Florida gig . . . and we have just leapt past the whopping credibility gap that's the basic foundation hole of *Some Like It Hot.*

Look at where and how the idea of drag is introduced. It's exposition disguised as gag, and it's rooted in character. Joe, the womanizer played by handsome Tony Curtis, runs into one of many women he's played too casually with, and her revenge is to play a joke on him. Jerry's reaction—desperate for work and the bigger worrywart of the two—is to briefly spin off into fantasy, which Joe (the audience-surrogate credibility monitor) ridicules. Nonetheless, it tells us everything we need to know (from wigs to names) about the logistics of drag.

Wilder and Diamond were looking for a strong rationale to justify their characters donning drag when they started work on *Hot.* They found it by making this choice a matter of life and death and by placing their story in the 1920s. Musicians on the run from gangsters gave the idea a credible foundation, and the time period cinched it. Like Viola's mustache in *Shakespeare,* matrons in flapper uniforms passed muster in those days (research), and in a world where deception and disguise ran rampant (sensibility—remember those coffins?), the ruse, as set up here, makes sense.

The writers of *Tootsie* clearly took a good look at *Hot,* because they applied the same principles to their drag movie's device. The very first shots of *Tootsie* show Michael Dorsey applying makeup, and the opening montage establishes this consummate actor as a first-class impersonator. Later, after establishing Sandy's failure to get the soap opera part despite Michael's coaching, an angry Michael confronts his fed-up agent, George. "No one will hire you," George says. Michael's retort—"Oh, yeah?"—cuts directly to a shot of a crowded city street, and upbeat soundtrack music trumpets the debut appearance of an oddly familiar-looking woman: it's Michael Dorsey in full-blown drag, en route to his audition to nab Sandy's part.

Imagine how cumbersome both *Hot* and *Tootsie* might have been without such savvy setups and payoffs. Both movies would've had to stop cold at their most exciting plot juncture to somehow explain their respective characters' seemingly miraculous transformations. And we wouldn't have bought it without all the plants these writers provided. Wilder and Diamond, by the way, prove their genius at such techniques way late at the back end of *Hot*—when the two bullet holes in Jerry's bass prove to be the telltale evidence that enables Joe and Jerry's pursuing gangsters to recognize them.

THE CREDIBLE RELATIONSHIP

These general techniques for sustaining believable stories go hand in hand with the credibility issues we cited in our discussion of characterization. Your protagonists have to be properly set up if we're going to believe in them as individuals. And just as important, *we have to believe that your two leads are an inevitable match.*

Just as a good screenwriter plants expositional material that will set up subsequent events (e.g., if everyone's talking about Sis's wedding in the opening scene, that wedding's going to factor somehow in the climax), a romantic comedy's writer has to provide the necessary plants for both protagonists, early on and within their relationship, that suggest a genuine affinity. We want to think of them as soul mates in the making.

In this regard, *Sleepless in Seattle* pulls one big fuzzy bunny out of its hat. It works a nice, satisfying meant-for-each-other riff the first time Annie hears Sam talking to Dr. Martha on the air, because Annie is able to second-guess many things Sam says and simultaneously speak the same words. In this "meet," their chemical equation is defined: he's missing "magic" and she's looking for the same. Then, later on, alone in her kitchen at night listening to a taped recap of Sam on the radio, Annie takes a knife to an apple and peels most of its skin off in one continuous pass. A few scenes after this one, trying to rekindle memories of Mom to his son Jonah, Sam recalls that "she could peel an apple in one long, curly strip."

Aha! we're meant to respond, that does it: Annie = Mom. Then, when Sam reads Annie's letter to him at Jonah's behest, it turns out that Sam and Annie both think Brooks Robinson was the best third baseman ever. Jonah seizes on this as "a sign," and Sam (note the use of hero as credibility monitor in this suspension of disbelief moment) objects: "*Everyone* thinks Brooks Robinson is the greatest." Further cinching the credibility issue to steer the audience in the right, anticipation-building direction, Sam goes on to show his son that Seattle and Baltimore are on opposite sides of the map: "*That's* a sign," he says.

The plot gets past such insurmountable difficulties by primarily employing Jonah and his girlfriend Jessica to bring about the inevitable Empire State Building climax. It takes magic, signs, fate, and the Hope of a Child to bring off the miraculous meeting, and the story works only because it ends precisely at the moment when Annie and Sam meet. One can envision any number of conversations transpiring in that elevator after the final fade-out ("I hope you're not one of those idiot Democrats," she/he says), which could have brought this star-crossed love to a quick, abortive end.

Sleepless's screenplay is actually a model of disbelief misdirection; it cannily raises so many logical objections to an Annie-and-Sam success that we're manipulated into wanting all the harder for the impossible to happen. But because the movie focuses almost exclusively on the pursuit, it gets away without clearly defining *why* he and she are meant to be. This is, of course, key to this great fantasy's universal charm; it plays into our belief that Somewhere There's a Someone, and that's all there need be to it.

Sleepless is a special, don't-try-this-at-home case. You are probably working with a scenario that requires your star-crossed lovers to actually spend some time face-to-face before your climax. And you'd better come up with something better than a well-peeled apple to make us believe they belong together.

What you can look to, as we discussed in Chapter 4 on character and chemistry, is your respective leads' inner lives. And how you get such necessary information about them onto the screen follows the same credibility precepts outlined here. You create rules for your protagonists' personalities that can be set up and paid off with a minimum of contrivance.

Generally, a character's behavior is the setup in that it tells us what we need to know about his/her inner conflict. A guy who's emotionally cut off stays in character at crucial junctures, as, say, Jerry Maguire does. Dorothy—a giver who keeps on giving emotionally until she truly feels rejected—dovetails nicely with Jerry. We see that she lacks the arrogant self-confidence he has in spades. We understand why she admires and loves him, and we understand why he needs her (he's got to free those cutoff emotions). At the same time, in their shared interests, dialogue, and sexual chemistry, we see that they're sympatico. The sum total of your leads' inner/outer chemical equation *is* the payoff in "coupling credibility."

What you want to avoid is a clunky, on-the-nose payoff that threatens believability. The revelation of a character's backstory late in the movie can be a dicey proposition: "My mom never loved me," he admits. "And I didn't have a father!" she cries, falling into his arms. David's (Richard Gere's) confessional bath-tub scene late in *Pretty Woman* is the good version of this ploy, since its execution is nimbly light-fingered. The rueful exec pokes fun at his own therapy (he learned he was "*angry, very angry*" at his father), and the knowing, sympathetic prostitute promises him more of her kind of therapy . . . while we know from her earlier bedtime confessional scene that she's basically a regular gal gone down a wrong path, more due to poverty than emotional scarring. Not much more need be said on-screen about how these two can help each other.

In romantic comedies, the idea of rules is especially key in creating viable story resolutions. Too often, a happy ending is too easily earned by having either or both characters abandon their supposedly vital priorities. If a woman who absolutely cannot trust a man who cheats on her forgives our hero for cheating under special circumstances, she may lose credibility, and we won't be satisfied by their walking off into the sunset together. Good romantic comedy characters are not so transformed by love that they're no longer recognizable; their growth is credible in its limitations. David in *Pretty Woman* doesn't quit his job under Vivian's influence; instead, he decides not to destroy but to help elderly exec Ralph Bellamy. He doesn't turn into a supersensitive goofball—but he does overcome his fear of heights (setup) long enough to ascend Vivian's fire escape and claim her (payoff) in the climax.

Balancing the incredible (true love) with what's credible is our genre's high-wire act. Apply these commonsense principles to both your character and plot development as you go. Credibility is the foundation of your dream house.

SUMMARY

A romantic comedy's world needs to be plausible. To establish credibility, a writer uses research to come up with the valuable facts that can suggest viable plot developments and provide telling details that will make characters and situations believable. Making a tonal choice about the material is another way to create a plausible world; a consistent sensibility grounds a story's characters in a specific reality, be it slapstick or sophisticated.

Credibility is built by setting up rules and adhering to them. Audiences will suspend their disbelief, initially, if an on-screen character acts as their surrogate in protesting the outlandishness of an idea and is then convinced to accept it. If the movie's world is fantastical, then its characters play on our real-life experience by investing the unreal with enough recognizable human behavior to make it tenable. But once you make your rules, you can't break them. An audience asked to suspend disbelief again and again won't stay with your story.

Screenplays set up their contrivances with *plants*—bits of dialogue, exposition, and so on that both seed future developments and create audience anticipation. Romantic comedies are particularly dependent on strong setups and payoffs to establish "coupling credibility"; we must believe that the leads belong together. Generally, their respective behavior sets up expectations that are paid off when the budding soul mates interact. But make sure your hero and heroine are not so transformed by love that they're no longer true to character.

Exercise: Starting-the-Draft Checklist

If you're presently getting into the first draft of your romantic comedy, you should be able to answer the following series of questions.

1. *Story concept*
   Can you pitch your movie in a sentence?
   Are there any other romantic comedies you can compare it to? What makes it different from them?

What subgenre or cross-genre is the movie in?

What's the hook of the story—the thing that will make it stand out from the romantic comedy crowd?

2. *Character*

What will the audience love about the female lead?

What does she want?

Which obstacles stand in her way?

What is her inner conflict?

What will the audience love about the male lead?

What does he want?

Which obstacles stand in his way?

What is his inner conflict?

Why do these two fall in love?

What does the relationship signify for her? For him?

What do they each stand to lose if the relationship doesn't last?

If there are significant supporting characters, what are their specific functions? In what way do they mirror the protagonists?

3. *Plot and structure*

Can you describe your story in three sentences that represent your three acts?

Describe each of your seven beats (setup, catalyst, first-act break, midpoint, second-act break, climax, resolution), using a single sentence for each.

Have you investigated some alternative developments and/or endings? Why does this story absolutely have to end the way it presently does?

4. *Theme*

Can you explain how your story—or some aspect of it—originated in your personal experience?

Can you state the axiom or question that the story explores?

(continued)

Exercise: Starting-the-Draft Checklist   *(continued)*

   Does the growth of your central character, or the lesson
      he/she learns, reflect this theme?
   Does the ending embody it?
   Do the subplots speak to theme?
   What does the coupling of your main characters signify?

5. *World and credibility*
   What's the world of your story?
   Have you defined its tone or sensibility?
   Have you defined the rules of situation, character, and
      event? Have you been consistently true to these
      rules?
   Do all your setups have payoffs, and vice versa?
   Why do we believe these two people have to end up to-
      gether (or apart)?

PART THREE

The Finer Points

CHAPTER EIGHT

The Art of Funny

INTERVIEWER:
Some of your comedies actually get pretty
grim at times . . . *Bringing Up Baby*, in its
later scenes . . . is lit almost like a tragedy.

HOWARD HAWKS:
Well, it was pretty sad for Cary Grant going
around on his hands and knees looking for
a bone.

S ome say comedy can't be taught. But after nearly a century's
worth of cinematic humor, there's certainly enough material
on hand to be analyzed and to identify guiding principles—
particularly in our own, form-repetitive genre. As the sports an-
nouncers say, "Let's go to the videotape."

The opening of *Bringing Up Baby* sends Professor David
Huxley, a paleantologist, onto a golf course to meet Mr. Peabody,
the attorney of a potential museum donor—only to be distracted
from his business agenda when the mischievous socialite Susan
Vance plays David's golf ball. Susan so confuses and distracts
David that he loses Peabody. Later, when David comes to rejoin
Peabody at a fancy restaurant, he's justifiably unnerved to run
into Susan again; within minutes, Susan has wreaked havoc, caus-
ing David to fall on his own top hat and to be wrongfully accused
of purse snatching. David flees. But informed by a psychiatrist
that "the love impulse in man frequently expresses itself in terms

of conflict," Susan now thinks David's interested in her, and, intrigued, she refuses to let him get away.

As he attempts an escape down a staircase, she grabs hold of his tails—ripping the jacket right up his back. David turns to look at her. "Oh," she says, "you've torn your coat." A maddened David now backs Susan, who's babbling excuses, up the stairs. "Will you do something for me?" he asks. "A needle?" she suggests. No, David explains, he wants to play a game: he'll put his hand over his eyes, he'll count to ten, "and when I take my hand down, you will be gone." Miffed, Susan at last turns on her heels and stalks off—but the hem of her glamorously trailing evening gown is caught under his foot, and its rear panel is ripped off, exposing her legs and underwear.

Susan, unaware of this, airily tells David off as he comes after her, not giving him a chance to explain what's happened. Thus she's startled and incredulous as, desperately trying to spare her embarrassment, he keeps clomping his top hat over her rear end every time she nearly exposes herself to the packed dining room. "You've made a perfect spectacle of yourself," she declares indignantly, and finally, David gives up. As Susan walks away, she reaches behind for her nonexistent train—and suddenly grasping her predicament, backs up hastily to a nearby pillar, tremulously demanding that David do something.

David gets behind her. "Get closer!" she cries. "I can't get any closer," he says. "Now, are you ready? Be calm. Left foot first . . ." And now, embracing Susan round the waist, a flustered David in ripped tails starts walking her quickly forward through the crowded restaurant. Their jerky lockstepped movement, with him crammed tightly against her, makes them look like a surreal burlesque windup toy, their routine rendered all the more idiotic by how fast they're going and by David having jammed his dilapidated top hat back on his head. It elicits laughter from the other patrons and bewilderment from the just-arrived Mr. Peabody. As the obscenely mechanical unit marches past him, David calls, "I'll be with you in a minute!" before disappearing through a revolving door.

When I show a clip of this scene to students, they invariably laugh. When asked, why is this funny?, some cite the performances. And, sure, both Kate Hepburn's dizzy delivery as Susan and Cary Grant's exasperated David add a lot to our enjoyment. Others hone in on the walk itself, which is certainly comical. But the laughs start much earlier. How come?

THE REVERSAL PRINCIPLE

The scene takes place in a swank eatery that caters to fashionable clientele. Tuxedoed Grant and evening-gowned Hepburn are part of a moneyed milieu where mature adults evince sophistication, grace, and urbanity. What goes wrong with this picture is everything, obviously, but let's identify the unifying throughline. Do Grant and Hepburn act their ages? Is their behavior sophisticated? Are their movements graceful? Is their exposed underwear and mimed parody of walking copulation what we expect to see in civilized society?

No way. The dynamics of this scene stem from both the people and the place becoming the opposite of what they're supposed to be. Adult Grant and Hepburn act like children. Their sophisticated conversation gives way to silly slapstick. Though they enter as flesh-and-blood humans, they exit like nuts-and-bolts robots. And though a high-toned urban nightspot is their arena, they reduce it to a sort of vaudeville playpen. Every premise in the situation has been reversed.

The principle of *reversal* is the crux of most comedic encounters. The element of surprise that a reversal supplies is what enlivens a joke (e.g., "Last night I shot an elephant in my pajamas. How he got into my pajamas, I'll never know"). The screwball comedy (and the romantic comedy that grew out of it) is founded on a reversal: the woman as romantic aggressor. So it's not surprising to find that the predominant humor in such movies is based on the same principle. Our scene from *Bringing Up Baby* is primarily funny because of its interlocking reversals:

1. *Adults become children.*

2. *Sophistication turns to silliness.*

3. *Humans become mechanical.*

4. *Urban goes wild.*

These four reversals are central to our genre. You'll find them from the 1930s on into contemporary romantic comedies. Still operative as well is the reversal at the genre's foundation:

5. *Feminine becomes masculine (and vice versa).*

Baby is replete with riffs on this gender reversal, including a scene in which Cary Grant is forced to run around in a woman's frilly bathrobe and another where Katharine Hepburn lights up a stogie, impersonating a tough-talking gangster.

Comedic reversals of a subtler stripe are embedded in the fabric of our nightclub scene from *Baby,* from its basic structure ("he tries to get away from her" becomes "she tries to get away from him"), on through its dialogue (the punch line of David's inviting Susan to play a game with him is that he doesn't want to play with her at all), right down to its props (the pillar against which Hepburn at first nonchalantly leans later becomes her desperately sought refuge).

Although variations on such reversals crop up in all kinds of comedies, the scene from *Baby* illustrates a secondary principle that's even more particular to the romantic comedy. Why do you suppose the creative team behind *Baby* chose to enact their romantic leads' routine in the midst of a crowded restaurant? For the same reason Crystal, Ryan, Reiner, and Ephron set their justly famous Sally-fakes-an-orgasm scene in the middle of a bustling delicatessen—yet another reversal:

6. *Private matters become public.*

On its primary level, a romantic comedy is a comedy about mating. Its core joke—an inescapable, cosmic one—is that in the sphere of romantic relationships, human nature inevitably yields to animal instinct. So it stands to reason that romantic comedies are rife with situations where the laughs come from exposure: sexual matters and secrets of the body are held up to public ridicule. Try to pretend you're above all that, the romantic comedy says, and you'll find out how much you're not.

Let's turn to another principle method of provoking laughter—one that is, in a sense, a conceptual reversal.

BE SERIOUS

Surely you've had the pleasure of telling a friend about a harrowing, horrible experience you had—and getting a good laugh out of it. As time passes, our new perspective on what was once terrible transforms it into something laughable. Time = distance. This is what's meant by the old maxim, "Comedy is tragedy plus time." A corollary to this idea is best expressed by a formula attributed to Mel Brooks. What the master comedian supposedly said was, "You fall down a flight of stairs. That's comedy. I get a hangnail— that's tragedy."

In other words, if a terrible event happens to us, the suffering is all too real, but if it happens to someone else, our psychic removal from it engenders humor. Comedy can be cruel, and never so cruel as when it comes to this basic truism. The distance between one person's personal experience and another's point of view is often what makes an audience laugh instead of weep. But how do you apply this to your work in progress? Simply put, one of the vital secrets to being funny is to make sure your characters are as serious as they can be.

Which is funnier: a clown who winks and giggles as he hits a banana peel and falls on his butt—or a stuffed-shirt executive, his suit and demeanor immaculately dignified, slipping on the same peel? Obviously the businessman gets the bigger laugh, because he's taking himself so very seriously. Similarly, the characters in your piece have to be wholly invested in who they are and what they're trying to accomplish to maximize the humor that develops when their identities are made to appear ridiculous and their goals become infernally unachievable.

Hawks was fond of telling interviewers that when Kate Hepburn began shooting *Baby,* she evidently thought that "acting funny"—hamming her scenes up with cute mannerisms and mugging—was the way to go, until the director and her costar showed her otherwise. As reported in Todd McCarthy's bio, *Howard Hawks,* she later said: "Cary Grant taught me that the more depressed I looked when I went into a pratfall, the more the audience would laugh." In this same regard, Hawks's quote about how sad Grant was, down on all fours digging up a bone, is apropos. Generally, *the characters in your comedy are not in on the joke.*

Think of Buster Keaton's ever stoic deadpan in the face of direst calamity. Or consider Bill Murray caught in his neverending *Groundhog Day;* you may laugh, but he bears the tortured visage of a man who's living a nightmare. Aspiring comedy writers too often think that their characters have to act funny—that is, come out with quips and comic bits. On the contrary, their intentions need to be very serious. *Funny* is a leading lady who says something in deadly earnest during a situation that makes the line wildly inappropriate.

Although a character who's witty can often be an asset to a romantic comedy, more often than not, humor comes out of credible characters behaving believably in a given situation. We then take them as seriously as they take themselves, while we (from our comfortable distance) are afforded the luxury of laughing at the fix they're in. The Hugh Grant character in *Four Weddings* often says funny things, and his ability to poke fun at himself makes him all the more endearing, but his remarks usually come out of extreme embarrassment. His famous what-have-I-gotten-myself-into monologue, where he declares his love to the Andie MacDowell character by quoting the Partridge Family, is a case in point. What makes the moment funny is his pained self-awareness of how ridiculous he sounds—while his intentions are as serious as a marriage proposal.

The great comedy writer Neil Simon resents being typecast as a writer of one-liners; he's actually famous for *cutting* jokes that he feels take away from the truth of a character's emotional response. Take your characters' dilemmas seriously, and make sure they do, too. Your biggest laughs may come out of their most serious, deeply felt moments.

MAKE THEM HURT

With this in mind, comedy writers love to push the envelope. When screenwriter-director Audrey Wells (*The Truth About Cats and Dogs*, *Guinevere*) spoke to my class a few years ago, she claimed that nothing is funnier than misery. "Steep your characters in pain—make them miserable," she said, and added, "Then after they've really suffered, make them happy."

Words to live by for a romantic comedy writer, sadistic as they may sound. Because although audiences are distanced enough to find a character's serious discomfort amusing, they also identify with it. We're sympathetic to someone in pain because we've experienced such pain ourselves. In a sense, sharing the pain is one of the functions of comedy.

For this reason, when it comes to getting your characters in trouble, practically no trouble is too awful. The nice thing about comedy, as opposed to tragedy, is that some sort of happy ending is assured. Thus, even if blood gets spilled, generally the results won't be fatal. Though you don't want your protagonists to be rubberized, cartoon-invincible Wiley Coyotes, you can (and should) make them suffer fates worse than death, because ultimately they will bounce back. And the audience will groan and laugh in sympathetic recognition because that's what they expect. All this anguish will be rewarded.

So don't shy away from the truly excruciating. Ben Stiller's zipper accident in *There's Something About Mary* is one obvious example. Anyone who's ever caught a little skin in a zipper could relate. The huge laughs elicited from Ben's catching *that* skin came out of the truly awful intensity of his pain.

There's another reason that pushing the pain envelope makes sense for a writer: torture is effective. Sadly, sometimes real pain is the only thing that will elicit honesty. And writers, like not-so-benevolent dictators, like to string their characters up by their thumbs—because, in between crying for mercy, that's when they're most likely to tell the truth. Cornered and suffering, your characters will come out with their most outrageous statements—outrageous because they're honest.

Pain + truth = funny

When we laugh at Grant and Hepburn's humiliation in *Bringing Up Baby*, we're laughing at our own worst fears coming true. What's also significant about this principle, from a screenwriter's point of view, is how such an embarrassment affects your protagonists. *Bringing Up Baby*'s demented two-step exit through a revolving door is immediately followed by one of the few instances when this madcap movie sits still (as Grant later says to Hepburn, "In moments of quiet I'm strangely drawn to you, but there haven't been any quiet moments"). Hawks cuts to a shot of surprising domestic tranquility: Hepburn sewing up Grant's ripped tuxedo jacket while he sits beside her, almost calmly explaining his Peabody predicament. The subtext of this juxtaposition is that no matter how excruciating their public exposure may have been, the experience has somehow brought them a little closer together.

This special kind of earned intimacy is typical of romantic comedy relationships. Both man and woman have been exposed. But instead of alienating them, being in this nightmare together puts them on equal footing and even creates a tacit bond: they're the special ones who've shared a little hell and lived to tell about it. Film historian Molly Haskell has a great quote about the dynamic of such couples: "From their moment of humiliation—their metaphorical nudity—they work their way back to salvation."

This idea of mutual humiliation as a source of humor is a mainstay of the kind of comedy we're writing.

DEFINE YOUR TONE

In Chapter 7, we saw how making a tonal choice—having a guiding sensibility that permeates the world of your romantic comedy—was an asset in establishing credibility. In addition, just as a familiarity with our genre's subgenres and cross-genres can be helpful in working out your plot and characterizations, a familiarity with comedy forms can help you focus and sharpen the humor in your romantic comedy.

Jerry Lewis's pratfall will seem completely out of place in Noel Coward's drawing room. So, as you develop your story, try to get a feel for the specific tonal world it wants to live in. Classifications for comedy forms are pretty loose, since each form tends to mix it up a bit, but generally, comedies fall into one or more of the following categories: *farce, satire, parody, black comedy, sophisticated,* and *comedy drama.*

Farce: From the finely tuned construction of *What's Up Doc?* to the gross-out antics of *There's Something About Mary,* the foundation of farce is physical humor. But while slapstick is its distinguishing characteristic, what powers farce is blatant improbability. Farces shove outrageous contrivances in our faces and revel in their ridiculous complications (e.g., French bedroom comedy, with its cast popping in and out of closets, or commedia dell'arte's wild disguises and deceptions). Often peopled with broad-stroked caricatures who exist as disposable figures of fun, the best farces wreak their havoc with fully dimensional humans.

Satire: Where farce makes fun of anything within range, satire skewers a specific milieu or belief system. Satire delights in exposing bad behavior, excoriating the hypocrisies, vices, and follies of its targets, from showbiz (*Bowfinger*) to the afterlife (*Defending Your Life*). Satire's primary weapons are irony, sarcasm, and biting wit of a more verbal or conceptual variety. Its tone tends to be arch, knowing, and cynical.

Parody: A close kin to satire, the parody form is even more specific. Parodies are satirical *imitations* of a given entertainment or subject. Thus, *Romancing the Stone* takes affectionate aim at the romance novel, just as the *Austin Powers* movies send up James Bond. Often, certain characters in comedies are parodies of famous people or amalgams of same; for example, *Austin*'s Dr. Evil is apparently part parody of producer Lorne Michaels.

Black comedy: So named because it takes on ostensibly serious, grim, or taboo subject matter and treats it comedically (e.g., *Dr. Strangelove* making a joke out of nuclear holocaust), this form utilizes a deadpan, arch-ironic sensibility in which people enact or endorse the most hideous behavior without guilt or self-awareness. Due to its mean-spirited flavor, this category is not natural to romantic comedy. A classic of this kind is *A New Leaf*, in which a man who keeps trying to kill his mate to inherit her money falls in love with her in the end. Another example is *The Graduate*.

Sophisticated: As the pie-in-the-face routine is to farce, the stinging comeback is to sophisticated comedy. Verbal wit is the potent artillery of this form, which often inhabits a highfalutin social milieu where such rarefied conversation can be credibly sustained. Such repartee is what distinguished early Lubitsch (*Trouble in Paradise*), but in our current to-hell-in-a-handbasket linguistic climate, it's tough to bring off in contemporary settings (Eric Rohmer's Gallic milieu aside), which is why its province is more often period (e.g., *Sense and Sensibility*).

Comedy Drama: Maybe the trickiest yet timeliest form, with tragicomedic modern life making laughter and tears too easily interchangable, this hybrid approach seems to be striking a resonant chord with the mainstream. Favoring realistic characters in a realistic world, with inner issues getting a full frontal workout, this form wears its emotions on its sleeve. The challenge of managing the shift from one mode to the other within one story has been successfully met by Woody Allen (*Crimes and Misdemeanors*) and James Brooks (*As Good as It Gets*).

Obviously, every form employs techniques from other forms. *Pillow Talk*, though a farce, is also verbally acute (sophisticated). There are elements of parody in a satire like *The American President* (the Michael J. Fox character is clearly George Stephanopoulos). And *The Truth About Cats and Dogs* would have to be identified as sophisticated, or "clever farce."

But the essential point to bear in mind while crafting your romantic comedy is that once you've started down a particular tonal path, there is no turning back. *A given tone sets up specific expectations,* so an audience will be alienated if those expectations aren't fulfilled. Occasionally, a critic may knock a movie for "descending into farce." This indicates that the movie didn't start off in obviously farcical mode. It's similarly difficult to turn from flat-out farce to tragedy.

Set us up properly, define your tonal rules, and we'll follow you without protests. Thus *Shakespeare in Love,* as we've noted, establishes a tone that encompasses both farce and speedy verbal wit in its opening minutes; we quickly know what kind of a movie we're in. If your comedy drama is going to routinely switch gears, have it do so within the first ten minutes. A moment's slapstick amid the sophisticated humor of your opening scene will prepare us for that major food fight in the third act.

THE COMEDIC SET PIECE

Speaking of food fights, you might want to have one.

Every action-genre movie has a major scene or sequence that's essentially a big fight, utilizing the bigger toys and the biggest explosions. Every thriller has its protagonist-in-a-nail-biting-near-death-encounter-with-the-lethal-antagonist beat. A musical has musical numbers. So it shouldn't surprise you that in addition to some scene that delivers full-blown romance, a romantic comedy is generally expected to have at least one scene or sequence that's laugh-out-loud funny.

There's no rule of thumb about the when and where of such set pieces. *Breakfast at Tiffany's* swinging soiree (complete with hat set on fire and doused by highball) occurs roughly toward the middle. Asta the terrier's mirthful custody battle in court comes very near the beginning of *The Awful Truth*. You should be able to find at least one opportunity in the context of your conflicts and complications to open up the script a little and let big laughter in.

The thing to be avoided is a comedy routine that has nothing to do with the central characters, plot, or theme. Although a set piece sets itself apart by virtue of its virtuoso effect (sustaining laughter by building from small jokes to memorably large ones), it should arise organically from the fabric of your larger story. Thus, when *Notting Hill's* William, mistaken for a journalist, endures the humiliating absurdities of a silly movie's press junket, this set piece arises from an important plot beat (Anna invites him to see her at her hotel), and is in fact topped by a plot beat climax: just as the exhausted William tries to make an exit from this hellish-hype labyrinth, he's called into one more room . . . where Anna awaits.

Sometimes a formal device (e.g., jump-cutting through time to create a set-apart montage as the latter *Hill* sequence does) helps organize and motor a set piece. *Some Like It Hot* features a classic set piece that achieves its momentum and major laughs by crosscutting. As Joe (Tony Curtis) uses a vintage reversal technique to seduce Sugar (Marilyn Monroe) on a borrowed yacht, pretending that kisses have never had any effect on him, we cut away to the ballroom where the yacht's owner Osgood (Joe E. Brown) is forcing an alarmed Jerry-as-Daphne (Jack Lemmon) to dance. Each scene gets progressively steamier, with "Daphne" and Osgood's tango acting as satiric counterpoint to Joe and Sugar's foreplay. Finally, Joe's successful reversal (Sugar's done all the se-ducing) is topped by Jerry/Daphne's reversal: he's gotten totally into the dance and is sweeping the floor with Osgood.

In shaping a set piece, an approach like *Hot*'s may prove use-ful, combining two or more scenes for contrasting comedic effect. But whatever your ultimate angle, consciously comb your story for potential set-piece situations. Such a sequence, when properly built, will enliven your romantic comedy and give your audience the belly-laugh release they desire.

THREES AND TOPPERS

Comedy writers are often the first to admit that their craft is more instinctual than scientific. There is no definitive Book of Rules for gags (and believe me, I've looked). But when it comes to the specifics of engineering a joke, principles we've been applying all along continue to be relevant.

A good setup leads to a better payoff. As Steve Martin noted in one interview, paraphrasing director Frank Oz, if you want to get a laugh by having a ladder fall on a character, then you have to credibly establish that ladder's presence in the scene, along with its physical relation to the character and justifiable reasons for ladder and character to collide.

To study physical humor, steal from the best: hours spent with Keaton and Chaplin can be the most fun schooling imaginable. Two recognizable structural patterns you may pick up on are *the principle of three* and *the topper*.

Threes: Half the jokes that are longer than one-liners operate on this principle. A kangaroo walks into a bar and orders a drink; he does it again; on his third visit, the punch line is delivered. Why? Simple. The first instance is random (man pokes baby in stomach, baby giggles). It's only part of a setup. The second time establishes a pattern (man pokes baby in stomach again, again the baby giggles). Now we're truly set up, with expectations in place. The third time is the payoff (man pokes baby in stomach, baby spits food in man's face). (1) No pattern is evident; (2) sequence is established; (3) a twist occurs.

Comedic movie sequences are often built on interlocking versions of this structure. The climax of *What's Up Doc?* is a masterpiece of "threes" in action. There are three vehicles involved in the chase that makes up Bogdanovich's virtuoso set piece, and you'll notice (if you can stop laughing) that it's the chain reaction of three-patterned payoffs (the third time a parked van is hit, the third time the glass-pane carriers seem to escape disaster) that yields sustained hilarity.

Toppers: On second thought, the preceding man-and-baby gag is missing something. What would make the gag's payoff even funnier? Sure, baby spits food in man's face, but add a beat for the man's reaction, and . . . baby giggles again. That's what's known as a *topper* (or *button,* or *capper,* or *sting*); it's a twist added to a gag's payoff to earn an additional laugh. It works for three-structured jokes, but it's effective for single-stroke or one-two punch gags, too.

In *Tootsie,* Michael-as-Dorothy hears from Julie that she wishes, just once, a guy would be honest enough to say, "I could lay a big line on you, we could do a lot of role playing, but the simple truth is, I find you very interesting and I'd really like to make love with you." Later at a party, Michael gets a chance to meet Julie as himself, so he attempts seduction by quoting her verbatim. And Julie throws a drink in his face. Funny! But what gets the bigger laugh is Michael's reaction. Humiliated and dripping, he backs away from Julie and uses the back of an unsuspecting guest's suit jacket to mop off his face.

Leave no good gag untopped. The added surprise of Michael's anarchic ingenuity rebounds off the first gag's energy, building on one laugh to engender another. Be alive to the comedic possibilities surrounding your jokes; you may have seeded an added, unexpected payoff. An audience loves it when they've had one good laugh only to be rewarded with another. The line everyone remembers from *When Harry's* orgasm-in-the-deli scene is "I'll have what she's having." That's the topper.

To examine all of the proceeding "art of funny" precepts in action, let's take a stroll through a classic that's generally considered the acme of romantic comedy. (Note: In the synopsis that follows, numbers in brackets refer to the seven major plot beats.)

· ·

CASE STUDY

The Lady Eve

Written and directed by: Preston Sturges
Leads: Henry Fonda and Barbara Stanwyck
Released by Paramount Pictures in 1941 (94 min.)

Log line: A female con artist sets out to bilk a beer tycoon, but falls in love with him instead; when he rejects her because she's a crook, she wreaks a fitting revenge.

Synopsis

Scholarly naturalist Charles Pike (Henry Fonda), wealthy son of the Pikes Ale Pikes, and his companion Muggsy (William Demarest) leave a tropical expedition and boat for civilization, a boxed snake in tow. On the steamship that stops to pick them up, cool customer Jean (Barbara Stanwyck) and her monocled dad, Col. Harrington (Charles Coburn), a pair of con artists, size up innocent Charles as their next mark. [1] That night in the dining room, Jean watches every woman on board make an unsuccessful play for Charles, then snags him herself by tripping him and guilting him into accompanying her back to her cabin to repair her broken heel. [2] Jean's perfumed wiles captivate Charles, while she finds his earnest honesty compelling. After the Colonel lets Charles win some money from him at cards (setting him up for a big payback), suspicious, protective Muggsy tries to find out who Jean really is. Charles is falling for Jean hard, according to plan, but what disrupts the usual sting is that Jean has fallen for him, and she now wants to be the good girl Charles thinks she is. [3]

Though Dad's determined to win back his money and more, rebellious Jean vows to outplay him. Despite Jean's best efforts in outcheating the Colonel, he manages in her brief absence to fleece Charles out of $3,000. Jean insists that Charles's check be ripped up, and the Colonel obliges (just having some fun with his future son-in-law). But Muggsy has obtained photos of Jean and her dad from the ship's purser, identifying them as pro gamblers. Charles, refusing to believe Jean's protests that she really loves him, breaks up with her. Jean, devastated, finds small consolation upon learning that the Colonel palmed Charles's check; she decides to get even in a more diabolical way. [4] Disguised only by a British accent, Jean poses as the Countess Eve. When she's introduced into the Pikes's social circle by a fellow con man, she overcomes a flabbergasted Charles's initial perplexity (while Muggsy insists, "It's the same dame!") and wins his heart a second time. The bamboozled, love-stricken Charles proposes. [5]

On their honeymoon night, the Lady Eve confesses that despite her pedigree, she's no virgin. Her long line of lovers so appalls Charles that he abandons her, leaving Jean victorious . . . but oddly unhappy. [6] Through lawyers, Charles refuses Eve's request that he see her in person in lieu of an expensive divorce and announces he's going overseas. He boards a steamer, where he's overjoyed to run into Jean-as-Jean again. Having learned his lesson ("the best ones aren't as good as you think they are, and the bad ones aren't as bad") he gratefully embraces her, unaware that it's really their third time around. [7]

. . . .

Always on the critics' short list of auteur Sturges's finest films, *The Lady Eve* is a genre paradigm. Its combination of sophisticated verbal humor and slapstick vaudeville vulgarity, the way its glamorous production and glossy sheen of directorial irony play against the genuine heart beneath its surface, and the enduring attraction of its pitch-perfect performances all reward many a re-viewing. So what makes its laughs endure?

Be Serious   Talk about a straight man—Hank Fonda in *Eve* is about as earnest and straight (and gullible) as they come. Charles Pike truly never is in on the joke, whether it's while father and daughter cardsharps are batting eight aces around under his nose or when he's headed to the altar with a totally bogus Brit. In fact, a lot of our enjoyment of the story stems from watching this man (who takes himself and appearances too seriously) get his come-uppance. Charles enters the picture as an innocent rube of the absentminded-professor variety, but in his immediate rejection of Jean, he reveals a somewhat priggish, small-minded side. Sensing his innate decency, we root for his ultimate transformation into a matured, redeemed good guy. But we take malicious delight in his continual humiliation because of his anything-but-comedic sensi-bility—he's just asking for it.

And Jean, in giving it to him, turns out to be just as serious in her emotionality. Although she comes on as both jaded and play-ful, with a wisecracking veneer of who-cares cool, in the presence of Charles's gee-whiz innocence Jean reveals a softhearted core. Charles allows her to indulge her own dreams of true romance, which is why, when she's abruptly denied them, her devastation goes so deep. Her furious intent on revenge is what powers the movie's midpoint ("I need him like the ax needs the turkey"). Though Eve can't help an occasional giggle at Charles's expense, she's so this-time-it's-personal serious that her victory over Charles leaves her, as Sturges's narrative notes, "neither laughing nor triumphant."

Thus both leads have more depth to them than their nearly caricaturish setups (snakelike predator and her out-of-it prey) ini-tially imply. All the film's characters exhibit the same sobriety of purpose. The Colonel wants his money. The put-upon Mr. Pike wants his breakfast. Fun is the last thing on anyone's mind, down to the last butler and footman. That's largely what makes their various predicaments so funny.

Make Them Hurt   Pre–cute meet, as Charles climbs aboard the steamer from his skiff, Jean, watching from a few decks above, drops her half-eaten apple on his head. This bonk on the noggin is merely a love-tap prelude to Charles's later hardships. When Jean trips him in the dining room, it's the first in a series of falls. There's a total of four more (including his penultimate dive into the mud), plus two spills and three bad bumps in the movie's second half alone. Add the subtler but no less agonizing torture Charles endures when, after he's been up the Amazon for a year, Jean cuddles up to him in her stateroom, arousing him to his gentlemanly brink and then shooing him out the door. Even this pales next to the horror he lives through on his wedding night, as Eve catalogs the virtual battalion of lovers who've been with her before.

We may be a little disturbed, at first, by Stanwyck's wicked persecution of Fonda, but by the middle of the movie, when Charles reveals his jerkishness, we identify with her completely and revel in the revenge. This is because Jean's wound—psychic, not physical—is palpable in that midpoint. Each of Charles's sprawling indignities is subsequently made doubly amusing; we're free to laugh at him, not just because he's making a fool of himself, but also because we've felt her pain.

Define Your Tone   Given its penchant for both knockabout physical humor and virtuosic verbal wit, *Eve* might seem to risk tonal schizophrenia. Yet there's a consistency to the tone that anchors even its wildest comedic riffs. It stems from Sturges's own sensibility. His point of view—embodied primarily by Stanwyck's character but also by every other character in the film's universe except the steadfastly straight Fonda—is *ironic*.

A dispassionate remove permeates every scene, where no one says exactly what they mean, creating a comedic edge and tension, since the slick, sharp surface is constantly at odds with the deeper emotions underneath. The dialogue crackles with arch and sardonic commentary, as in this exchange between the leads: "Snakes are my life, in a way," says Charles, and Jean replies, straight-faced, "What a life." The last exchange between hero and heroine caps this tone perfectly, as Charles, reunited with Jean, protests that he shouldn't be in her cabin, "because I'm married." "But so am I, darling," Jean replies. "So am I. . . ."

Irony permeates the major plot twists. It's ironic that Charles won't believe Jean at the moment she's more honest than she's ever been—ironic that in her moment of supposed triumph, having gotten even with Charles, Jean is totally forlorn. There are elements of farce throughout (the fake Lady Eve contrivance), satire (Jean's impersonation skewers the pretensions of the upper class), and parody (swindler Sir Arthur's absurd explanation of twin sister Jean's existence is a parody of melodramatic potboiler romances). But an ironic tone is what creates the film's comedic consistency. It's even evident on the sound track, as Sturges has Wagner's love-death theme from *Tristan and Isolde* play during Charles's wedding-night nightmare.

Comedic Set Pieces   *Eve* is rife with memorable sequences. The cute meet is a tour de force for Jean, as she sits at a table with her dad and, holding up a compact mirror, observes a parade of women trying to attract Charles's attention while he sits at a table behind her trying to read a book. The specificity in Jean's caustic running monologue, a delicious litany of foolish female behavior, gives the set piece its kick, as in Jean's frisky imagining of one female pursuer's totally bogus come-on: "Why, for heaven's sake, aren't you Fuzzy Oathammer I went to manual training school with in Louisville?"

Comedy set pieces don't get much better than the crucial card game played by Charles, Jean, and the Colonel. A silent battle of wits between two expert cheaters unfolds, while brittle conversation provides ironic counterpoint. Each time Dad pulls a fast one, his daughter outtricks him, and all the while Charles is blithely unaware that anything untoward is going on.

The later dinner-party sequence is a definitive set piece, as Muggsy, hell-bent on getting a good look at this countess, grabs a tray from an indignant butler to maneuver his way closer to her. It ends, naturally, in all the roast beef and gravy pouring over Charles's shirt. Each of these set pieces, expertly constructed around single settings, employ physical and verbal gags to build toward explosive payoffs.

Threes and Toppers   *Eve* has its share of threes. Mr. Pike, annoyed that no one's served him breakfast, rings his service bell, rings it more furiously the second time, and the third time, improvises a set of clanging cymbals out of the silver serving dishes.

Charles goes through three suits on the night of the dinner party. Suspicious of Eve, he takes a face-first stumble over a couch and a pratfall in the hall, then has to change his clothes; the serving platter fiasco in the dining room, caused by Muggsy's suspicions, requires another change; finally, when Charles stops being suspicious (due to Sir Alfred's bogus twin-sister story) and stoops to help Eve free her dress from a chair leg, he straightens up right into a tray held by a servant and spills a full coffee service over his nice white (and last) suit. The intensity of each humiliation is what tweaks the mounting hilarity: Charles lands with his face in an hors d'oeuvre dip, is nearly suffocated by the wall-hanging he brings down in fall number two, is garnished with roast beef and gravy at the table, and tops it all off with coffee—on his head.

Toppers abound, but perhaps the most satisfying is the film's final line. Right on the heels of Charles and Jean's but-I'm-married-so-am-I exchange, a nice laugh in itself, the cabin door shuts behind them . . . and a moment later is opened by Muggsy. He hurriedly slips out of the cabin, shuts the door, then mutters once again, "Positively, the same dame!" End of movie.

Reversals   Like *Four Weddings* and other ingeniously packaged romantic comedies we've cited, the formal brilliance of *Eve* is most apparent in an inventive structure; despite hitting the standard seven beats within a conventional three-act form, the movie appears to be done in two acts: "Charles and Jean's shipboard romance" is followed after a brief interlude by "Charles and Eve's Connecticut romance." Each half is a six-beat story that mirrors the other, both ending in crisis. The seventh beat of resolution acts like a coda capper for both parts. But Part 2 is actually a perverse reversal of Part 1, comedically parodying its progression.

In Part 1, Jean's intentions are honorable, which in itself is a reversal in premise: the con artist decides to play it straight. In Part 2, she enacts virtually the same scenes and situations with exactly the opposite intent: she's out to make a fool of Charles and break his heart.

This comedic symmetry of reversal is also found in the use of matching Buddies: Muggsy, looking out for Charles's best interests, sabotages his romance. The Colonel, looking out for Jean's best interests, fleeces Charles, thus unwittingly colluding with Muggsy to break up the couple. In *Eve*, the supposed allies become the antagonists.

Specific reversals within gags and set pieces abound. Charles is transformed from sophisticated adult to silly child, with wild chaos overtaking urban decorum practically every time the dame or the Lady walks into his life. But Sturges's ironic use of reversal is most apparent in his canny scene construction. Jean's dining-room scene gets its ultimate topper from a sly reversal. While every woman in the room throws herself at Charles, trying to get him alone, Jean merely sticks her foot out, and Charles falls to the floor at her feet. Made to feel guilty for breaking her heel, he volunteers to accompany Jean back to her room for a change of shoes. After blithely dismissing his "My name is Pike" ("Oh, everybody knows that, nobody's talking about anything else"), the one woman who seemingly had no interest in meeting this millionaire waltzes out of the rival-filled dining room on his arm.

At a brisk 94 minutes, *Eve* is a model of economy. Able to get us into a character and a plot point in a single line (Jean, observing Charles's arrival: "I hope he's rich; I hope he thinks he's a wizard at cards"), *Eve* has nary a wasted shot in its entirety, and many are packed solid with comedic setups or payoffs. Sturges's piquant, uniquely specific dialogue enables him to quickly etch vivid characters (e.g., the Colonel's "Let us be crooked but never common" reprimand to Jean in that same introductory scene). But the story is also glued tightly together by a thematic subtext.

From the animated snake that wiggles and winks its way through the opening credits (and is shown too pooped to move in the film's "The End" card)—and the use of Charles's real snake Emma as a recurring gag—to the apple Jean drops on Charles and the ubiquitous "falls" taken by this latter-day Adam, *Eve* has a cohesive Edenic motif. This is, after all, the story of a man whose eyes get opened by an already fallen Eve.

Dame and Lady are in fact the same, and Sturges's inspired use of all these comedic techniques makes this movie just as compelling—and laugh-provoking—sixty years after its debut.

Comedy is of course subjective. One person's laugh may be another one's shrug. But these basic principles should help you with your comedy craft. The thing not to lose sight of is that romantic comedies *are* comedies.

The lack of a specifically comedic approach is what weakens a movie like *Runaway Bride*, making it, despite its star-driven success, lightly likable at best. Beyond its video recap of Maggie's first three weddings, *Bride* has no true comic set pieces. It has a dearth of palpable male lead "hurt" (other than a bad hair-dye job and getting thwacked with the occasional newspaper, Ike sails through most of the movie unmussed), and its overall tonal fuzziness (i.e., a sentimentality somewhat at odds with its screwball premise) also contributes to the movie's humor remaining muted and sporadic.

You want your audience to laugh—loudly and often. The executive who guffaws at a romantic comedy spec script is the one who makes sure it gets studio attention. A romantic comedy that keeps its audiences amused is the one that generates word-of-mouth box office upon its release—and whose stature, like *Eve's*, continues to grow over time.

What the enduring romantic comedies have in common is that their jokes are rooted in some sort of truth. Their laughs are laughs of recognition. We've taken that fall . . . felt that horrible kiss-off . . . been that silly for the sake of love.

According to Hawks (in McCarthy's bio), that weird, mechanical, burlesque duet walk by Hepburn and Grant in *Baby* was based on the time a very embarrassed Grant, finding his fly undone while out at the theater, got it caught in midzip on a lady's dress. The two of them had to be pliered apart by the theater manager. So if you're looking for comedy, try looking at life: some of the most outrageous movie gags have come out of a deeply felt personal experience.

SUMMARY

A central principle of all comedy is the use of a reversal—a surprising turnabout in position or direction that subverts an audience's expectations. In romantic comedies, we often see, for example, adults acting like kids, sophistication turning to silliness, the feminine becoming masculine (or vice versa), and private matters being exposed in public.

Comedy is also rooted in its characters taking themselves seriously. Writers play upon this by inflicting as much cruelty on their protagonists as possible. Ironically, the more sober the characters and the more pain they're in, the more truth and humor that's likely to emerge from their situations. Romantic comedies use mutual humiliation as a means to unite their besieged couples and maximize the humor in their plight.

It's necessary to define your comedic tone. Farce, satire, parody, black comedy, sophisticated, and comedy drama are the basic varieties that can be mixed or matched—but you must be consistent. It's also important to employ comedic set pieces in your romantic comedies, since a prolonged sequence that delivers big laughs is a vital ingredient for success. Certain time-honored structural devices, such as the use of threes and toppers, are also helpful in shaping the humor of a piece. But the bottom line is honesty: the deepest laughs come from situations that audiences recognize as being true-to-life.

CHAPTER NINE

Being Sexy

Sex is only interesting when it releases passion.
JOHN BOORMAN

What is erotic is our passion for the liveliness of life.
DIANE ACKERMAN

When Kathleen Turner and Michael Douglas are en route to their inevitable date with bedroom destiny in *Romancing the Stone*, we see everything we'd expect to see: he dances her around a plaza under a starlit sky, which, as the dance gets hotter and heavier (accented by soaring strings), erupts into fireworks above the couple. Ultimately, they're the only dancers standing still, lip-locked in their embrace while the rest of the crowd whirls around them. Cut to two candles flickering above a bed . . . followed by a pan down to our movie stars, postcoital beneath chastely arranged sheets. The only thing missing, in terms of checking off your cliché list, would be an interim shot of waves crashing on a rocky shore.

Since *Stone* is a parody, these images are appropriately tongue in cheek. But sadly, your average American movie today shows the same dearth of imagination when given this story beat to play. A slow dissolve from a silhouetted kiss to a close-up of a hand clutching a sheet in passion, dissolved again to an artfully composed morning-after tableau . . . this is the kind of Hallmark Card version of foreplay, lovemaking, and afterglow you'll usually see. The assumption is that the sex was perfect—too divine, in fact, for us to be privy to—and now we can get on with the plot.

What a waste! Did we learn anything about either character? Did anything really happen between them, beyond the exchange of endearments and precious bodily fluids? Did what happened reflect what the movie's about, thematically?

On the other hand, one major mainstream movie that made millions and reaped a couple of Oscars, Cameron Crowe's *Jerry Maguire,* had one of the longest, steamiest first-kiss scenes in recent cinematic history. But when you take a close look at that kiss (as we will shortly), you'll find that it's not just about sex. The excitement of this scene comes out of character, plot development, thematic subtext, dialogue, and sure, some sizzling physical chemistry, but above all, something else—the something else that enlivens the most memorable erotic encounters: *intimacy.*

Naked flesh is one thing, but naked vulnerability—the scary/exciting transcendant connection that happens when two lovers really expose themselves—means so much more. The exploration and enjoyment of this kind of intimacy is the great secret weapon of the romantic comedy genre. In this chapter we're going to see how smart moviemakers have created cinematic intimacy—before, during, and after the act of love itself—and we'll explore ways you can achieve it on the page.

METAPHORICAL FOREPLAY: CREATING EROTIC SUBTEXT

In a sense, romantic comedies are nothing *but* foreplay, their plots posing the question: When are these two people going to get over themselves and into bed? But in the specific art of getting your characters into horizontal harmony, there are really two kinds, or two levels, of stoking and sustaining sexual tension.

The first is metaphorical. It's about sex on an unconscious level—your leads are already in the dance and they only half know it, or are only half willing to know it. *Implicit* foreplay yields a special kind of suspense, the tension created when the A story rubs up against the B story, or where one is actually a metaphor for the other.

Take a memorable scene from James Brooks's *Broadcast News*. Fledgling TV news anchorman William Hurt and producer Holly Hunter have been flirting and feinting, trying to resist the erotic current that's crackling between them, when a suddenly breaking story puts him live on national television for the first time. From her microphone in the control room, Hunter has to feed Hurt incoming bulletins as he sits facing the TV camera on the studio floor, her voice literally in his head via an earpiece tucked in his ear.

As she prompts and guides him, slipping him information seconds before he needs it, her forefinger hovers over the button on the console that's labeled with his name, tapping and rubbing it with unconscious affection when he takes her direction well and improvises a good line to the camera ("that's good," she murmurs, "real good").

The sexual subtext is unmistakable. It resonates metaphorically (your classic experienced-woman-initiates-a-virgin situation), while at the same time, the scene bristles with archetypical romantic comedy tension (private matters intruding on a public situation). They're simultaneously the cool, unflappable reporter working with a seasoned pro while millions look on and an aroused couple whose mating dance is shifting into higher, hotter gear.

What's gone on is so palpably exciting, in fact, that right after his successful performance (he's scored!), Hurt rushes into the newsroom, flushed and wired, to grab Hunter's chair and pull her toward him, crowing: ". . . you knew just when to feed me the next line, you knew the second before I needed it, there was like a rhythm we got into—it was like great sex!"

Indeed. And it's not long after this pivotal moment that things get physical. But let's pause here to observe the principle in action. In romantic comedy, there's nothing sexier than *sublimated* sex. When we know, and our leads can feel, the nearly out-of-control impulses simmering underneath a seemingly placid surface, the most mundane actions (and plot beats) become glamorous and exciting. In the context of Brooks's well-constructed scene, that console button is a lot more than a piece of plastic.

A similar dynamic infuses the clinching-the-big-business-deal scene in Mike Nichols and Kevin Wade's *Working Girl*. As Harrison Ford and Melanie Griffith maintain an admirable cool, business-suited and briefcase-armed on the opposite side of a desk from some intimidating corporate sharks, we're well aware that pulling off this delicate negotiation is the culmination of their relationship thus far. A lot of the scene's enjoyment stems from watching these two in concert, working their prospective clients, never breaking a sweat as they deftly leap over unforeseen obstacles and force the deal to a close. Their smooth, savvy teamwork reads "made for each other."

Which is why, when Nichols cuts from the silence of the office meeting to the financial-building stairs, where Ford wordlessly stops midflight to pull Griffith into their first passionate clinch of the movie, it seems so well earned. These two have just performed, with precision and panache, a feat made of equal parts expertise and bluff that's going to net them millions. After playing that high-stakes hand so poker-faced, this erotic explosion is inevitable. Note, too, that it's not so easy to find a location in the modern urban environment where an embrace can still raise eyebrows. The lobby of a staid, high-toned Wall Street enterprise is one of the few, and that private-gone-public frisson is what gives their clinch its extra charge.

At its most blatant, the metaphorical or implicit approach to foreplay can easily degenerate into mere silliness. *Ghost* may have made a bundle, but it's hard to watch the infamous fun-with-clay scene with a straight face: Patrick Swayze wrapped around Demi Moore with a leeringly phallic, dripping wet clay pot between her legs seems more like a *Saturday Night Live* parody than a romantic encounter one can take seriously. This is somewhat due to lack of real subtext. The let-me-help-you-throw-that-pot device doesn't come out of any credible tension arising in a workplace or home environment, it's a transparently sexual gambit; there's really nothing else going on in the scene.

But generally, sexualizing an environment—creating an erotic subtext where we don't expect to encounter it—is often what gives a romantic comedy its heat. Savvy use of implicit foreplay speaks to a basic tenet of the genre: it's got to be about more than just sex.

FOREPLAY II: GETTING EXPLICIT

When Jerry Maguire (Tom Cruise) takes his assistant Dorothy (Renee Zellweger) out for their first date, both are aware that an all-important line is being crossed. They're moving from the workplace into what could be a romantic relationship, and their night out is suffused with tension raised by the question: How far across that line are they going to go? So, after dinner, Jerry takes her home, walks her to the door, where—with her kid and a baby-sitting friend right inside—the moment of truth arrives. "Well, this would be goodnight," he says, handing her the styrofoam container of Mexican food leftovers. "Goodnight," she says, trying to smile her way past the awkwardness, and . . .

What? What would you do, given the assignment? With such a familiar plot beat to deal with, how do you get from here to the place that the plot's demanding you must go (i.e., Dorothy's bedroom)? Playing it straight and simple is bound to disappoint; you can't have him lean in, kiss her goodnight, trust that it's a hot one, and dissolve from there. Not with so much invested in this moment and such vulnerably human characters (the winner-suddenly-turned-loser and the gamely-sticking-her-neck-out-helpmate) at your disposal.

Let's look at what Cameron Crowe did (note: bracketed passages in italics are transcriptions from the finished film). Jerry says "I'll see you tomorrow." Dorothy nods, but they don't move. They linger. She reaches up to straighten his collar. Jerry leans in to kiss her goodnight, veering cheekward, and something in the formalness of the gesture makes her stiffen, so . . . he stops . . . backs up. They look at each other.

On impulse she grabs him and pulls him close. Kisses him. It's a good one.

> DOROTHY
> Well, goodnight.

> JERRY
> G'night.

But they don't move. [*His hand caresses her cheek . . . moves down her neck . . . slides her sweater from her shoulders . . . both his hands play with the thin straps of her dress, and*] He pulls her closer by her straps. They break.

> [*They're startled. They both laugh.*

> JERRY
> *Oops!*

> *Their laughter quiets. He holds up the straps.*

> JERRY (cont'd)
> *I'm gonna fix this.*

> DOROTHY
> *Good idea.*]

It's a *very* good idea. Because what follows is the last thing you'd expect to see from this standard moment, as Jerry kisses his way over her upper chest while taking his time in retying the straps around her neck: it's about a man seducing a woman by *dressing* her. The erotic electricity it provokes, complete with a squirming Dorothy breathlessly trying not to melt into a puddle of arousal, is so potent that despite choice dialogue (Dorothy: "I think you should come in, or not come in, depending on how you feel." Jerry: "Same to you." Dorothy: "No, I have to go in. I live here.") the outcome is a foregone conclusion.

Consider how specific the choices are: the location (right outside the door with Dorothy's son within) emphasizes the high stakes simmering in the subtext; single mom Dorothy stands to lose a lot by jeopardizing an already precarious job should this tryst go south, and at all costs, son Ray can't be hurt. The choice of dress is key, since the straps business (spaghetti thin, tying at the nape of Dorothy's neck) is the motor of the scene. The redressing versus undressing is imaginative, and so is Dorothy's bold, risky move at the top of the scene. We don't expect to see her grab Jerry, since it so goes against the grain of her usual behavior, so this reversal is a nice surprise. Given the length of this good-night-kiss scene (from her grab to their "let's do it" is just under three minutes of uninterrupted erotic play, which is long by American mainstream standards), there's a lot of information compacted into the one beat. Everything we need to know about both characters' conflictedness (her yearnings and hesitations, his sense of being in over his head but going for it) is so clearly delineated *within* three minutes, that this material never needs to be restated.

The scene's intensity is self-evident (it takes only this one prolonged kiss to drop-kick our couple into bed), and it has integrity. Every element in the scene arises organically from what's come before. But in its broad strokes, what makes the scene cook is how character and theme drive the erotic tension. It's about the exciting but dangerous shift in this couple's power structure, symbolized by Jerry's manipulation of Dorothy's clothing. And the glue of it is the *intimacy* that arises from their mutual vulnerability—acknowledged in that laugh they share when his "being sexy" yields a broken dress strap.

Humans being human—this is what an alert romantic comedy writer tries to capture on the page.

HAVING SEX: DON'T STOP THE PLOT

Given the mainstream's apparent squeamishness about sex, opting for the old "their shadowy figures melt into tangled sheets and . . . FADE OUT" routine might be a screenwriter's safest bet. But do you really want to be safe?

Hope not. Safe is what makes many of the lifeless scripts floating through Hollywood so easy to dismiss. And a romantic comedy that skips over the truly hot stuff when the plot's demanding it be dealt with is kind of like an action-adventure movie that leaves out its biggest explosion. The audience for *Lethal Action* wants to see that giant fireball propel an action star into space, and the audience for a romantic comedy is going to want some sort of erotic payoff after all that built-up sexual tension. They may want it discreet, inferred, slyly symbolized—but that all-important "It" *is* going to have to be dealt with, somehow.

So what are you going to do? There's such a thin line between suggestive and salacious that even Jean Luc Godard, that Picasso of cinematic trailblazers, once said that a movie about what really goes on between a man and a woman in a bedroom could never be made. There are also some industry realities. Most stars don't do nudity, and most studios aren't happy to get R ratings (it sometimes reduces a picture's box office potential). Nonetheless, say the arc of your brilliantly constructed story demands that, in a pivotal plot beat, the two leads actually get naked and roll around together. What are your options?

A good rule of thumb is to remember that in real life, most people don't shed their character and personality when they shed their clothes. In real life, many people actually reveal *more* about who they are when the lights go out. In real life, *when people who are emotionally involved with each other have sex, the plot doesn't stop.*

In fact, it usually thickens. Things *happen* in bed. Many of us have had some of our greatest laughs, our most profound emotional moments (and even some of our scariest ones) while between the sheets—all grist for the comedy mill. So if your characters have to go there, give them something to do beyond a Playboy Channel approximation of the ultimate orgasm. To tweak the old joke, *Is sex dirty? Only when you're doing it right,* let's posit that in a romantic comedy, sex is worth doing only when you're making it meaningful.

To see how a savvy screenwriter gets the most out of an intimate physical encounter, let's look at one of those handful of genuinely erotic American movies, albeit written by Frenchman Jean Claude Carriere (adapting Polish Milan Kundera), Phil Kaufman's *The Unbearable Lightness of Being.*

In this film, the womanizer played by Daniel Day Lewis has a wonderfully kinky mistress in Lena Olin. A scene midway through the story finds them in the throes of passionate sex . . . but how passionate is it? Olin is atop Lewis, watching their glistening bodies in the mirror by the bed (its presence a nice touch, in what it succinctly tells us about this couple's sexual predilections). She catches Lewis, not knowing he's observed, surreptitiously checking his watch before again lying back beneath her.

Olin's hand reaches past Lewis's writhing shoulders to snatch one of his socks from the floor and, even as his yelps of pleasure grow louder, crumples it up. Cut to Lewis, fully dressed but for one bare foot, impatient and perplexed at his sock's mysterious disappearance. "You must have come without it," says Olin. "I wouldn't wear only one sock, would I?" replies her exasperated lover. "You've been very absentminded lately," Olin notes, eyes glistening with amused satisfaction. "Always in a hurry. Always looking at your watch."

As indeed he is at that very instant . . . until he looks over at her in sudden comprehension.

It's a beautifully crafted little moment. The substance of the scene could be translated as "Lewis's mistress realizes that he seems to have grown a little bored with her and contrives to make him stay longer than he'd intended so she can find out why." Carriere, via Kundera, has *used* their sexual coupling—which, after all, is clearly the core of their relationship—to make the point as vividly, as concisely as possible. The scene certainly is about sex. But it's simultaneously about a lot more.

MAKING SEX SEXY

Okay, you may say, but what if you've got a scene on your hands that really isn't supposed to be about anything *but* sex—a scene where the big beat is simply: "Ohmygod! they're finally doing it?" Maybe you'd even like to leave it out altogether, but you sense, after such a big buildup in the story thus far, that some erotic moment, however obligatory, has to be filled in on the screen.

We turn to Paris, to Jean-Charles Tacchella's *Cousin, Cousine*. In this gem of a romantic comedy, Marie-Christine Barrault and Victor Lanoux play two distant cousins who, left to their own devices because their mates are philanderers, become close friends. A romantic attraction brews between them, and ultimately—since their respective mates and the entire family already assume that they must be sleeping together—they decide to become lovers.

Marie and Victor plan an assignation. They meet in the afternoon and go to a hotel that a friend of Victor's "used to bring girls to," only to find that it's been demolished. Victor thinks there may be another place around here. This time, they're in luck, as the door is answered by a quintessentially Gallic character: a coolly appraising, overly made up, and exotically dressed concierge whose every movement, even as she's matter-of-factly demanding cash payment before handing over the key to their room upstairs, reeks with knowing suggestiveness.

Once upstairs, the couple—two tourists in the House of Love—make a quick silent tour of their accommodations. She turns from looking into the bathroom to face him, across the room, and pronounces it "fabulous." They smile. He then flings his bag playfully to the floor. She tosses her shoulder bag. Still smiling, they hurry into each other's arms. They kiss, standing there in a warm, loving, fully clothed embrace.

What follows is a montage, a series of isolated moments leapfrogging across time. Here's what makes up the big sex sequence in *Cousin, Cousine*.

We see a dark screen with an overturned lamp in the foreground and hear Victor: "We broke the lamp." The camera pans to the bed, where he lies face down in his pillow. Beside him, Marie gently strokes his back and notes "I scratched your back." She bends down to kiss the wound.

Cut to Marie, naked, laughing in Victor's arms. He dumps her unceremoniously on the bed and announces: "Fourth round!"

Cut to Victor lying on his back in bed, Marie sitting up, moving with delighted anticipation to grab his foot: "Let me cut your toenails. I want to." She does. He puffs contentedly on a cigar and observes: "It's almost dark outside." She wonders what time it is; as she snips, he picks up his watch, announces "6:40." He lies back down, puffs. She clips.

Cut to Victor and Marie lying side by side, heads over the bed's edge. The concierge phones to find out if they intend to keep the room for the night. Marie nods happily. Victor says "Oui." Told that the establishment serves food, they order some.

Cut to Marie, looking radiant, smiling down at Victor. "This time, our families are really worried."

Cut to looking like naughty schoolkids, the couple huddling with the sheet pulled up to their chins. A knock at the door. Victor calls "Entre!" The concierge sashays slowly into the room, bearing a tray with wine and food. Victor instructs her to set it down and thanks her. They discuss payment; the concierge says tomorrow is all right and saunters, smiling, from the room.

Cut to blackness. A yelp from Marie: "Turn on the light. I'm lost!" From the bed, Victor turns on the still overturned lamp. Whatever Marie is doing, it makes him laugh.

Cut to Victor sitting in the bathroom tub, Marie soaping his back. "As a boy, I wanted to be a tramp," Victor says. "My parents wouldn't let me."

Cut to Marie and Victor sitting up in bed, dimly lit. He's writing on a little pad. "Cut your rabbit into pieces," dictates Marie, "let it marinate for two hours. Make your marinade with . . . three spoonfuls of olive oil . . . two lemons. . . ."

Cut to Marie lying on her back in bed, face up. Victor leans in slowly, very tenderly kisses her lips, then one eyelid. She smiles.

Cut to Victor and Marie cuddling against their pillow, eyes closed in the soft dawn light. Suddenly Marie sits up. "I fell asleep!" She looks at him. "Are you angry?" Victor murmurs, "Yes. Very angry." Smiling, she nestles into his arms, strokes his chest.

Cut to a hotel waiter coming in bearing a breakfast tray. "Good morning. Is everything all right?" Marie and Victor are sitting up in bed, sheet modestly arrayed. They simply watch him. "Need anything?" No reply. "Do you intend to stay a bit longer?" Victor: "Yes, we do." The waiter sets down the tray, smiles . . . "Enjoy your Sunday!" . . . turns and exits, shutting the door.

Cut to Marie and Victor zooming down a Parisian street on his motorcycle. It's dusk.

Note that in the entire sequence, there were mere seconds of partial nudity, en passant, and that the total amount of actual graphic sex observed was . . . zero.

And yet the montage is undeniably *sexy*. Partially enhanced by the charming performances of both leads, who strike just the right note of childlike wonder in the midst of their very adult activities, the sequence resonates with a unique combination of wry humor and poignant eroticism. Each detail has been picked out to express a different aspect of this couple's closeness, from Victor's playfully macho "Fourth round!" declaration (saying all we need to know about the intensity and depth of their lovemaking) to

Marie's sweet "I fell asleep!" (which goes right to the emotional heart, endearingly, of how precious their time together really is).

The concierge's ooh-la-la attitude adds a nice comedic subtext to the sequence. She puts some nudge-wink salaciousness into an experience that's clearly pure and healthy, and in this she echoes the main thematic thrust of the movie, which places these two innocents in opposition to a cynical, unromantic world. And underlying the montage, giving it a cohesive structure, is the plot beat's congenial, amused stoking of story conflict: "This time, our families are really worried," muses Marie happily, in the couple's sole reference to that domestic world outside their own—while afternoon gives way to evening . . . night . . . morning.

Along the way, we get precisely the kinds of behavior—the toenail clipping, the exchanging of recipes—exhibited by human beings who are being truly intimate with each other. The love between them is unspoken but palpable. Ironically, by putting in these moments that your average mainstream romantic comedy leaves out, *Cousin* achieves a credibility and a closeness to the characters in its sex scene that no amount of sweaty-handed sheet-clenching and silhouettes-in-fadeout could deliver.

DOING IT DIFFERENTLY

The key is using your imagination. *Cousin* makes its obligatory sex scene interesting by turning it inside out: everything *but* the sex is what gets the most attention.

If you're looking for a way to enliven and deepen your script's first big physical encounter, a logical storytelling component to explore is *world*. What's the location? What can you use in setting, atmosphere, time of day, or weather to make it as special as it can be?

A further way to pursue distinctive choices is to investigate *character*. That's what Audrey Wells did in *The Truth About Cats and Dogs.* In this filmic variation on *Cyrano,* low-self-esteemed radio talk-show host Janeane Garofalo uses gorgeous model Uma Thurman to pose as her, because she doesn't want to deal with having hunk Ben Chaplin (who's infatuated with her on-the-air personality) dump her when he sees what she really looks like.

The screenwriter's problem: How can I get my two leads into a sexual situation, to up the stakes, when the plot demands that Ben not be with Janeane face-to-face? Her solution, simple but perfect, evidently came out of examining what she had in her characters. Janeane's a radio talk-show host who takes live phone calls from people with pet problems. In fact, she's most comfortable, she really shines, when . . .

The phone-sex scene in *Cats and Dogs* is a model of smart convention-tweaking. Its credibility is rock solid; once Ben calls and Janeane refuses to go out with him (her front, Uma, is unavailable), it stands to reason that Ben, not giving up easily, would suggest having their date over the phone. They met on the phone (he was a caller with a troublesome dog), and, afforded the luxury of not being seen, Janeane is happy to talk to him from a comfortable distance.

The sequence that follows is reminiscent of *Cousin* (with recipe comparisons and a mutual bath, albeit in split-screen separate apartments). By the end of their evening, sharing poetry, music, and intimate thoughts, both are feeling close to each other and aroused. This marathon phone call—enlivened by funny cutaways to their respective pets—leads to a mutual pleasure taking that plays anything but raunchy and obscene. It's phone sex, but it's well motivated and well executed, especially by normal gal Garofalo, whose I-can't-believe-I'm-doing-this hysteria adds a nice loopy vulnerability to a genuinely intimate scene.

So take a tip from Ms. Wells. Mine your characters: their homes, workplaces, hobby spots. Think about what in their world suggests an offbeat, but appropriate, situation where a unique, meaningful sexual encounter can take place.

Or where it can't. Sometimes, *not* having the sex that's supposed to be had can be even more erotic.

My particular favorite "coitus unrequitus" scene comes from a
romantic dramedy, *Two for the Road* (script by Frederic Raphael):
Audrey Hepburn and Albert Finney, right in the radiant bloom of
having fallen madly in love, with only one week together before
they have to part, make the fatal error of falling asleep together
on a sunny beach. Cut to their hotel room, as two lobsters contemplate their horrific reflections in the mirror. "What do we do?"
moans Finney, through clenched teeth (for even the smallest
movement is painful). "Stand very still," says Hepburn, "for several days." But they don't want to stand very still. What ensues is
an amusingly sexy sadomasochistic ballet, as they strain to kiss,
wincing, murmur frustrated endearments, and finally—"To hell
with it," sighs Hepburn, "It'll only hurt for a minute"—literally
dive into bed. End of scene.

Think about what huge obstacles you can put between your
leads and their devoutly desired consummation. That's another
way to leap from the mundane to the magical.

CLIMAX

Of all the difficult beats to portray, for players as well as writers,
orgasm's got to rate way up there on the scale. By comparison,
death's a piece of cake. Sexual climax is such an intimately private
thing, that one risks losing an audience (and embarrassing an
actor) if you write it even minimally wrong. To tweak an old
actor's adage ("Dying is easy, comedy is hard"), "Dying is easy,
coming is hard."

Discreetly panning away from this moment of truth is still an
oft-used technique. The principle to remember, as with all these aspects of "the act" on the page, is this: use it or lose it. Most of the
time, your sex scene's not going to require the big finish (think again

of *Cousin*'s approach) to make its point. But if for some reason you have to go all the way, find a way to do something with the moment.

Humor's one good way to go. In *Bull Durham*, when Susan Sarandon and Kevin Costner are in the throes of bathtub love-making and approaching climax, writer-director Ron Shelton makes a wry comment on the traditional concept of such cinematic cliché moments. He pans from the lovers, whose rocking momentum is making waves, to the group of candles burning on the tub-side table. Water from the tub splashes over the candles, putting them out, and the audience laughs appreciatively at this sly parody of the old waves-breaking-on-the-shore metaphor for sexual fulfillment.

AFTERMATH: HEIGHTENING BONDS, CONFLICTS, AND CHARACTER

Okay, they've done it. And you've navigated your characters smoothly and imaginatively through some often treacherous terrain, hopefully mining some plot subtext and/or deepening a characterization or two in the process. Your impulse is probably to get the hell out of there and quickly head for the plot proper.

Hold on. Even if you've dealt with the sex deftly, and especially if you gave it short shrift, don't be in such a hurry to get everyone back into their clothes. Because, think about it, what's the effect, if the sex has been meaningful, on your lead couple? What's there even more of to take advantage of than was there before? *Intimacy*.

You now have your two leads in the screenwriting equivalent of a Sodium Pentothal session. They're more vulnerable, more open, more likely to share secrets with you, each other, and the audience than they've ever been. How either or both react to having just had someone rock their world is a moment worth exploring. Why squander such an opportunity?

The traditional good use of an aftermath scene in romantic comedies is to *heighten conflict*. One of the most memorable examples of this occurs in the swivel scene (second turning point) of *When Harry Met Sally*. Harry and Sally have spent two-thirds of a movie proving that men and women can't be friends because sex always screws everything up. But when Harry comforts Sally, who's devastated because her ex is getting married, friendly affection takes a sudden turn into genuine lust. Director Reiner does a slow dissolve from this couple's first-ever passionate kiss to a close-up of Harry, flat on his back in Sally's bed with his eyes wide open in what-have-I-done terror, while she, wearing a smile as wide as all outdoors, happily nuzzles him, oblivious.

The slow zoom-out from Harry's frozen visage gets a big laugh (everything we need to know is so perfectly captured in his facial reaction), and the scene that develops from here is ripe with intense discomfort. Sally cheerily offers to get them some water, and Harry is barely able to squeak out his acquiescence. When she returns to the bedroom moments later, Harry's already running scared, having apparently been transformed, in the interim, from best friend to total stranger.

An equally effective variation on the aftermath pushes the plot in a different direction by *heightening the bond*. Let's take another look at *Working Girl*. After that implicit foreplay scene in the financial building, it goes amusingly explicit, with Harrison Ford and Melanie Griffith so eager to get into bed that they're stripping off their clothes as soon as they're through the apartment door—a scene, by the way, that features a great laugh-earning moment of intimacy as Ford, that man among men, gets stuck in his still half-buttoned shirt and can't get out of the damn thing. Once they're past that hurdle, he hoists her into his arms and out of the frame, the camera lingering on their discarded clothing strewn across the floor.

Cut to Ford, a bedcover wrapped round his waist, in the hallway paying a delivery boy for takeout food. In the ensuing aftermath scene, he quickly discards the bags to return to the bed so he can kiss and embrace Griffith, who's happily tousled beneath the sheet. She reaches up to caress his chin. "How'd you get this scar?" she asks. "Some guy pulled a knife in Detroit," he tells her. "Really?" "No," he replies, grinning sheepishly, "I was nineteen and I thought it'd be cool to have a pierced ear and my girlfriend stuck the needle through and I heard this pop, and fainted and hit my chin on the toilet." She laughs. "And you've been telling that story ever since?" Ford shakes his head. "You're the only one who knows the true story," he says.

Every lover's fantasy, amplified—even better than one of those "I've never done *that* [erotic act] with anyone else before" riffs; Ford has just revealed a little more of himself than we've seen up until now. Screenwriter Kevin Wade then tops the moment by upping the stakes further, as Griffith wonders what happened to the girlfriend, and he jokingly says "No, I had her . . . disappeared." What's inferred in the subtext of their dialogue is that from here on out, Ford's current girlfriend is history. Thus, a turning point of another kind: this couple's lovemaking has led directly to a commitment.

A third valuable use of the aftermath scene is for *character revelation* or development. If you've been looking for a moment where you can give us a glimpse of a character's inner life to reveal his/her deeper, formerly hidden needs and desires, the afterglow zone is a logical choice.

Unbearable Lightness achieves this quite poignantly in a brief, wordless morning-after scene between Daniel Day Lewis and Juliette Binoche. Though we know he's a seasoned womanizer who's more or less encouraged country mouse Binoche, a nurse at a provincial clinic, to visit him on a whim, we don't know that much about Binoche—who's turned out to be surprisingly sexually voracious in a seduction scene where she turned the tables on Lewis and decimated his apartment in her zeal to make love.

Their morning-after begins with Lewis shutting off his alarm, moving to get up from bed—then realizing he can't, because Binoche, fast asleep, has a firm grip on his hand. Even unconscious, she's not letting go; he tries to tug loose, but she only hangs on more tightly. Lewis the doctor, true to *his* character, resorts to a ruse born of his knowledge of human reflex: he nudges a book into Binoche's palm, and she accepts this substitute, holding onto it as he slips his hand free. What we've learned of Binoche, instantly (the depth of her investment in her new lover) is one thing. But Carriere and Kaufman add an interesting grace note: Lewis, as he carefully guides Binoche's fingers into place around the book's binding, kisses her knuckles with a surprising tenderness. So we learn something new about Lewis: some emotion has been kindled here, and this new lover may not be just one of an indifferent series.

The continued intimacy found in the aftermath of an act of love can be worth its weight in screenwriting gold. Dig deeper into your characters, and see what you find.

SECOND TIME AROUND: RAISING STAKES

Just when you thought it was safe to lock the bedroom door behind you, you might find, due to the dictates of your plot, that your characters have to (i.e., they want to!) come back for more. What then, other than new positions, can you do with a repetitive beat like that?

Well, consider the consequences of such activities in real life. What's the difference between a one-night stand and a night that becomes two, three, or more?

Cousin, Cousine brings its lovers back for another assignation a bit later in the movie. Again, there's that charming Gallic blend of whimsy and sophistication; when Marie pulls off her blouse in their hotel room, it's to reveal that she's covered with tattoos, having swiped a play-tattoo pencil from one of her kids. As the sequence unfolds in bed, *après amour*, she uses the pencil to draw on Victor. They talk about his work, some upcoming jobs. As he tattoos her, they speak of traveling; they'd like to go somewhere together. "Some day, you must make me cry," she tells him further on (she can't seem to do it on her own). He promises to try. The scene culminates with them in the tub, furiously scrubbing themselves and each other to no avail. The play tattoos won't come off! Laughing and soaping, "Teach me to dance," she entreats him. "I want to learn the new ones . . ."

What's different?

Subtle but simple: this couple has left the Now. Where their earlier first-bliss idyll existed outside of time (time's expansion being its subtext), the outside world is beginning to impinge on their private world. Now there's a future to consider. It's touched on lightly, indirectly, but clearly things must be, and already are, moving forward.

Second times are about *raising stakes*. If you and your lovers need to go there again, go with a purpose. The second (third or fourth) round is good place to make your statement about what's changed—in the relationship, in the situation, or, if this is the beat required, what hasn't changed yet but needs to.

Again, the general principle applies: for romantic comedy couples, it can't be just about sex. If there's more sex going on, something else must be going on as well. So use the act to illustrate the action.

SUMMARY

The most important thing about your movie's intimate encounters is that they *be* important. The lovemaking should matter. A good way to make it matter is to approach the act's before, during, and after with all the energy and imagination you'd apply to your most important dramatic beats. The best way to deepen the experience is to use your erotic situation to further the plot and develop character.

More crucial than establishing pure sexual heat is creating a genuine sense of intimacy between your lovers. They should expose more than skin. After they've "known" each other, we should know more about them and about where the movie is going. You can leave out the graphic stuff if you leave in the revelatory vulnerable, quirky-scary stuff. That's what being sexy in a romantic comedy is really about.

CHAPTER TEN

Designing Dialogue

Good dialogue can't take the place of the motor of the story. If people are just standing around saying cute things to each other, it isn't enough.

DONALD WESTLAKE

The story is being carried by the shots. Basically, the perfect movie doesn't have any dialogue.

DAVID MAMET

What writer doesn't enjoy writing dialogue? With all that white space around it, it fills up pages fast. If you're on a roll, dialogue can carry you right through an entire act. But as a reader, I sometimes think dialogue ought to be largely off-limits to screenwriters, stored in a high-security vault, like plutonium. Like plutonium, it's a supremely powerful commodity that can, with the proper technological support, blow millions of people away—so you don't want it falling into the wrong hands. In the wrong hands, dialogue just puts people to sleep.

Too many writers don't really understand its purpose, but David Mamet, a writer perhaps best known for his dialogue, clearly does. His preceding quote, a seemingly perverse statement, speaks to a fundamental truth about movies: they're a series of shots that tell a story. Ideally, each shot should move the story forward, answering the audience's primal question: What happens next? Any dialogue included in a shot has to provide part of that answer.

Good movie dialogue isn't there to fill up space, it's there to do a job.

The screenwriters whose voices are distinctive enough to earn them latitude in this regard have done a lot of damage in their day. Quentin Tarantino is a brilliant crafter of conversation, but you can't imagine how many truly awful couple-of-tough-guys-talk-pop-culture-while-loading-their-guns spec scripts the studios saw in the wake of *Pulp Fiction*. And many an aspiring romantic comedy writer's love of Sturges and the rapid-fire blather of *His Girl Friday* has led to screenplays that are rife with tedious male and female talking-heads scenes.

But wait a second, you may say, what *about* all those wonderful talk-heavy romantic comedies we know and love? Isn't witty banter what we expect and want from such movies?

Yes . . . and no. Dialogue can be fun, amusing, even brilliant, but it has to be *functional*. Good romantic comedy talk does something for the story.

WHAT DIALOGUE CAN DO

1. The first and foremost function of dialogue is *to move the story forward*. Dialogue is a primary means of activating conflict. This doesn't mean, as Mamet takes great pains to point out (in his book, *On Directing*), that dialogue is narration. You don't have Mary set eyes on John for the first time and tell Trudy, "Hey, I think I've found the incredibly attractive hunk I'm finally going to have my firstborn child with." What moves the story forward can be two syllables uttered under Mary's breath with the right inflection (e.g., Mary sees John. "*Hel*-lo . . . !").

2. Dialogue can carry plot, and it's also good at providing the necessary information that must be conveyed before the plot proper gets under way. Mary sees John and, never taking her eyes off him, murmurs to Trudy: "This dance is singles-only, right?" Dialogue *sets the scene*.

3. But this is only one of two kinds of exposition that's often needed in scene construction. Continue Mary's conversation with Trudy as follows: Trudy answers Mary's question with an affirmative nod. Mary, still eyeing John, asks, "How long have I been divorced?" Now we're utilizing another expositional function: dialogue *reveals the past.*

4. Where these three uses of dialogue are largely concerned with matters of plot/structure and conflict, an absolutely vital function of dialogue is its ability to establish and sustain characterizations. Here comes John, who's noticed Mary's interest. Whether he says, "How do you do?" or "Yo, babe!" will tell us a lot. Dialogue *reveals character.* Inflection, accent, grammar, and all the many aspects of human speech come into play here, but certainly vocabulary (i.e., choice of words) is a crucial indication of who your movie's people are.

5. John says, "Yo, babe," winks at Mary, and continues past her to pick up a brewski, apparently his prime objective. Mary grimaces in disgust and turns to Trudy. "I swear," she says, "this mind-body problem is going to be the death of me." Dialogue *reveals theme.* It shouldn't be fortune cookie–like in its obviousness, but dialogue can, in many subtle and effective ways, speak to your story's axiom or area of interest. *Tootsie's* recurrent "friends" motif is a case in point.

6. Yet another function of dialogue deals with the world of your movie. If Mary reacts to John's "Yo, babe" with a roll of the eyes and a Valley-speak-inflected "What-*ev*-er," then mutters "Dork!" to Trudy, that's one kind of movie; if instead she licks her lips, murmurs "I hope he's got type O . . ." and smiles to reveal two gleaming fangs, we're clearly in another. Dialogue sets the mood and *defines tone.*

7. Finally, dialogue, instead of moving the story forward, can merely suggest or forestall forward momentum for dramatic purposes. John is distracted by someone else and doesn't approach

Mary. Mary mutters, "C'mon, it's getting late," and a puzzled Trudy looks at her wristwatch. "Not that clock," Mary says, and taps her lower belly. "This one." Dialogue *creates tension* and suspense, often via someone's acknowledgment or avoidance of a conflict.

Given these seven disparate (albeit often overlapping) functions, it's not surprising that the one rule concerning dialogue most familiar to writers of film and fiction alike is: *dialogue should do more than one thing at a time.*

> Mary walks into a diner where Joe sits devouring a
> piece of apple pie.
>
> MARY
>
> Hi, Joe.
>
> JOE
>
> Oh, hi, Mary. How's it going?
>
> MARY
>
> Pretty good. Especially since I can see you
> just lost our no-sugar diet contest.
>
> JOE
>
> I guess so.
>
> MARY
>
> You don't seem too happy about it.
>
> JOE
>
> Well, I never thought you'd find me here.
>
> MARY
>
> Too bad. Want to pay up now?

Any alert screenwriter could accomplish the same beat in one quick exchange:

> Mary enters the diner as Joe's devouring a piece of
> apple pie.
>
> MARY
>
> Just one slice?

JOE

Gol-dernit!
   (Sighs)
All right. . . . Got change for a twenty?

The lack of greetings telegraphs a friendship; people caught in an embarrassment are prone to involuntary displays of emotion. This kind of compression also introduces, however clumsily, a clearer sense of character: Joe's evidently not a guy who curses, and he doesn't sound like an urbanite. And if Mary had said, "Merely a single serving, is it?" we'd know she and Joe were probably not from the same ethnic background.

Dialogue that isn't revealing character as it moves the story forward (sets the scene, reveals the past, etc.) has no reason to live.

LESS IS MORE

A general principle in screenwriting scene construction is "come in as late as you can and leave as early as possible." In our post-MTV age, when some movie scenes take all of a second to make their point and move on, this is especially true for the crafting of cinematic conversation. A corollary to the "do several things at once" principle is "do it economically."

And bear in mind that while speech is a primary source of information (expositional or emotional), what *isn't* said is equally revealing.

"I'm thinking Charlie Bimbohead is the right man for this job," says Ben. Two executives exchange a quick glance. "Absolutely," one replies. What's been left out of the exchange is implied in a simple narrative direction, and the omission of any discussion also nails down the characterizations: Ben's the boss, wielding real power, and the exec's a flunky (only a true brown-noser would be so quick to unequivocally agree).

A screenwriter wanting to fill us in on the specific whys and wherefores of the situation might follow this scene with another. Cut to the hall. Exec 1: "Can you believe that our shit-for-brains boss is giving a worthless skirt chaser such a choice gig?" Exec 2: "I not only can believe it but will say nothing to jeopardize our own cushy positions by illiciting his ire." Clearly, the same objective could be reached another way:

EXEC 1
Bimbohead?! Well, great minds . . .

EXEC 2
Uh-huh. Meet you in the VP sauna?

Brevity is not always the point. *The Remains of the Day*, Ruth Prawer Jhabvala's admirable (if at times excruciating) adaptation of Ishiguro's novel, is replete with conversations that are like long, elegant waltzes on the grave of a relationship. But the dialogue between its hopelessly repressed protagonists creates a screamingly emotional subtext by virtue of *what is left out.*

The same principle applies not only to dialogue exchanges, but to entire scenes. Mamet may be going too far in his definition of a "perfect movie"; speech is so much a part of human expression that the contemporary film medium shouldn't be denied it. Still, it's certainly true that screenwriters are always confronted with a choice: to say it or to show it. You decide—what is the best means of expression for a given beat?

Romantic comedy writers are too often prone to letting dialogue carry their scenes. But the smart ones, like Richard Curtis, know the value of rewriting even one's choicest lines right out of a scene if it will serve the story best. Here is what Curtis originally intended for the midpoint of *Four Weddings*, in the key scene (from the shooting script reprinted in *Scenario*, vol. 1, no. 1) where Charles and Carrie, having slept together a second time despite her now being engaged to another man, wake up the morning after:

INT. CARRIE'S BEDROOM—DAWN
Dawn coming in Carrie's bedroom.

> CARRIE
> I think it's time you went.

> CHARLES
> But it's five in the morning.

> CARRIE
> And at nine in the morning my future
> mother-in-law comes round. We're
> discussing bridesmaids.

> CHARLES
> You're right. I've got very little to
> contribute on that one.

Silently Charles dresses. Watches her. She looks back
at him.

> CHARLES
> You see, this is my whole argument against
> marriage—even when I'd found the right
> girl—I'd keep bumping into you.

Her hand comes up and waves him goodbye. He
hesitates and then turns to go.

There's nothing ostensibly wrong with the scene as written, and a more stubborn writer, enjoying his little joke about bridesmaids and the eloquence of Charles in explaining his feelings, might have argued that the scene was essential. But Curtis, who wryly admits to seventeen rewrites on *Weddings*, evidently saw the wisdom of another approach. Here is the scene as published (by St. Martin's Griffin) after the movie was released, reflecting what we all saw on screen:

INT. CARRIE'S BEDROOM—DAWN

Dawn coming into Carrie's bedroom. Love theme
plays. Charles and Carrie lie awake in bed together.

Cut to Charles putting on his wedding coat. He
watches Carrie as she lies, half-awake, half-asleep. At
her most beautiful. Her eyes open. A long moment.
Then quietly he leaves the room.

That "long moment" is a quintessential less-is-more example.
Curtis and director Mike Newell evidently realized that in the
context of their story as a whole, (1) one more joke about the inappropriateness of Charles and Carrie's relationship and/or about
weddings in general wasn't necessary (and was perhaps even a
flogging of that horse), and (2) Charles's fairly direct expression of
his feelings for Carrie was actually a bit *too* much, since if he
seems too self-aware and demonstrative at that moment, his later,
more dramatic declaration of love could seem anticlimactic. Such
conversational boldness also puts too much emphasis on Charles's
side of the equation (Carrie says nothing) and raises the credibility issue (why *aren't* they being more direct with each other about
this romance?).

As the scene plays on-screen, it's amazing how much
poignant ambivalence and ambiguity—helped of course, by some
nice lighting and that "love theme"—seems packed into the long
moment when Hugh Grant and Andie MacDowell simply look at
each other. In fact, the very lack of dialogue at this crucial moment in the movie serves to maximize its conflict. Say something!
the audience silently entreats these lovers. Is he really going to
walk out the door, just like that . . . ? He is. And the movie's hook
(a tantalizing sense that this man and woman *are* a couple, but
just can't own up to it) sinks in deeper, as we now wait to see how
the impossible/inevitable will be made to occur.

Interesting to note, from a writer's point of view, that Curtis
and his team arrived at the more satisfying "less" moment after he
had written the "more." Part of what makes the scene work as it
stands is that Curtis had played through Charles and Carrie's possible conversation, and he was intimately familiar with each character's thoughts, feelings, and attitudes. This is the screenwriter's

duty—you find the truth of the moment and write it as fully and richly as you can. But once the discovery is made, you may find that removing a few words, lines, or an entire scene is the most effective means of dramatizing your beat. That's the art of "less is more."

The *story line* is more important than the "good line."

EMOTIONAL CLARITY

Because Richard Curtis is one of our finest living masters of pithy, laugh-out-loud dialogue, we can take him to task on his discarded scene. As Curtis himself would be likely to admit (he's as marvelously self-deprecating about his work, in print, as his Hugh Grant characters can be on-screen), Charles's original midpoint dialogue is somewhat guilty of a screenwriting cardinal sin: we would say that it's too "on the nose."

Inference, intimation, and innuendo are techniques dear to all screenwriters, but in the romantic comedy genre, they're truly prized. When we're dealing with matters risky and risqué, with sexual and emotional intimacy, then sly double entendre and wry understatement are our stock-in-trade. Howard Hawks coined a term for it back in the 1930s; he referred to the sort of dialogue Ben Hecht and others wrote for him as "three-cushion" dialogue, meaning that, as a billiard ball bounces from one side of the table's felt to another before going in the hole, the point of a scene would be hit to one side, another, and yet another—without ever being directly articulated.

This is not to suggest that your characters ought to beat around the bush. But credible, complex, and compelling characters tend to speak more obliquely than squarely—as do their real-life counterparts on occasion. That's what makes them interesting. Witness our introduction to Fiona, at *Weddings'* first wedding. She gets the movie's first actual sentence of dialogue, after the opening montage's infamous string of expletives, when Charles rushes into his seat beside her:

FIONA

There's a sort of greatness to your lateness.

CHARLES

Thanks. It's not achieved without real
suffering.

The affection and sly wit intermingled in Fiona's line—as well as the immediate deadpan response in kind from Charles—goes a long way toward setting up a friendship that goes, as we eventually discover, deeper than even Charles suspects. Fiona doesn't say "I know you're always late because I'm conscious of everything you do, finding you as attractive as I do." That would be on the nose. What's deftly squeezed into Curtis's line, however, is a subliminal hint of those feelings, not entirely disguised in this casual backhanded compliment.

Remember how smart you are as an audience, and then write for someone as smart (or smarter) than you. We don't need to be hit on the head with plot beats; the lightest tap can go quite a distance. Good dialogue does this—hints at what's really going on without giving the game away.

Unless it's time to do just that.

Screenwriters who are justifiably leery of being too on the nose sometimes fall into the other kind of dialogue-writing folly. Too much wordplay can lead to obtuseness and obscurity, and to exasperation for your audience. While appealing to their intelligence is one thing, you're also trying to hit them where they live—in the gut. So every now and then, there's nothing more effective than having characters really make their feelings felt.

This is what gives Fiona's confession, late in the movie, its undeniable force. That this woman, who can go one-on-one with Charles in batting witticisms back and forth, is finally driven to a straightforward declaration of love makes the moment as significant as it could possibly be. Similarly, when Jerry Maguire, not a character ever given to being up front and personal when it comes to his emotions, tells Dorothy, "You complete me," we're nearly as bowled over as she is by the raw honesty of what he's admitting.

In both cases, specificity is what takes the onus off what could seem to be too on the nose. Fiona, even in her naked vulnerability, winds up her statement on a bittersweet, self-mocking note that's totally Fiona-esque ("It's always been you, since first we met oh so many years ago. I knew the first moment. Across a crowded room— or lawn in fact."). And Jerry Maguire is, of course, repeating the words that Dorothy herself had to translate for him from the hand signals made by a mute couple they once met in an elevator.

But the point is, romance comedy writers can't shy away from the big emotions their characters inevitably experience. One of the reasons people come to these movies is to share those feelings. So your dialogue has to have, above all, *emotional clarity*. Whether your character is tap-dancing around the truth in an amusing, less-is-more exchange, or finally baring her innermost soul, the dialogue is there to make the feelings felt.

This is the secret weapon of all good dialogue. Why resort to spoken words anyway, given the arsenal of cinematic storytelling techniques at a screenwriter's disposal? Because dialogue is perhaps the most effective storytelling component for *using feelings to express information*. Exposition uttered in anger, character revealed in a moment of heartbreak, the joke that earns laughter because it's breaking incredible tension . . . these are some of the truthful moments we treasure in our favorite romantic comedies. So make sure your dialogue is doing as much as it can do.

SUMMARY

Good dialogue is functional. It's there for a reason, and its uses are many. Dialogue can move the story forward, provide exposition (set the scene and reveal the past), reveal character, reveal theme, define tone, and create tension. Given its myriad functions, dialogue should always do more than one thing at a time.

It should also be economical. Often, when it comes to the verbal expression of a given beat, less is more; brief, maximally compressed dialogue can speak volumes through implication or through what's left unsaid. Sometimes screenwriters write a scene in dialogue to discover the truth of a moment and subsequently end up cutting out all the dialogue.

While writing too bluntly (i.e., verbalizing subtext) results in clumsily on-the-nose dialogue, and while romantic comedies do thrive on more subtle, wordplay-driven approaches, don't shy away from moments when characters can reveal their raw emotions in simple, heartfelt terms. Striking the balance between insinuation and naked revelation is part of the art of dialogue, a writer's best tool for using feelings to express information.

Exercise: Working with Dialogue

1. Here is a brief dialogue excerpt from a well-crafted romantic comedy. Read through it once, and then take a more analytical look at it. Answer the questions that immediately follow the excerpt.

In *Some Like It Hot* (by Billy Wilder and I. A. L. Diamond), this scene introduces the leading men: buddies Jerry (Jack Lemmon) and Joe (Tony Curtis). They're playing bass and saxophone, respectively, on the bandstand of a speakeasy, as Jerry speaks his first lines of the movie:

> JERRY
> Say, Joe—tonight's the night, isn't it?

> JOE
> (*Eye on tap dancer*) I'll say.

> JERRY
> I mean, we get paid tonight, don't we?

(continued)

Exercise: Working with Dialogue   (continued)

                              JOE
Yeah. Why?

                              JERRY
Because I lost a filling in my back tooth. I
gotta go to the dentist tomorrow.

                              JOE
Dentist? We been out of work for four
months—and you want to blow your
first week's pay on your teeth?

                              JERRY
It's just a little inlay—it doesn't even have
to be gold—

                              JOE
How can you be so selfish? We owe back
rent—we're in for eighty-nine bucks to
Moe's Delicatessen—we're being sued by
three Chinese lawyers because our check
bounced at the laundry—we've borrowed
money from every girl in the line—

                              JERRY
You're right, Joe.

                              JOE
Of course I am.

                              JERRY
First thing tomorrow we're going to pay
everybody a little something on account.

                              JOE
No we're not.

                              JERRY
We're not?

JOE

First thing tomorrow we're going out to
the dog track and put the whole bundle
on Greased Lightning.

JERRY

You're going to bet my money on a *dog?*

JOE

He's a shoo-in. I got the word from Max
the waiter—his brother-in-law is the
electrician who wires the rabbit—

Is there a conflict between Jerry and Joe? What do we learn about
their present situation? What's been going on in the recent past?
Is any tension created about their future? What do we learn about
Jerry's character? Joe's? What kind of tone is established? Given
that this is the opening scene for these buddies, is there anything
else we need to know about them?

2a. *For writers who've yet to begin a draft,* pick a scene from
your outline or beat-sheet, one that you've got a pretty good
sense of in terms of the beat it's meant to convey.

Write a draft of it in as pure a dialogue form as possible,
meaning restrict yourself to using only the most minimal, absolutely necessary stage directions. For example:

MARY

(Pulling out a gun)
Why not stick around?

Try to limit your length (and/or cut it down) to three pages at the
most. Now submit it to the seven-uses-of-dialogue test. Is every
exchange in the scene doing at least double duty? If not, what
makes a particular line essential to your scene? Revise until it
seems maximally functional.

(continued)

Exercise: Working with Dialogue *(continued)*

2b. For writers with a completed draft or draft in progress, pull a dialogue-heavy scene that's no more than three pages in length. Remove all the narrative. Does the scene work?

Put in the bare minimum of stage directions necessary (see item *2a*) and then submit it to the seven-uses test. Revise, cut, and combine until every line is doing at least double duty.

CHAPTER ELEVEN

Imagery—The Movie
in Your Mind's Eye

*I have had problems with writers because I find that I am
teaching them cinematics. A lot of writers . . . go by what is
written on the page. I have no interest in that. I have that
square, white rectangle to fill with a succession of images, one
following the other. That's what makes a film.*

ALFRED HITCHCOCK

*When I write a screenplay I describe a movie that's already
been shot.*

ROBERT TOWNE

Where are the romantic comedies of Scorsese? Malick?
Bertolucci? Polanski? Coppola? Today, when a cross-
genre free-for-all sensibility permeates both mainstream and indie moviemaking, you don't see auteurs from either
the quirky fringe (e.g., the Coen Brothers) or the center (e.g.,
Spielberg) adding a classic romantic comedy to the canon.

To be fair, few of the foregoing filmmakers have proven to be
adept at comedy, period. The drama, the adventure-and-action,
and the thriller movie have traditionally been the favored turf
of heavyweight directors. But while even the musical has attracted (in both cases, fatally) Coppola and Scorsese, our
genre—with the sole exception of the Woodman, who can filmically hold his own with the best—is remarkably weak in cinematic champions. What is it about romantic comedy that has

kept our most visually involving, cinematically inspired artists from taking a whack at it?

Some say it's the subject matter itself, which can seem too lightweight. But matters sexual and farcical didn't keep the dark and dour Ingmar Bergman from doing his wonderful *Smiles of a Summer Night*. And members of Hollywood's Golden Age pantheon did some of their best work in the form (see Hawks, Sturges, Wilder, et al.). You'll also notice that the biggest box office stars have rarely shied away from romantic comedy material.

No, the fault—to paraphrase Shakespeare, who excelled at such material—lies not with our stars, but with ourselves. I blame us—the writers.

The talking-heads romantic comedy has given our genre a bad rap. Coupled with its penchant for contrivance and the too-easily-achieved happy ending is the contemporary rom-com's dire habit of turning into television, theater or stand-up that's more like sit-down. When people think of our genre, they're likely to picture funny, flirtatious conversations over a dinner table. Somewhere in the back end of the past century, the romantic comedy seems to have largely forgotten that it's a *movie*.

Consider two exceptions, both monster hits. *Romancing the Stone* kicks cinematic butt. Mud slides, whitewater escapades, knife fights—even its obligatory he-and-she-forced-to-spend-a-night-together-in-close-quarters scene was enlivened by the quick decapitation of a snake. And *Shakespeare in Love*, for all its verbiage, *moves*. The story hits the ground running with that let's-burn-the-feet-off-a-theater-manager scene, whirls its way through swordfights, costume balls, and tavern brawls, and is still soaring (literally, over the shores of the New World) in its final fadeout.

These are movie movies. What both of these seemingly disparate romantic comedies have in common is an imaginative embrace of *imagery*. Both are genre hybrids (adventure/romance and period/romance comedies), so they get assistance from milieus that are naturally rich in visual opportunities, but the point is, they were clearly conceived with the big screen in mind. Or, to echo Robert Towne's quote at the beginning of this chapter, they were conceived on the screens of their writers' minds—they were *seen* as well as heard.

Would that this were the case with the majority of romantic comedy scripts floating around town. Unfortunately, many specs written in our genre read as if their writers had never even been to the movies. And though it's true that an exceptionally well-written romantic comedy that's dialogue-heavy can lead to a great movie (*Chasing Amy* is one such rule breaker), many of these scripts never get in front of a camera because they don't demand—or command—that medium. The criticisms "small" and "soft" are often code for: this doesn't have to be a movie (i.e., it might as well be on the stage or TV screen or in a short-story magazine).

Are you really thinking in pictures? Are you aware of all the many powerful techniques—from sound editing to color manipulation—that filmmakers have at their disposal in telling a story on the screen? Your romantic comedy doesn't have to be set on the Amazon River or in a medieval monastery to utilize cinematic storytelling. Brooklyn was all Spike Lee needed, given his electric imagination, to turn *She's Gotta Have It* into a memorable feast of imagery.

Working with images is an essential component of screenwriting, and thinking in imagery and film technique can enliven even the most seemingly mundane, character-driven story. If you want your romantic comedy to really deserve, and hold, the big screen, it helps to be familiar with everything that's in a moviemaker's toolbox.

Savvy screenwriters are well aware that what they are writing when they write a screenplay is essentially a blueprint. A veritable army of technicians, creative assistants, and performers (director of photography, editor, production designer, et al.) will transform what's on the page into that stream of moving images unspooling in the multiplex. All the more reason to be as specific—as visually acute and imaginative—as you can be when you're crafting those pages. For one thing, you want people who are reading your script to be excited by the movie it invokes in their minds. For another, you want the movie they see when they're reading to be as close as possible to the one you imagined when you wrote it.

EMOTION PICTURES

The more you think in terms of what film techniques can do for your story, the richer in imagery your story will be. And by *imagery*, I don't mean the kind of beautiful-happy-people-walk-down-an-empty-tropical-beach-at-sunset fare that's common fodder for airline commercials. What goes into effective movie imagery is not unlike what makes for good dialogue: memorable images evoke character, theme, story concepts, and above all, emotions.

A choice of camera angle, for example, can convey emotions and psychological subtext. A camera that looks up at the story's protagonist against a vibrant blue sky is saying "heroic," just as a high-angle shot both literally and figuratively "looks down on" a character. The choppy cutting you suggest on your page by writing a quick montage of action phrases ("the horse, rearing—John ducks—reins whip by") telegraphs the confusion and excitement of a sudden calamity.

Say your story beat is the dark moment when your heroine, despite her love for the hero, has decided she has to leave him. The two discuss her reasons, and then she's gone. On the page, you might have their poignant dialogue followed by a line of narrative: "Jane exits, leaving Pete alone."

But what does that tell us about the moment? How does each character feel, and just as important, how are we to feel about each of them? A cheap revision of the line might read: "Jane exits sadly, leaving Pete alone and forlorn." That's certainly clearer, but it's banal. And what does it conjure up in the mind's eye?

A multitude of options present themselves, however, if you

design a visualization of the moment that speaks to subtext. If Jane's exit so devastates Pete that his life stops in its tracks, you might want to compose a shot of him accordingly: "While couples in the crowded park rollerblade, toss frisbees to their dogs, and stroll in the sun, Pete is a solitary figure immobile on the bench." Is Jane leaving Pete because he's done something that diminishes him in her eyes? Then, as Jane ascends a hill, Pete might be "a tiny dark shadow on the bench far below her." What about Pete's perception of Jane? "The setting sun burnishes Jane's blonde hair and highlights her white dress as she walks away. She's like a candle that recedes, flickers, then disappears amidst the trees."

These on-the-nose enhancements aren't great writing, but the exaggerations are there to make the point: use pictures to tell your story and get your emotions across.

You're making a movie when you write, so filmic techniques of all kinds are up for grabs. There's a marvelous moment in Truffaut's *Shoot the Piano Player* when a character declares, "May my mother drop dead if I'm not telling you the truth," and Truffaut immediately cuts to a shot of a gray-haired matron clutching her chest and falling to the floor. He's back to reality in about three seconds, and the cutaway, which gets an audience laugh, is much more playfully visceral than any pedestrian treatment (e.g., shifty eyes) would be.

The more you visualize your scenes on the page, the more vivid the material becomes. The screenwriter's goal is to inhabit the moment as if it's happening before his/her eyes. Where are the characters standing, and what are they doing? Where's the audience in relation to them? What's being revealed in the frame—by light, by color, by design?

Of course, what you don't want to do is clutter up your text with literal shot descriptions. Scripts riddled with camera terminology ("we pan to . . .", zoom in for a close-up of . . .", camera revolves around him to reveal . . .") constantly interrupt the flow of the storytelling (and annoy any director reading such descriptions, since you're meddling in what's ultimately his field of expertise). The trick is to *suggest* shots and scene construction by first visualizing the pictures in your mind and then choosing your language carefully to imply what's meant to be seen on the screen. For example, consider these three shots:

1. At the far end of the cavernous ballroom, the silhouette of a tall, thin figure appears in the doorway.

2. It's clear how Bean "Pole" Baxter earned her nickname as her heels pause on the threshold and the silver barrette in her hair grazes the top of the doorframe.

3. The tiny crescent-moon scar under her left eye seems to glow in the light from the open door.

Obviously we've moved from long shot to medium to close-up, but the camera positions are only implied. Using this kind of descriptive language, you should be able to "pre-direct" your material when necessary without being unduly intrusive.

The primary function of such cinematic storytelling, beyond clarity of visualization, remains metaphorical. One resonant image can speak volumes, in the manner of a well-wrought haiku. Films that are truly alive to such poetic possibilities sometimes employ *image systems*—stating a theme through the use of an evocative metaphorical or symbolic image and then weaving variations on that theme throughout the story.

Moonstruck, for example, uses the moon as a visual touchstone. As the story progresses, its presence begins to seem truly mystical, like a magic talisman uniting the disparate characters into one lunar-bewitched family. At the same time, there's a secondary image system involving hands—specifically, one hand finding another. When you next see *Moonstruck*, check out how this simple but powerful visual concept enriches the story, from its first introduction (as Ronnie brandishes his isolated, wooden hand) through symbolic permutations (Mimi and Rudolpho reaching for each other's hands onstage at the Met) to its climactic use (as Loretta takes Ronnie's hand).

Imagery is the very essence of moviemaking, and a romantic comedy script that's strong in "emotion pictures" is far more likely to attract interest.

MOTION PICTURES

On a more pragmatic level, since we're hoping to make movies, not "stillies," your romantic comedy should keep moving—meaning that even if your characters have to be confined to one location, the eyes of your audience should be engaged and in motion (as opposed to drooping shut).

Just as visual metaphors can enliven your storytelling, scene settings can offer many a visual opportunity. Sam Mendes and Alan Ball's *American Beauty* milks maximum humor and pathos out of its suburban milieu. *Bullets Over Broadway* similarly takes advantage of the clash between its upscale theater world and its pool-hall/waterfront underworld.

Settings in turn suggest another helpful visual storytelling technique—what's known in the business as "business." Generally, any action woven in, around, and through dialogue will enliven the reality and content of a scene, so it's a good idea to give your characters something to do. The talky *When Harry Met Sally* is a virtual manual on this technique; witness Harry and Jess doing "the wave" as they discuss Harry's breakup at the football stadium, and Harry and Jess batting balls as they discuss Harry's relationship with Sally. In both cases, the business they're given creates additional humor for the scene. When Harry, shopping with Sally, seizes upon a karaoke machine to play with, this business even sets up and makes all the more awkward the scene's plot beat: Harry running into his ex, Helen.

In scenes where an obvious piece of specific business doesn't present itself, visually conscious screenwriters help dialogue along through *wallpapering*, creating a backdrop of visual interest for an otherwise static scene. A talk-on-a-bench scene where *Splash*'s Tom Hanks talks to mermaid Darryl Hannah is wallpapered with an ice-skating rink full of active skaters. *My Best Friend's Wedding* sets a crucial scene between Julia Roberts and Dermot Mulroney against a major-league baseball game in progress. Similarly, writers employ a walk-and-talk device for dialogue-heavy scenes that might otherwise go inert. *Sleepless in Seattle* is just one of hundreds of romantic comedies with its respective Buddy scenes (Hanks with Reiner, Ryan with O'Donnell) beginning out on the street before ending up at the lunch table.

Sleepless also makes an effective use of *mood painting* in its scenes that feature still-grieving widower Hanks. We know that Seattle's prone to showers, but take a look at the myriad shades of gray infusing all the sets (from office to home to street) this character occupies, wearing subdued and muted-color clothing to match. Similarly, the cold metallic light of old black-and-white movies playing on a TV screen becomes the symbol of a heroine's misguided affection (she's in love with her boyfriend's ghost) in Anthony Minghella's *Truly, Madly, Deeply*.

Finally, romantic comedies in particular can always use an action sequence to keep their "movieness" alive and kicking. While you may not want to contrive an out-and-out action set piece that wreaks havoc with your story's tone (*The Fugitive*'s train wreck would derail your average romantic comedy), an activity that arises naturally enough from your characters' lives or livelihoods can be helpful. *Four Weddings*, having established its Scottish fiancé for Carrie, delivers a boisterous Scottish dancing sequence amidst wedding sequence number 3, using it as a tacit catalyst for the collapse of supporting character Gareth. Simply putting a character on wheels livens things up in *Arthur*, as Arthur, unhappy without his beloved, goes speeding round a racetrack. A similar gambit gets used in the admirably quirky coming-of-age romantic comedy *Rushmore*, when hapless protagonist Max flies a toy plane by remote control to work off his existential angst.

All of these strategies function best when they have *integrity* (arise organically from the material). A patriarch who's a master chef is the anchor for *Eat Drink Man Woman*, and thus this clever ensemble romantic comedy is replete with mouthwatering food-preparation scenes that are as visually arresting as a train wreck or its ilk. Look to your characters and their environments for visual keys and devices. Above all, keep *looking*. See that imaginary movie in your mind, then describe it on the page. If your visual storytelling is inventive enough, you might even snag the interest of one of those elusive auteurs.

Speaking of which, let's take a brief tour of a bona fide romantic comedy masterpiece to see how one of America's finest cinematic storytellers utilized all of these techniques—and more.

....

CASE STUDY

Annie Hall

Screenplay: Woody Allen and Marshall Brickman
Director: Woody Allen
Leads: Diane Keaton and Woody Allen
Released by United Artists in 1977 (92 min.)

Log line: A neurotic comedian recalls his poignant and amusing relationship with the equally neurotic aspiring singer who eventually outgrew him.

Synopsis

Stand-up comedian Alvy Singer talks to the audience of his midlife crisis in the wake of his breakup with Annie Hall. He recalls his childhood in Brooklyn; he's always been a social misfit, prone to fantasy, and afraid of death. [1] We pick up his relationship with Annie when things aren't going well [2], which leads to flashbacks showing how neurotic behavior sabotaged his first marriage. We then hopscotch through time, from the early bliss of his romance with Annie, back to the dissolution of his second marriage, to Alvy and Annie's first meeting—introduced by Alvy's best friend Rob and his date, playing doubles tennis. [3]

Alvy and Annie begin dating, with him supporting this low-self-esteem-plagued woman in her first stabs at becoming a professional singer and encouraging her to further her education. Though they're very much in love, Annie can't relax in bed without smoking marijuana, and Alvy's threatened by her moving into his apartment and the commitment this signifies. A visit to her uptight WASP family (contrasted with Alvy's boisterous ethnic brood) tacitly underlines the essential differences in their sensibilities, and soon Alvy's jealousy of Annie's relationship with an adult-education professor leads to their breaking up. [4]

After some unhappy time spent apart, Annie summons Alvy to her apartment (rescuing him from a weird one-night stand) to kill a spider; they end up reconciling and vowing never to part again. But their second honeymoon becomes short-lived as Annie's career gets a lift from big-time record producer Tony Lacey. Annie and Alvy visit Los Angeles, where die-hard New Yorker Alvy can't abide the lifestyle his transplanted friend Rob is enjoying, but Annie's exposure to such fun in the sun only serves to highlight her unease with Alvy. On their way home they decide their relationship is over and break up again. [5]

Alvy's unable to find happiness with another woman, and flies to L.A. to ask Annie to marry him, demanding she return to New York. But Annie refuses. [6] Back in Manhattan, Alvy tries to work out his disappointment through writing about the romance. After some time, he and Annie meet as friends and part amicably. The present-day Alvy is philosophical about relationships, which he sees as absurd, but necessary. [7]

Note: The "Anti-Beats" of Annie Hall. Seven-beat analysis of the film is particularly academic because the original script, a sprawling 140-plus-page mass of material, was never intended to be a romantic comedy. The Alvy-Annie throughline was created by Allen, Brickman, and editor Ralph Rosenblum in the course of editing a two-hour-plus rough cut (a general autobiography of Alvy Singer) down to its current, refocused form.

Interestingly, what the team wrought yields beats that support a kind of antiromantic arc. They make ironic sense for a story whose *joyful defeat* is the dissolution of a relationship. Thus, part of the setup is news of the romance's failure. The structural *cute meet* introduces us to the couple at their relationship's nadir, showing us why it didn't work as opposed to why it did. The catalyst turning point is the couple's own cute meet, reversing the usual expectations of a romantic comedy first-act break (the *complication* is their becoming attracted to each other when we know they're doomed to part).

The other beats follow form: a midpoint *hook* tacitly establishes that Alvy and Annie can't and won't end up together. The *swivel* is a decision to break up that we on some level actually support. The *dark moment* is Alvy's irrational marriage proposal, which Annie sensibly refuses, and the *resolution* is a tacit understanding that the breakup was for the best.

· ·

What remains perhaps most impressive about this Woody Allen classic, when viewed today, is how little its filmic innovations have aged. In retrospect, we can see just how pervasive an influence *Annie Hall* has had on the genre—so much so that even now, no romantic comedy writers and/or directors (and, for that matter, few filmmakers in any genre) have taken the form much further.

In its freewheeling trajectory in and out of reality, fantasy, past, present, subjective points of view, and various filmic mediums (from animation to black-and-white documentary), Allen's "little" movie has proven to be a sort of tabula rasa for the contemporary urban comedy, be it romantic or ensemble sit-comic (one can't, for example, imagine *Seinfeld* without it). And what's daunting (if not depressing) is that some two dozen years after its release, many romantic comedy writers are still struggling to come up to the standard that *Annie Hall* set in 1977.

While the movie is chock-full of memorable dialogue, its visual inventions are what make it so uniquely entertaining. Allen's visual approach to his material didn't come from nowhere. As we've noted, he was heavily influenced by the European cinema of the 1960s. An acknowledged fan of Bergman and Fellini, Allen had already progressed, filmically, from the amateurish first-feature flatness of *Take the Money and Run* to the assured, faux-epic pictorial grandeur of *Love and Death*. But he put various techniques already familiar from cutting-edge foreign films to use in his latest work for good reason. Allen's intention, according to quotes in a number of texts, was to convey on-screen what it was like to be inside comedian Alvy Singer's mind.

Given this conceptual premise, the form of *Annie Hall* seems all the more sound and profound. Not unlike one of Allen's own nightclub stand-up monologues, the movie sails through a series of stream-of-consciousness riffs, closer to the jazz improvisations near and dear to this clarinetist than a linear, earthbound traditional narrative. It helps, of course, that Singer/Allen's mind is a funny, fascinating place to be and that the basic melody he weaves his variations on is a love song to a uniquely appealing character.

So what does this sort of subjective reality look like? Take just one moment among many: the scene that portrays Annie, in bed with Alvy, literally splitting into two Annies—one who remains entwined with Alvy (Annie's body as sexual object) and one rising from the bed to sit on a nearby chair and contemplate doing some drawing (Annie's mind). Allen expands on this already intriguing conceit by having Alvy acknowledge the presence of Annie's second self and talk to Annie-in-bed about her being so "removed."

The same idea could be conveyed in fiction, in poetry, and perhaps (with the use of body doubles) onstage, however clumsily. But not with the same immediacy and effectiveness. Clearly, this is quintessential cinematic storytelling. The story beat has been conceived and executed by taking advantage of those qualities unique to one medium: film. The screenwriter is thinking in moving pictures.

Filmmaking Language   The opening *shot* of the movie, while not revolutionary (Groucho Marx, Jack Benny, and George Burns all used this technique), establishes the movie's unconventional sensibility, as Alvy Singer "breaks the fourth wall" by addressing the audience directly. The brisk *flashbacks* that follow the first, more lengthy flashback scene with young Alvy in the doctor's office establish the *editing rhythm* of the story, with *jump cuts* leaping through time and space. We enter Alvy's schoolroom through a slow *pan*, moving from one teacher at the blackboard to another, and this shot concept creates a purely *filmic space* as three separate times are combined into one by the camera's seamless movement. *Sound editing*, meanwhile, carries Alvy's monologue forward, into a flashback that becomes *filmic fantasy* as the grown-up Alvy occupies the same space and time as the childhood Alvy. The sequence is topped by one of the movie's most memorable gags, as the children recite their grown-up, present-day occupations for the camera, including a young Joyce Carol Oates–type who announces that she's "into leather." We cut to *video footage*, a manipulation of medium offering us a glimpse of Alvy's success as a comedian on TV, then cut to Alvy's mother in *flashback/fantasy* again, dressed in her 1940s clothes, clearly situated in that era as she talks to us in the present day.

So many rules of conventional narrative time and space have been broken in the film's opening ten minutes that we're now prepared to go anywhere with our narrator. And we do—into two masterful *split-screen* sequences (the contrasting families and the dueling therapy sessions), *animation* (Alvy's "Wicked Witch" fantasy), *subtitles* that convey unexpressed thoughts, and virtuoso *montages* that compress years of time into minutes.

Allen's achievement, considering how he's dealing so freely with "reality," is that the movie nonetheless delivers a realistically portrayed, emotionally effecting relationship between two fully realized flesh-and-blood characters. He's aided in this by the subtler, more conventional use of *lighting, color,* and *production design* throughout.

Director of photography Gordon Willis, who only a few years previously had virtually patented the contemporary conception of period lighting in the golden, sepia-toned *Godfather I* and *II* (and continued doing some of his most outstanding work with Allen for years afterward, including the shamefully under-appreciated *Zelig*), utilized a gorgeous palette in *Annie Hall,* with images at times elegiac (the deep blue "magic hour" moment on the pier) and at other moments farcically bright (the Hollywood party at Tony Lacey's house). The art direction of Mel Bourne and costume design of Ruth Morley fill out and deepen the movie's canvas, from Alvy and Allison Portchnik's early 1960s liberal-intellectual-couple apartment with its brass bed, book stacks, and Aubrey Beardsley print on the wall to the perfect posthippie professional garb worn both in and out of bed by Pam, the space-cadet reporter played by Shelley Duvall.

Emotion Pictures   *Annie Hall* is visually arresting at every turn, and certainly there are individual images that resonate with emotion. There are a number of contrasting worlds and before-and-after linkages. Annie's first nightclub sequence, for example, with her appearing pale and tremulous at the microphone amidst garish purples and blues during her ultimate nightmare of a club audition, in vivid contrast to the later nightclub scene (one of the movie's longest uncut takes), a lovingly respectful portrait of Annie as a matured singer, bathed in velvet blacks and the warm reddish glow of accomplishment . . . the split-screen therapy session, its set decor a virtual short-story portrait of Annie and Alvy's respective sensibilities, with their physical behavior and dialogue underlining the ironic exasperation felt by two people going through the same experience—but experiencing it totally differently . . . Alvy's explosion of hostility in the L.A. parking lot, crashing from car to car, cross-cut with flashes of the bumper cars he drove as a kid . . .

Rosenblum and Allen make a poignant montage of the movie's more overtly romantic moments at the climax, and what's most telling is the final image, which speaks to the story's subtle but pervasive *image system.* When Alvy and Annie have parted for the last time on an Upper West Side street corner, the camera holds on a view of what has been, all along, a significant supporting character in *Annie Hall:* New York City.

Manhattan looms large in this movie. The edges of its canvas are filled with New York cars and cabs, tourist sites, athletic clubs, bars, restaurants, downtown streets, movie theaters, and parks. A near-constant stream of quirky pedestrians act as figures of fun for Annie and Alvy to comment on in Central Park and as Greek chorus–like individuals solicited by Alvy for advice, even offering him news uninvited, like the man on the street who informs Alvy, late in the film, that Annie is now living happily with Tony Lacey in Los Angeles.

The pervasive presence of the city, and Alvy Singer's association with it, make the contrast of sunny L.A. all the more surreal. The separate-worlds subtext underscores our view of Annie when she angrily confronts Alvy at their abortive Sunset Strip lunch date; where the New York Annie had that wide-eyed apologetic innocence, hiding behind her bag and racquet in the tennis club lobby, the L.A. Annie hides her eyes behind tinted sunglasses, defiant and opaque in the chilly Hollywood sun. She even articulates the idea overtly, accusing Alvy of being, like the city, an island unto himself.

Alvy-as-Manhattan, full of brilliant comedic hostility and restless neurotic energy and not going gentle into any good night, is the implicit central metaphor of *Annie Hall.* The equation of his horn-rimmed glasses with the many-windowed skylines filling out the frame is what gives the movie its extra thematic kick. It makes Allen's follow-up film, after the experimental *Interiors,* seem absolutely inevitable: *Manhattan* begins with one long cinematic/poetic paean to his muse.

Motion Pictures   On a purely technical level, *Annie Hall* is replete with visual storytelling devices that keep the action active. The long take that starts on an empty sidewalk while Alvy and

Rob's conversation begins off-camera, is one of many walk-and-talks. Even here, Allen pushes the envelope; a walk across the sand dunes of eastern Long Island, utilizing a voice-over conversation between Alvy and Annie, never does introduce the characters on-screen, preferring to take a shared-subjective point of view, as if we are Annie and Alvy walking. Backstage bustle serves as wallpaper for the first Allison Portchnik flashback, just as her clipboard and pencil give her plenty of business for that scene. The bright light, saturated candy colors, and contrived clothing mood-paint the Los Angeles sequences. And while there are few stand-alone action sequences, certainly Alvy's wild car ride in Annie's VW qualifies, along with other brief moments such as the preceding tennis game.

The combustion between visual invention and verbal gag is the very essence of *Annie Hall*'s greatness, and one of its scenes in particular has become a paradigm for the kind of talk-plus-action scene we think of now when we think of romantic comedy: Alvy and Annie versus the lobsters.

Why the murder of innocent crustaceans should provoke such affection and merriment may be one of life's cruel mysteries, but there's no denying that this delightfully absurd interlude embodies everything a romantic comedy screenwriter would want from a couple-in-love scene. Though the embarrassment Alvy endures here (fear of lobsters doesn't rate high on anyone's shortlist of manly qualities) is private rather than public, the shared humiliation (Annie's nearly as helpless, initially) creates a moment of closeness for the couple that even occasions an impromptu photo session (the stills later show up framed on the wall of Annie's apartment). The physical humor of Alvy's squeamish ineptitude as he tries to capture their fleeing dinner is topped by his typically quick verbal wit ("Talk to him!" he beseeches Annie, "You speak shellfish!"), and what could have been momentary business becomes the scene's real activity.

It's a vivid illustration of the life-is-what-happens-to-us-when-we're-busy-doing-other-things principle, as work becomes play, and joy (from where? for what?) transforms the mundane into something wonderful. Their laughter and ours arises from a recognition of what is so tenderly, ridiculously human in us humans. It's a celebration of the foolishness of our fears.

That Annie, in reaching for her camera, is aware (as are we) that "these are the good old days" gives the scene a subtly poignant subtext. Allen plays on this toward the movie's end in perhaps its most painful moment, as Alvy pathetically tries to replicate his and Annie's Hamptons experience with a woman who just doesn't get it. But *Annie Hall*'s original lobster hysteria, reprised in the ending's fond montage, remains one of its most beloved scenes. An ideal romantic coupling—two lovers enjoying each other being themselves—is etched in eternally amusing imagery.

That's cinematic storytelling.

SUMMARY

Romantic comedy screenplays that avail themselves of the full arsenal of filmmaking techniques stand a better chance of holding the big screen. Utilizing options of cinematography, editing, production design, etc., can enliven our often dialogue-immobilized genre. Screenwriters, by visualizing a movie in their minds, can suggest shooting and cutting ideas on the page without using technical language that distracts readers.

Imagery, when vividly evoked, brings out the emotional values in a scene, and much psychological and thematic subtext can be expressed by an imaginative visual metaphor. Some movies employ image systems, working variations on thematic material embodied in an "emotion picture" (e.g., the moon and the reaching hands used in *Moonstruck*). Alert screenwriters also employ a number of technical devices to add interest to their talk-heavy stories, such as wallpapering, business, and action sequences. Such visual aids should be organic to the material.

Exercise: Working with Imagery

1. Mike Nichols's eye-opening direction of Buck Henry and Calder Willingham's *The Graduate* was filled with visually exciting ideas, not the least of which is a now-famous match cut that still has film lovers extolling Nichols's cutting. What many don't realize is that it was the screenwriters' edit.

Ben Braddock, in the midst of his passionless affair with Mrs. Robinson, goes swimming in his parents' pool:

> At the waterline. Ben surfaces, and in one movement, pulls himself up on the raft and—
>
> Cut to:
>
> Int. Taft Hotel room—Night—lands on top of Mrs. Robinson on the bed. He stays on top of her for a moment.
>
> MR. BRADDOCK'S VOICE
> Ben—what are you doing?
>
> Ben turns toward us and looks.

"I would say that I'm just drifting," Ben answers his father—who's peering down at him from the side of the pool—as if he were still atop his partner. Henry and Willingham's disjunctive design then gives way, and we're into a scene at the pool, but for a wonderful few seconds of cinematic suspension, we've been inhabiting the center of a metaphor, simultaneously saddling two time-and-space frames, drifting with Benjamin across a bitterly meaningless moment of his life.

Scan your romantic comedy for such metaphoric opportunities. Do you have any leaps to make across your characters' complex lives? Any comments that could be made through the juxtaposition of disparate images? Are you thinking about the cuts from scene to scene? The visual equivalents of key phrases in your dialogue (e.g., "drifting")? The laughs you might get with a witty manipulation of time and space?

2*a*. Take the dialogue scene you worked on at the end of the last chapter and reconceive it in visual terms.

Using *no dialogue*, rewrite the scene to express the same plot beat and emotional values.

What can you suggest through camera angle, shot composition, and point of view? Can you make the moment more visually intense through sound manipulation? Lighting and color?

Is there a visual metaphor that can get your beat across? Are there characterization points that can be expressed through visual means?

2*b*. Compare your two versions of the scene. Now see if you can revise the scene a final time, combining the most effective moments of both. Use the maximally evocative images and the most expressive pieces of dialogue, substituting imagery for dialogue and vice versa to avoid repetition.

Ideally, this version of your scene should end up being the shortest and most vividly felt.

PART FOUR

Completing Your Draft and After

CHAPTER TWELVE

Deepening Your Craft

W hen it comes to basic writing skills, one thing is true of romantic comedy and every other movie genre: for any screenplay to make the successful transition from pile of paper to successful commercial commodity, it's got to be well crafted.

Screenwriting is a peculiar science, with peculiar hazards. Many a wonderful story concept has gotten stuck in development limbo because of politics or timing, and many a horrific script has gotten fast-tracked into production because of the same factors. But I've never heard of a screenplay that didn't get bought because it was written too well. With this in mind, let's look at your primary craft task: finishing your draft.

WHAT FIRST DRAFTS ARE FOR

Every screenwriter has his or her own method of getting through the pages. Most work from an outline, beat sheet, or stack of index

227

cards, but some are more free-form than others. One writer I know says that she dives into a draft at whatever scene she finds easiest to start with and writes from there, though she tends to work backward—knowing her ending before she begins. Ron Bass employs a small staff of researcher-writers who often map out an entire draft from first scene to last, according to his specifications, before he puts his own pencil to yellow pad.

However detailed or loose you like to play it, the ultimate object is to realize your story from start to finish—without stopping to rewrite or edit as you go. Get it all out first. Go with every impulse, no matter how absurd it may seem. "I can't have them say (do, think) *that,*" is to me a wonderful thought. You can and should make your characters do whatever occurs to you in the chaos of creation. First drafts are good testing grounds for all ideas. Have the courage to be bad. Something awful in a first draft can lead to an idea that's truly brilliant. Take the risk!

Creativity doesn't come out of a can, which is why that push-through energy may occasionally fail you. On days when a script that's been a congenial pussycat suddenly climbs up your back and whomps your head with a stick, step away from the draft altogether and let your unconscious take over. When you're truly immersed in a story, amazing things will suddenly come to you, lightning bolt–like, during your "time off"—when your conscious mind suspends its obsessive controlling.

Whatever your methodology, if you're doing it right (like a human being, not a computer software program), there are bound to be unforeseen developments—surprises either delightful or appalling. Chances are, the draft won't adhere exactly to your original intentions (or, if it does, this conformity may turn out to be troublesome). But whether the changes that occur in the writing are incremental or catastrophic, there are two things the first draft of a script should accomplish. The first, which is usually a done deed as soon as you type your final *Fade-out,* is to have the damn thing out of your head and on the page where you can get a look at it. *First drafts are for finding out what you're writing about.*

Only when you see your movie on the page for the first time do you have the unique opportunity of seeing what it says. Are the protagonists true to your conception of them? Do they end up where you wanted them to be? If so, does the ending really speak to that personal-but-universal thematic concern that got you started on this story in the first place? Do you have a second act? These are the kinds of questions a first draft answers. At the same time, such answers yield different kinds of questions (e.g., "What was I thinking?").

The second thing a finished first draft should accomplish is comparable to a doctor's diagnosis: *First drafts are for finding out what your problems are.*

What may have seemed sound on an index card has turned out to be shaky on the page. A leap you took with one character has left another in the dust. Something that was supposed to provoke laughter now seems more likely to bring out the handkerchiefs. Used properly, first drafts are great metal detector–like instruments. They show you which areas require digging, whether what's under the surface turns out to be silver or scrap metal.

A first draft that identifies both what it's about and what its problems are is the most valuable thing a screenwriter can have— even if the resulting revelations lead you to a paper shredder. The late playwright Mark Houston nailed it when he offered his definition of this part of the process: "A first draft," he said, "is just something to change."

Of course, it's hard to change something if the thing itself is un- defined—incoherent, murky, unclear. Which brings us to a craft issue of paramount importance.

CLARITY: THE BASIS OF GOOD STORYTELLING

After perusing close to 4,000 screenplays in my past decade of work, I've noticed two things that consistently create bumps in the reading road. If I'm confused at any point and have to stop and reread a passage to understand what's going on, it jars my involvement in the material. And if I'm not emotionally affected by characters because I don't understand what they're experiencing, it removes me from the world of the story. *Clarity in communicating actions and emotions is a key attribute of a successful draft.*

When it comes to clarity, every screenwriter walks a paradoxical tightrope, balancing inference and explicitness. We're told "show, don't tell," but at the same time, the audience has to understand exactly what's going on. While the what-you-see-is-what-you get rule holds true (what's on the screenplay page should reflect only what can actually be seen or heard on the screen), make sure that what we see is what you see. There's no room for ambiguity.

I once suffered through an exhaustive story conference about the midpoint in a romantic comedy of mine, optioned by a producer who just didn't get the point of this crucial scene. We went over protagonist Jake's character arc, invoked subtext, and talked structure until I questioned my own sanity, but it wasn't until I let slip a phrase in passing that I finally saw the lightbulb go off over the producer's head. "Oh," she said sheepishly. "I didn't realize Jake was walking down a *ledge*."

The fault wasn't hers, but mine. My narrative was a word or two off the mark (not calling a ledge a ledge)—enough to create a small-but-serious bump, which could easily have been avoided. Exactly what is going on in the action of your story must be absolutely clear.

A reader's involvement in your story also depends on his/her empathy for your characters, and this is created by another kind of clarity: *emotional clarity*. It's not enough to give your characters great depths of feeling and fascinating emotional complexities. Your reader and your audience have to understand—specifically—what those emotions are.

This is a trickier exactitude. Again, the screenwriter walks that tightrope between text and subtext. To show too much may seem melodramatic. But in this arena, it's usually better to err on the side of clarity. We get inside our protagonists, as opposed to watching them from a removed distance, when we identify with what they're feeling—and we do this in a linear way. Alert to detail, we pick up cues as we watch them go through a story, doing a kind of subliminal emotional math. If anything's fuzzy or missing from our equation, the figures don't add up. And we no longer care about what's happening to the character as we'd care about something happening to us.

Say that you introduce protagonist Melanie, en route to work in morning rush hour traffic. We can see she's in a hurry, driving fast and a bit recklessly. She cuts off a car and gets honked at, but ignores the driver and continues on. Racing across her office building's crowded lobby, she dashes through the just-closing doors of an elevator and, emerging on her busy floor, hustles through a labyrinth of people with requests and messages, making short shrift of them all until she arrives at her office. With a nod to her assistant, she's through the door to her inner sanctum. There's a glorious bouquet of fresh, still-wrapped red roses on her desk. Melanie looks for a card and finds none. Taking a moment's pause for the first time that morning, Melanie inhales the scent of one rose, eyes closed. Then she flips on her intercom, opens her Rolodex, and jumps into work mode.

On a superficial level, this description may have achieved its objective if the beat is that Melanie rushes to work to see if there's another gift from her secret admirer. But how are we supposed to feel about Melanie? A reader who's particularly peeved by inconsiderate drivers is already annoyed with her. Another, who works in an office, is offended by Melanie's apparent disregard for her colleagues. Even a relatively bias-free reader may perceive her as a workaholic. None of them, at any rate, have been made privy to Melanie's inner thoughts and feelings. They're guessing, and they may be guessing wrong.

Fine, the screenwriter might say, that's just the way she is. Melanie never shows her feelings until she falls in love—that's my whole point in this setup!

Wrong. We have to bond with a protagonist—especially with a potentially unsympathetic one—as soon as possible. In this regard, the description is rife with missed opportunities. Could we fill in the blanks without compromising the writer's conception of Melanie? Of course we could.

A driver who's fast and reckless could be angry, frightened, drunk. Melanie, given her situation, could be eager and distracted, "her mind on something other than the road," her expression dreamy (soft, spacy). Choose a reaction to that honk from the driver she's cut off: "Melanie winces, glancing apologetically into her rearview mirror, but the incident is soon forgotten as she accelerates, the shadow of a smile stealing across her face."

A closer look at Melanie's arrival reveals that the writer hasn't even truly delivered the story beat. How do we know she's rushing to work today, as opposed to any other day, specifically because she expects flowers? Give the receptionist some business: "The receptionist, surprised to see Melanie, glances at the clock." Carry the idea through Melanie's walk to her office, while creating more sympathy for her ("short shrift" can be managed deftly, charmingly, cleverly as opposed to arrogantly, coolly, officiously—depending on how your character interacts with each coworker). A quick "You're early today!" from someone isn't verboten, especially if Melanie's mute-but-friendly response telegraphs that she "doesn't reveal herself."

Melanie's assistant is useful. Say she's *not* surprised to see her boss in early, which suggests additional exposition (e.g., these gifts have come before). Give her a subtle nod in the direction of the office ("it's in there") and Melanie a pleased expression (there's collusion and a tacit friendship between exec and assistant). And finally, the rose moment itself can be tweaked in any number of ways to suggest something more specific in this burgeoning romance and Melanie's feelings about it (the slow caress of a flower petal with forefinger or cheek suggests sensuality, while an expression that becomes almost childlike gives us a different insight altogether).

I dwell on the point because it's such an important and too-often-overlooked aspect of the read. We have to care about your characters, and screenplays that are emotionally resonant become so through an accumulation of information. Just as you want to be crystal clear about the action in your story, you want to create empathy through the clarity of your characters' emotions. That's the basis of good storytelling.

Your first draft should communicate its story values clearly. Now let's explore the ways in which practiced writers make those values snap, crackle, and pop.

CRAFT ENHANCERS

One hidden goal of any screenplay is to be un-put-down-able. Readers and writers often talk about a story having "great energy," some kind of momentum that carries you from start to finish. Such energy doesn't necessarily require fast action and major pyrotechnics. It can even be evoked subliminally through choices of vocabulary and syntax.

One mark of an amateurish draft is the use of passive tense. "The gym is buzzing with activity. Jerry is standing on line. He is waiting for a machine to be free, and looking over the schedule of yoga classes." And I am putting down this script, because life's too short. Such passive writing sucks all the energy out of a simple beat, whereas "The gym buzzes with activity as Jerry, waiting for a machine to free up, looks over the yoga schedule" at least keeps us reading on to the next one.

Low energy is the result of passive craft. It comes from a writer not being alert to the liveliness inherent in every moment. What follows, distilled from my lifetime of viewing, reading, writing, and analysis, are five *craft enhancers*—keys to energizing a screenplay. If we think of a script as a living thing, then these are writing vitamin/mineral supplements composing a protein drink, so to speak, that will make your work healthy, fortify its strength, and give it a longer-lasting life.

1. *Specificity.* Mark Twain once said that the difference between the right word and the almost right word is the difference between lightning and the lightning bug. The most memorable lines in movies are justly remembered because the choices the writers made were specific, and this applies to visual images as well. Ben Braddock being offered "plastics" as the code for success in *The Graduate,* the shape of Cameron Diaz's sperm-gelled hairdo in *Mary*—the greatness is in the details. The more plot-specific and character-specific your beat is, the more effective it will be. Specificity is the difference (in terms of costume, makeup, and persona) between Beetlejuice and a beetle.

2. *Invention.* Here are some superlatives that critics and audiences (and script readers) all too rarely get to use: *fresh, imaginative, surprising, ingenious, original, inspired.* Jaded by the tried and true, we love it whenever a writer takes a truly inventive approach. Whether it's an ingenious structure (*Unfaithfully Yours*), an unconventional character (the gay buddy played by Rupert Everett in *My Best Friend's Wedding*), or an inspired concept (*Zelig*), invention is vital to comedy. The idea of "twist" comes from this kind of imaginative thinking. Thus, any gag powered by a creative device (e.g., *Austin Powers'* Mini-Me) makes a far stronger impression than a formulaic one.

3. *Compression.* Brevity's the soul of wit, and overlong, overwritten screenplays don't sell. The best comedies tend to be lean, clean machines. They don't waste words nailing their beats and jokes. Just as pressurized coal yields diamonds, writing that's compressed breeds energy and excitement. Cutting material to its essence and compressing time and space help to create a seamless, exciting ride. The opening of *Broadcast News* sets up its three protagonists (defining who they were as kids) in three deft scenes that total four and a half minutes. *Groundhog Day* turns Andie MacDowell's rejections of Bill Murray into a swiftly accelerating montage of slaps. When you deliver maximal information in record time

(i.e., come in late and leave early) for every scene, what you get is fast, furious, and funny.

4. *Intensity.* Along with "be serious" and "make them hurt," "take it past the limit" could be another writing maxim to live by. It's not that a romantic comedy must employ wretched excess to earn big laughs or tears, but that its best moments are generally the ones which are genuinely, deeply felt. Evoke intensity through the senses; one minute of excruciating comedic torture that we can almost smell, taste, and touch can be worth half an hour of clownish pranks. Use the passion of your protagonists (witness the first Nicholas Cage/Cher "leave nothing but the skin over my bones!" coupling in *Moonstruck*). Make sure your beats are as visceral as possible; story energy can be born of its characters going the supreme physical and spiritual distance.

5. *Integrity.* Aristotle put it best: "The structural unity of the parts is such that, if any one of them is displaced or removed, the whole will be disjointed and disturbed. For a thing whose presence or absence makes no visible difference is not an organic part of the whole." A necessary dramatic moment will leave a gaping hole in a scene if it's removed. Conversely, a gag that doesn't fit (doesn't organically arise from its surrounding material) has got to go. Integrity applies to the entire fabric of a romantic comedy. Its quirky, contemporary teen-speak characterizes *Clueless* from first line to last. The comic book convention scenes that bookend *Chasing Amy* help make it "of a piece." Unity is a vital component.

To see how these five craft enhancers work in microcosm, let's analyze one gag: "The Tongue," from *Tootsie*.

Half an hour into the movie, Michael-as-Dorothy, prepping for his first appearance on the soap opera set, is told that elderly actor Van Horn kisses all the women on the show—they call him "The Tongue." Sure enough, as a now doubly nervous Dorothy waits for her on-camera entrance, the lecherous Van Horn introduces himself. "We're up next," he says, and gives his mouth a generous spray of Binaca. Determined to thwart Van Horn when they play their scene together, Dorothy suddenly improvises, showing the first glimmer of the outspoken "Tootsie" to come: Van Horn makes his move, and she hits him with her clipboard. Scene completed, a relieved Dorothy bears with director Ron's reprimand, happy she got away with it—and Van Horn, saying he loves her work, welcomes Dorothy to the show by grabbing her and kissing her long and hard.

Specificity (it's unique): we get a visceral charge from that squirt of Binaca. *Invention* (we can't predict it): thinking Michael has escaped, we're surprised by the kiss when we least expect it. *Compression* (we get it fast): a finite unit set up and paid off in one under-five-minute sequence. *Intensity* (we can feel it): what could be more intense than a tongue in the mouth? *Integrity* (it feels right): while the sequence packs in an amazing amount of story development (setting the entire Ron-Julie-Michael subplot in motion), the Tongue threat is its throughline, beginning with Michael's hearing Van Horn's nickname and ending with Van Horn's parting Binaca squirt, heard offscreen as Michael stands shell-shocked by the surprise kiss.

The sum of these five craft enhancers operating in any beat, scene, or story arc is a kind of density—a richness and a lively energy that makes a work hold up to repeated scrutiny.

REWRITING

Hemingway reportedly put the ending of *A Farewell to Arms* through thirty-nine rewrites before pronouncing it unimprovable. And he was no exception to a general rule, stated in the very accurate cliché: writing *is* rewriting.

Screenwriter Richard Curtis acknowledges in interviews having done more drafts of *Notting Hill* than *Four Weddings and a Funeral*'s seventeen. And that figure is par for the course in filmdom, primarily because it's a collaborative medium. Once you've put your romantic comedy through a number of drafts to satisfy your own standards, your script has to face—and reflect—the scrutiny of story analysts and agents, who are followed (God willing) by studio executives, producers, directors, and (God help you) actors. If you really think your written word should be sacrosanct, then you're in the wrong line. Go join that equally congested stream of wordsmiths stalled outside the doors of a book publisher (and see if it's any easier over there).

Most writers consider themselves blessed if a substantial percentage of their first draft makes it into the so-called final draft. They understand that writing a screenplay is a complex, ever changing process of problem solving. Through discovery, discouragement, and galvanizing flashes of insight, the movie evolves, and hopefully improves, the deeper the writer gets into the process.

Judging from some mainstream Hollywood products, the obverse is just as often the case. Rewrites—with a plethora of "ands" and ampersands in the multiwriter credits—have brain-deadened many a movie. Such credits, at times listing the names of six writers who never sat in the same room together, tend to give rewriting a bad name. It took all of them, one thinks, staring incredulously at the screen, to come up with . . . this? But such unfortunate occurrences shouldn't obscure the inherent value of revision. Rewrites are what led to, by whatever tangled skein of contributions, the glory that is *Tootsie*. Rewrites resurrected *Groundhog Day* from turnaround. Rewrites yielded—practically on the set—*When Harry Met Sally*'s biggest laugh.

The awful truth is, it's a rare screenwriter who is equally adept at every single story component. It's a rare script that gets shot almost as is. And given all the people who will try to reshape your material to reflect their own particular vision (be it brilliant or cross-eyed) en route to the screen, there's all the more reason for a writer to *do the necessary work*. You want the movie *you* envision to be as fully realized on the page as it possibly can be. And chances are, it's going to take more than a single draft.

That's why the smartest thing you can do when you're done with a first draft is get rid of it. Put it away! Give it to someone you trust who will lock it up in a deep dark vault and not bring it out—despite your subsequent screaming and rending of clothing—until the allotted, agreed-upon time has elapsed; a week is minimum, and a month is great. Why so long? Because right after completion, if you're anything like me or any other writer I know, you'll still be too close to the material to be able to comprehend what you've written. You'll either be giggling over your favorite gags or gagging over what was supposed to be a giggle, but either way, you're no help. You're the writer who just wrote this—how can you possibly be objective? Wait until you're the writer who wrote this, lo, so many days ago. It'll make things easier for both of you.

When you do confront the results of your first heated labor in the cool light of a later day, you should be able to assess what's working and what needs work. And since in our modern age most everything is salvageable, you will always have this draft on computer file and/or hard copy. Which is a good thing, as this will serve as psychological insurance for the absolutely necessary but often truly grisly job ahead. "Read over your compositions," said Samuel Johnson, "and, when you meet a passage which you think is particularly fine, strike it out."

Romantic comedy writers are suckers for the fine line. After all, one day's work might mean coming up with that "Great Funny Thing Everyone Wishes They'd Said to Her or Him." Should we hit on the ultimate bon mot, it could end up etched in stone. But one thing seasoned screenwriters know about dialogue is that it's almost always secondary to the higher priority: great repartee becomes useless dialogue if it doesn't serve the scene.

Knowing what the scene is about is a primary objective for any draft. The story is of paramount importance. The best joke in the world is your worst enemy if it gets in a scene's way. So when in doubt, strike it out. You can always put it back should you have second thoughts. Many screenwriters keep a file of deleted material, ready for use in a later project. Remember the "elevator to Hell" sequence in *Deconstructing Harry* (1997)? This routine existed, nearly verbatim, in an early draft of *Annie Hall*. That it surfaced in a Woody Allen movie twenty years later proves this principle: any material that doesn't serve your story should be removed—but don't throw it away.

A woman falls in love with a jeweled brooch, buys it, and begins to assemble the outfit that'll best set it off. This dress looks best, which calls for this pair of shoes, and then these earrings . . . and so on, until the ultimate smashing ensemble is created. The woman now looks better than she's ever looked in her life. Only one problem: the brooch doesn't fit.

It's a known phenomenon that the precious seed, the initial notion, that first great scene that originally inspired your story is often the very thing that has to go, as subsequent drafts define and refine your piece. Some writers call it "killing babies." But your jewels, if truly valuable, will survive to surface in another setting. "The wastepaper basket," said Isaac Bashevis Singer, "is the writer's best friend."

FEEDBACK

Self-evaluation is the first step. But can you always rely on yourself to be the most trustworthy and ruthless revisionist? This is what friends are for: to tell you the truth about your work without hurting you in the process.

Some writers keep their first drafts for their eyes only; they put that first outpouring through some necessary fixes before exposing the material to others. But getting a reaction to a self-revised first draft early on can be extremely valuable. To get a sense of what's working and what's not working, have at least two people read your material—three is even better. With three reads, you can form a consensus of opinion and won't be misled by having only one person's point of view. And it's good to give the draft to someone unfamiliar with the specifics of the story so that they come upon it fresh.

Bearing in mind that everyone's opinions are subjective and that not everyone—even a fellow writer—knows how best to read a screenplay, give your readers a specific focus. There's nothing more exasperating than wanting to find out important stuff (e.g., whether your ending works) and getting back a long-winded analysis of your grammar and punctuation, along with a list of typos. A list of typos might indeed be valuable at some other point, but if you have specific questions you want these trial reads to answer, there's nothing wrong with spelling them out.

Though you may not want to lead the witness too overtly ("Everybody hates my male protagonist, Egbert—tell me if you do, too"), there are craftier ways to get the feedback you're looking for ("See what you think of Egbert and Drusilla"). Another equally effective method is to ask your readers to jot down their questions about the characters and/or story as they read. Either way, you're making the reader a more active, helpful participant in the process and, hopefully, avoiding the horrors that can happen when a myopic reader is given carte blanche ("You can't set a movie in Chicago. Nobody wants to see Chicago. Every movie ever made in Chicago *sucks!*").

When receiving feedback, try not to defend or justify your choices. Just listen. Collate the various responses. Generally, if more than one reader has a comment about one particular moment, it's worth red-flagging. The tricky part is to understand what the underlying problem may be. It may not be the line of dialogue itself, but an action that's preceded it (or failed to); it may not be a fault with a character's behavior, but a lack of clarity in defining that character's motivation. We figure these things out over time through trial and error. But certainly, getting an honest, broad-strokes appraisal of your work is a necessary, valuable part of the rewriting process. And being able to deal with—and put to use—constructive criticism is another important craft skill to hone.

READER-FRIENDLY FORM

Finally, it helps to be familiar with screenplay form. There are many screenwriting texts extant, as well as academic courses and a plethora of published scripts (see the appendixes), that can show you the commonly agreed-upon professional format adhered to by most contemporary screenplays. These days, a ready-to-show draft is expected to run between 100 and 120 pages. The first ten pages are expected to establish the genre and tone of the story and identify a protagonist (with some significant plot point kicking in by around the tenth page). Here are a few tips on the subtler points of form from a working story analyst.

When you approach the industry, your first read, and the first line of resistance your script will encounter, comes from a professional reader, or *story analyst,* who reads and then "covers" your submission. *Coverage* is the one- to four-page document that includes pertinent info, log line, synopsis, and commentary on a script. No matter what you may be told, every script that is submitted to a studio, major agency, and/or production company is read by a reader. This makes practical and legal sense. Coverage is the easiest method of desseminating information about a script, and a reader's objectivity is helpful to all who may or may not read it further up the executive ladder.

Here's the biggest credibility stretcher I'll ever ask you to accept: the reader is not necessarily your enemy. Believe it or not, your average story analyst would like nothing more than to read a wonderful script that blows the top of his/her head off. *Home runs,* as we call them, are rare and exciting, and if we love a script, and our exec agrees with us, and if, lo and behold, someone buys the thing . . . then don't we look good? Many readers are writers themselves who appreciate good writing. The thing that makes us ornery is that 99 out of 100 submissions tend to be not so great. *Bad* writing is the coin of the realm in spec submissions; we see truly awful material on a daily basis.

Thus, to put it another way, the readers really want to like you—until you piss them off. What can often turn a reader from friend to enemy, sometimes by the bottom of the first page, are abuses of the following kind:

1. *Useless information.* Camera directions ("we *pan* from them and *dolly* slowly forward to . . .") are the province of the director. Unless you *are* the director, their presence is a distracting hallmark of amateurism. Similarly, keep casting choices ("she's a Sharon Stone type") to yourself; it's not your job and suggests a lack of writerly imagination. Specific music selections are equally dicey, since permission rights are notoriously problematic—and why are you wasting our time on such details when you're supposed to be telling us a story?

Try not to forget the what-you-see-is-what-you-get principle. The best character introductions give us, in one or two compact sentences, a vivid sense of who's on screen, with just enough inference to engender curiosity. (Ted Talley's intro to Jack Crawford in *Silence of the Lambs*, "He is haggard, haunted; his face is a road map of places we could not bear to visit" has become a justly famous paradigm of this technique.) Similarly, excessive backstory details (as well as those of setting), slow down the read and distract from the imaginary movie that must keep *moving* in the mind's eye.

2. *Chatter and hype.* Some blame William Goldman. The archly knowing style of his published *Butch Cassidy* screenplay in the 1970s gave lesser scribes permission to openly address the reader, in a tone somewhere between sardonic carnival barker and TV ad pitchman. "The biggest explosion you've ever seen" was Goldman's description of a dynamiting, and many scripts since have taken this often irritating tack to an abrasive extreme. A screenplay that's constantly nudging and winking ("From the looks of that dress, she's not thinking about going to church, if you know what I mean, and wait till you see what she's got on underneath!") makes a reader want to

give the writer a knuckle sandwich instead of a "Consider." A well told doesn't need hawking and unearned familiarity with audience.

3. *Clutter.* Finally, pay some attention to the physical look of your work upon the page. Any reader, whether a professional or a relative, will inwardly groan when faced with dense chunks of text. Plenty of white space, on the other hand, actually attracts the eye and psychologically encourages an upbeat reading experience. Generous spacing (narrative paragraphs less than half a dozen lines apiece and dialogue that's well within set margins) telegraphs a positive message: the writer is being respectful of the reader and has the story and form under control.

Adhering to these guidelines should earn you a fair, antagonism-free introduction to the industry's gatekeepers.

CHECKLISTS

After you've had some time to absorb the reactions to your script (a good stiff drink is sometimes helpful), if you haven't been entirely disabused of the notion that this is a story worth writing, you'll begin another draft.

Don't try to do everything at once.

If you're at all fond of lists (you know I am), making a pragmatic things-to-do one is the best prep for going into another draft. Once you've assembled such a list, culled from your own observations and others' feedback, you'll probably find that specific rewrite tasks fall into different categories, from large (you're killing a Bellamy) to tiny (you have to fix the rhythm of your heroine's witty comeback on page 103). The further you can break down your tasks and categorize them, the easier it will be for you to navigate your way through the pages.

...eenwriting components are interconnected ...ry, dialogue with character, etc.), it's often ...ch one out and assign a read of the draft to ...cture, for example, making sure your scenes ...per order and length, while leaving dialogue, im-..., and the rest alone. Later, you'll do a read-through for dialogue. At some juncture, you might test each scene against our craft enhancers. A little more specificity, for example, can go a long way.

It's all a lot of work, you may be thinking, but please accept this cautionary note: a script's first read is often its last. Don't think, "Oh, they (the producer, studio, etc.) can fix that if they want to." *They* (meaning most people on the buyer's side of the business) are deluged with material on a daily basis, and a couple of bumps early in a read are often enough to stop even a potential smash script in its tracks.

The rewrite process can be long and exhausting. But if you believe in your movie and early reactions are supportive, there's everything to gain and little to lose by putting in the extra time. People in the business are easily inclined to say no, given the investment that even a modestly budgeted romantic comedy suggests. Your job, however many rewrites it takes to get every comma correct, is to make them an offer so exquisitely conceived and crafted that they can't in good conscience refuse. To help you achieve that end, what follows is a checklist specifically designed to assist romantic comedy revisions.

Romantic Comedy Rewrite Checklist

Character and POV

☐ What makes your protagonists compelling and distinctive?

☐ Are their exterior goals clearly and specifically expressed?

☐ Are their interior emotions articulated?

☐ Do they each have vivid and intriguing entrances?

☐ Do they ever surprise us?

☐ Why do we root for these two people to end up together?

☐ What do they each stand to lose by falling in love?

☐ What will they specifically lose if the relationship fails?

☐ Whose movie is it?

☐ Are your supports genuinely functional?

☐ How do your supports mirror/contrast with your protagonists?

Plot and Structure

☐ Can your story concept be expressed in a simple log line?

☐ Do you have a clearly defined three-act structure?

☐ Are your seven beats in place?

☐ Is your protagonists' meeting indicative of their dynamic?

☐ Does the midpoint truly hook them together?

☐ Is the dark moment as dark as it possibly could be?

☐ Does the story start as late and end as early as possible?

Theme

☐ Can you express your theme in a simple sentence?

☐ Does it come from a personal place? touch on a universal truth?

☐ Does your protagonist's growth express your theme?

☐ Does the story's ending? Do the subplots?

☐ Have you used visual means to articulate theme?

World and Credibility

☐ Is the world of your story convincingly evoked?

☐ If we've seen this world before, what new aspects do you show us?

☐ Can you define the comedic tone you're employing?

☐ Have you broken any rules that you established early on?

☐ Do your setups pay off satisfactorily? with surprises?

☐ Why do we believe these two people are meant for each other?

Humor and Sensuality

☐ Are you maximizing reversals and surprises for humor?

☐ Do you have a comedic set piece?

☐ Have you been inventive with your intimate moments?

☐ Do your romantic encounters embody character? plot development?

☐ Are craft enhancers enlivening both intimate and comedic beats?

Dialogue

☐ Does your dialogue reveal character?

☐ Does it perform more than one of six other functions?

☐ Is it as sharp and succinct as it can be?

☐ Is it too on the nose?

☐ Can you remove it and make your points through other means?

Image

- ☐ Does your story move, literally?
- ☐ Are you telling it visually?
- ☐ Have you used visual metaphors?
- ☐ Do you have action sequences?
- ☐ Are you using every available cinematic technique you can?

CHAPTER THIRTEEN

Romantic Comedy—
Today and Tomorrow

At the end of the last century, a new gospel spread through-out Hollywood: with the lack of any superexplosive guys-with-guns blockbusters in the box office top ten, the action movie was pronounced officially dead, and agents all over town encouraged writer clients to come up with comedy spec scripts. In particular, due to the success of *Runaway Bride* and *Notting Hill,* the word was, "it's a really good time for romantic comedy."

In truth, it was a really good time for Julia Roberts. And, to go out on a very short limb, let me predict that by the time you're reading this, some moneymaking action movie will be said to have "reinvented the genre," and those same agents will be singing a different tune, especially if a high-profile romantic comedy has re-cently tanked. As in fashion, where the hems seemingly go up and down on a yearly basis, everything in the movie business is cycli-cal. But just as skirts themselves have been with us for a hundred years, romantic comedy has had remarkable staying power. In a sense, it's the movie equivalent of that simple black dress which never really goes out of style.

Same as it ever was? Or constantly evolving? If there really is such a thing as a "modern" romantic comedy, *Chasing Amy* would seem to be it, but as we saw, in structure it was actually much like all that had come before it. What felt modern (i.e., cutting-edge as opposed to conservative) was its milieu (a slacker world of gay bars, comic book stores, low-rent diners, and arty loft apartments) and its sensibility. Vulgar, sweet, sophomoric, and wise beyond its youth, *Amy* pushed old-fashioned romantic comedy silliness in a more serious direction, taking on issues of faith and liberalism. Its frank sexual discussions gave its audience a sense that they were hearing themselves on the screen, uncensored—and in this sense, it brought the form closer to "real life." But has the genre really changed?

THE MODERN ROMANTIC COMEDY

Lipstick lesbians. Lovers-turned-stalkers. Mobster's daughters. Dysfunctional-family escapees, multidivorcées, extraterrestrials. . . . These are some of the boys and girls currently losing and getting each other at the multiplex. "We have met the weirdos and they are us" is one conclusion. At the same time, the foibles of just plain folks falling for each other is an ever successful romantic comedy subject.

There's a delicious contradiction at the core of most contemporary moviemakers' approach to the romantic comedy: as much as we want to debunk the myth, the myth is what we want. But if *Chasing Amy* indicates anything about a subtle but pervasive shift in the template at the top of the twenty-first century, it's that we want more truths acknowledged in the course of our dreaming. We want the happy ending, but we want the bitter realities articulated. The unlikely but star-crossed lovers do go into their clinch at the end, but there could be a psycho lining them up in his rifle crosshairs (*There's Something About Mary*). And, in spite of a true love being given its due, hero and/or heroine may well end up alone (*Shakespeare in Love, My Best Friend's Wedding*).

Nonetheless, the basic time-honored belief system (of love as a positive, transformative force) remains intact. No matter how gender-bent the characters may be, however raunchy the dialogue may get, the subtext is the same: the questions may be exasperatingly complex, but love is still the answer.

That love is good remains inarguable. But it's the threats to sustaining love, in our disaster-prone modern life, that often make today's romantic comedies look schizophrenic in their attempts to have this cake and eat it; witness the preponderance of alternate-reality movies like *Sliding Doors* (she dies—she lives!). Certain cross-genres will never be the same: one just could not make another *The American President* after Monica-gate. The cross-genre approach in general, however, continues to thrive; Austen-esque projects continue to materialize, and the teen romantic comedy refuses to chill out.

The straight-up, traditional form is just as hardy. But what makes a well-crafted romantic comedy that's "modern" (i.e., alive to the uninhibited, often black-humored cultural moment) truly competitive? What makes it a hot commodity?

APPROACHING THE MARKETPLACE

Just as Freud's years of research and work led to the plaintive cry, "What does a woman want?," it seems that all my classes on this subject inevitably end in a student's query: "What are the studios looking for?" So I asked Stacey Snider, former head of production and now chairman of Universal Studios, what she looks for in a romantic comedy, besides the words "Julia Roberts is attached."

"The kind of script that will interest a Julia Roberts or a Cameron Diaz, which are not the wacky, contrived ones," Snider said. What gets her attention are "those ideas that everybody relates to—stories rooted in experiences that people remember from their own lives." She cited *My Best Friend's Wedding*, produced during her tenure at Sony, as a screenplay whose central character predicament got ten assistants relating similar stories concerning the specter of marriage. "Everybody had at one time or another the person they thought of as their backup. He'd be the one, if nothing else worked out." Seen from this perspective, the film asked: What would you do if you were about to lose your backup partner? "If you can ask what-if," Snider offered, "and more than a few people say, 'Yes, I've thought about that,' then you know you're onto something." *Never Been Kissed* was another romantic comedy she saw as having a core idea (an adult goes back to high school) that was very relatable: "It was about wanting to be able to do it over again."

For those of us working in a genre that's never entirely shed its screwball origins, such straight-pitch thinking should serve as a heads-up. What the studios want (read, what the best minds in the business believe the public will buy) is not the high jinks, but the humanness. What Snider and her colleagues are looking for in a romantic comedy is an idea that hits a common chord.

This is borne out by the green-lighting of a project that attracted a star who'd formerly shunned the romantic comedy genre. Mel Gibson made the very successful *What Women Want* for Paramount, in which, after an accident, a chauvinistic man is suddenly able to hear the thoughts of every woman he meets. Here's a what-if that's immediately intriguing. Men would love to have that power, and women are amused by what such a premise suggests (what would it be like, for one thing, to be so totally understood—nirvana, or a form of rape?).

It harkens back to theme. A romantic comedy that pokes at provocative truths, that speaks to the issues floating about in the consciousness of our common experience, is the one that will stand out from the crowd . . . and ultimately gather one.

WHAT ROMANTIC COMEDIES ARE FOR

Trends come and go. At the time of this writing, having people talk directly to the camera is the new fad in romantic comedy and character-driven features and TV shows ("new," that is, unless one remembers the opening of *Annie Hall*). Next year, who knows? But for you, the writer, it really doesn't matter. Your job isn't to second-guess the latest style, but to deliver something far more important: an authentic experience that people will respond to.

Audiences go the movies for a variety of reasons, but there's no denying that film is one of the most effective mediums for enabling people to *have their feelings*—to experience the full range of emotions we all carry inside of us and the cathartic effect of letting such feelings loose. The romantic comedy hones in on one particular, vital emotional experience. It's one of the few forms of contemporary entertainment in which characters are allowed to give free rein to their sappiest, gooniest, most exalted expressions of love—and the people watching get to share those feelings.

This is not a small matter.

This is, in fact, secretly what people really want from a romantic comedy: they want to feel what it's like to love and be loved . . . without being embarrassed. They want to be deeply moved, and at the same time, they want to laugh at the ridiculousness of giving in to such feelings. They want to believe in love and its transforming power, and simultaneously they want to enjoy how absurdly *human* we all are in our most innocent, vulnerable head-over-heels moments of believing.

Underneath the slapstick, snappy banter, and outrageous contrivances, your romantic comedy must get to the heart of what makes us human. To fulfill your audience's desires (and even inspire them), show your characters *being human*—having the courage to make utter idiots of themselves in the name of love.

Homo sapiens are possibly the only living creatures that are really good at doing this. And they can be beautiful to see in the act. Capture some of *that* on the page, and the rest (from reader-friendly first pages to a quotable closing line) becomes secondary. Deliver that and you're doing all of us some good.

At its best, the romantic comedy lets us articulate our most intimate feelings in ways that approach poetry. "Love don't make things nice," Ronny Cammareri tells Loretta Castorini in *Moonstruck*. "It ruins everything, it breaks your heart, it makes things a mess! We're not here to make things perfect."

They're standing outside the door to his apartment building, the cold making his breath visible. Snowflakes glitter and melt in Loretta's dark halo of hair. "Snowflakes are perfect," he goes on, "The stars are perfect. Not us, not us! We are here to ruin ourselves and to break our hearts and love the wrong people and die! The storybooks are bullshit. Now I want you to come upstairs and *get* in my bed!"

Ronnie holds out his gloved wooden hand. "Come on," he murmurs, "Come on . . ." Her lips quiver, soft strains of *La Boheme* swell in the wind as her hand takes hold of his, and . . .

It may not be Shakespeare, but it's good enough for me. And if this book has asked a lot of you in seeming to raise the screenplay standards bar awfully high, it's because a dozen or so romantic comedies have been that good. The movie that's funny, sexy, and uses credible characters with compelling conflicts to explore a provocative truth is no impossible dream.

So why not try to achieve that rare and wondrous thing, a story with brains, soul, and beauty—a story that has it all? Isn't that what we're hoping for when, bumbling and stumbling against the odds, we go looking to find true love?

100 Noteworthy Films of the Romantic Comedy Genre and Beyond

Such an overview can't include every film that fits the genre profile. These are not necessarily the best or my personal favorites; *Pretty Woman* is neither, but because it is the biggest moneymaking romantic comedy of all time, it's one of 100 . . .

> Noteworthy films: indicating those with some specific value, contribution to the genre gene pool, and/or historical significance
>
> Of the romantic comedy genre: films with a romantic relationship as the focus of their central story, primarily comedic in tone
>
> And beyond: films combining genres—many of the most interesting and successful romantic comedies being hybrids.

Accordingly, *You've Got Mail*, despite its small charms and large box office returns, is not included, since it's a blip on the larger genre screen, whereas the bracingly original *She's Gotta Have It*, often overlooked on such lists, is one of our genre's first to feature African-American leads. *The Graduate*, stocked in some video stores under "Drama" and technically a black comedy or social satire, is listed because its subversion of stock romantic comedy elements makes it a provocative subject for study.

Key

> *Title*   (Director, *Writer*, Lead couple)

> \+   Classic: generally acknowledged as the cream of the crop

> O   Sleeper: not so well known but well worth a look

> →   Cross-genre: movie that combines genres, or movie from another genre with strong rom-com interest

> *   A top-grossing movie of its decade

1930s
Precursors

1931

> *Private Lives* (Franklin, *Coward*, Shearer-Montgomery)

1932

> O   *Trouble in Paradise* (Lubitsch, *Raphaelson*, Hopkins-Marshall)

> *Red Dust* (Fleming, *Mahin*, Harlow-Gable)

1933

> *She Done Him Wrong* (Sherman, *West-Thew-Bright*, West-Grant)

> *Design for Living* (Lubitsch, *Hecht*, Hopkins-Cooper-March)

The Screwball Era

1934

+   *It Happened One Night* (Capra, *Riskin*, Colbert-Gable)

    Twentieth Century (Hawks, *Hecht*, Lombard-Barrymore)

→   *The Thin Man* (Van Dyke, *Hackett-Goodrich*, Loy-Powell)

1936

+   *My Man Godfrey* (La Cava, *Ryskind*, Lombard-Powell)

○   *Theodora Goes Wild* (Boleslawski, *Buchman*, Dunne-Douglas)

→   *Swing Time* (Stevens, *Lindsay-Scott*, Rogers-Astaire)

1937

○   *Easy Living* (Leisen, *Sturges*, Arthur-Milland)

+   *The Awful Truth* (McCarey, *Delmar*, Dunne-Grant)

+   *Nothing Sacred* (Wellman, *Hecht*, Lombard-March)

1938

+   *Bringing Up Baby* (Hawks, *Nichols-Wilde*, Hepburn-Grant)

○   *Holiday* (Cukor, *Stewart-Buchman*, Hepburn-Grant)

1939

○   *Midnight* (Leisen, *Wilder-Brackett*, Colbert-Ameche)

    Ninotchka (Lubitsch, *Wilder-Brackett*, Garbo-Douglas)

Emerging/defining talents: Ernst Lubitsch, Frank Capra, Leo McCarey, Howard Hawks

1940s
The Golden Age Peaks

1940

+   *His Girl Friday* (Hawks, *Lederer/Hecht*, Russell-Grant)

+   *The Philadelphia Story* (Cukor, *Stewart*, Hepburn-Grant-Stewart)*

O   *The Shop Around the Corner* (Lubitsch, *Raphaelson*, Sullavan-Stewart)

1941

+   *The Lady Eve* (Sturges/*Sturges*, Stanwyck-Fonda)

The War Years

1942

    Woman of the Year (Stevens, *Lardner*, Hepburn-Tracy)

→ *I Married a Witch* (Clair, *Pirosh-Connelly*, Lake-March)

1943

    The Miracle of Morgan's Creek (Sturges/*Sturges*, Hutton-Bracken)

Postwar

1947

→ *The Ghost and Mrs. Muir* (Mankiewicz, *Dunne*, Tierney-Harrison)

1949

+   *Adam's Rib* (Cukor, *Kanin-Gordon*, Hepburn-Tracy)*

Emerging/defining talents: Preston Sturges, George Cukor, Ruth Gordon, Garson Kanin

1950s
Transition

1950

Born Yesterday (Cukor, *Kanin*, Holliday-Holden)*

1952

○   Pat and Mike (Cukor, *Kanin/Gordon*, Hepburn-Tracy)

1953

Roman Holiday (Wyler, *Dighton/Hunter*, A. Hepburn-Peck)

1954

+   Sabrina (Wilder/*Wilder-Lehman*, A. Hepburn-Holden-Bogart)

1955

→   To Catch a Thief (Hitchcock, *Hayes*, Kelly-Grant)

○   Smiles of a Summer Night (Bergman/*Bergman*, Andersson, etc.)

1958

→   Gigi (Minnelli, *Lerner*, Caron-Jordan)*

1959

+   Some Like It Hot (Wilder/*Wilder-Diamond*, Monroe-Curtis-Lemmon)*

Pillow Talk (Gordon/*Green-Richlin*, Day-Hudson)*

Emerging/defining talents: Billy Wilder (with I. L. Diamond and/or Charles Brackett), Vincente Minnelli

1960s
The New Sophistication

1960

+ *The Apartment* (Wilder/*Wilder-Diamond*, MacLaine-Lemmon)*

1961

+ *Breakfast at Tiffany's* (Edwards, *Axelrod*, Hepburn-Peppard)

→ *A Woman Is a Woman* (Godard/*Godard*, Karina-Belmondo)

1962

Divorce—Italian Style (Germi/*Germi*, Sandrelli-Mastroianni)

1963

→ *Charade* (Donen, *Stone*, Hepburn-Grant)

The Nutty Professor (Lewis, *Lewis*, Lewis-Stevens)

1964

→ *My Fair Lady* (Cukor, *Lerner*, Hepburn-Harrison)*

1967

+ *Two for the Road* (Donen, *Raphael*, Hepburn-Finney)

Barefoot in the Park (Saks, *Simon*, Fonda-Redford)

→ *The Graduate* (Nichols, *Henry-Willingham*, Bancroft-Ross-Hoffman)*

1968

O *Stolen Kisses* (Truffaut/*Truffaut*, Seyrig-Leaud)

1969

→ *Bob & Carol & Ted & Alice* (Mazursky, Wood-Culp-Cannon-Gould)

Emerging/defining talents: Blake Edwards, Stanley Donen

1970s
The Modern Era

1971

○   *A New Leaf* (May/*May*, May-Matthau)
    Claire's Knee (Rohmer/*Rohmer*, Cornu-Brialy)

1972

+   *What's Up Doc?* (Bogdanovich, *Henry/Newman/Benton*, Streisand-O'Neal)*
    The Heartbreak Kid (May/*May*, May-Matthau)

1975

○   *Shampoo* (Ashby, *Towne-Beatty*, Christie-Hawn-Grant-Beatty)*

→   *Swept Away* (Wertmuller/*Wertmuller*, Melato-Giannini)

1976

+   *Cousin, Cousine* (Tacchella/*Tacchella*, Barrault-Lanoux)

1977

+   *Annie Hall* (Allen/*Allen-Brickman*, Keaton-Allen)*
    The Goodbye Girl (Ross, *Simon*, Mason-Dreyfuss)*

1978

→   *Heaven Can Wait* (Beatty, *Beatty-Henry*, Christie-Beatty)*

○   *Get Out Your Handkerchiefs* (Blier/*Blier*, Laure-Depardieu-Dewaere)
    Same Time Next Year (Mulligan, *Slade*, Burstyn-Alda)

1979

+   *Manhattan* (Allen/*Allen-Brickman*, Keaton-Hemingway-Allen-Murphy)

→   *10* (Edwards/*Edwards*, Andrews-Derek-Moore)

Emerging/defining talents: Neil Simon, Woody Allen, Elaine May

1980s
Cross-Genre Reigns

1981

+   *Arthur* (Gordon/*Gordon*, Minnelli-Moore)*

1982

+   *Tootsie* (Pollack, *Gelbart/Schisgal*, Lange-Hoffman)*

1984

→   *Splash* (Howard, *Ganz/Mandel/Friedman*, Hannah-Hanks

     Sixteen Candles (Hughes/*Hughes*, Ringwald-Hall)

+   *Romancing the Stone* (Zemeckis, *Thomas*, Turner-Douglas)*

1985

→   *Prizzi's Honor* (Huston, *Condon-Roach*, Huston-Nicholson)

     Purple Rose of Cairo (Allen/*Allen*, Farrow-Daniels)

1986

+   *Hannah and Her Sisters* (Allen/*Allen*, Farrow-Caine, etc.)

→   *Something Wild* (Demme, *Frye*, Griffith-Daniels)

O   *She's Gotta Have It* (Lee/*Lee*, Johns-Hicks-Lee)

1987

+   *Moonstruck* (Jewison, *Shanley*, Cher-Cage)*

     Roxanne (Schepisi, *Martin*, Hannah-Martin)

+   *Broadcast News* (Brooks/*Brooks*, Hunter-Hurt-A. Brooks)

→   *The Princess Bride* (Reiner, *Goldman*, Wright-Elwes)

1988

     Working Girl (Nichols, *Wade*, Griffith-Ford)

→   *Bull Durham* (Shelton/*Shelton*, Sarandon-Costner-Robbins)

1989

○ *Say Anything* (Crowe/*Crowe*, Skye-Cusack)

○ *The Fabulous Baker Boys* (Kloves/*Kloves*, Pfeiffer-Bridges)

+ *When Harry Met Sally* (Reiner, *Ephron*, Ryan-Crystal)

Emerging/defining talents: Rob Reiner, Nora Ephron, James Brooks

---

1990s
Pushing the Envelope

1990

+ *Pretty Woman* (Marshall, *Lawton*, Roberts-Gere)*

1991

→ *Defending Your Life* (Brooks/*Brooks*, Streep-Brooks)

1993

+ *Sleepless in Seattle* (Ephron, *Ephron/Arch/Ward*, Ryan-Hanks)*

+ *Groundhog Day* (Ramis, *Rubin*, MacDowell-Murray)

→ *True Romance* (Scott, *Tarantino*, Arquette-Slater)

1994

+ *Four Weddings and a Funeral* (Newell, *Curtis*, MacDowell-Grant)

1995

→ *Sense and Sensibility* (Lee, *Thompson*, Thompson-Grant)

→ *Clueless* (Heckerling/*Heckerling*, Silverstone-Rudd)

○ *Before Sunrise* (Linklater/*Linklater*, Delpy-Hawke)

1996

+   *Jerry Maguire* (Crowe/*Crowe*, Zellweger-Cruise)*

○   *The Truth About Cats and Dogs* (Lehman, *Wells*, Garofalo-Chaplin)

1997

+   *Chasing Amy* (Smith/*Smith*, Adams-Affleck)

     My Best Friend's Wedding (Hogan, *Bass*, Roberts-Mulroney)*

+   *As Good as It Gets* (Brooks, *Brooks/Andrus*, Nicholson-Hunt)*

1998

→   *There's Something About Mary* (Farrelly, *Farrelly/Decter-Strauss*, Diaz-Stiller)*

+   *Shakespeare in Love* (Madden, *Norman-Stoppard*, Paltrow-Fiennes)

1999

     Notting Hill (Michell, *Curtis*, Roberts-Grant)

Emerging/defining talents: Cameron Crowe, Kevin Smith, Richard Curtis

---

2000s
An Open Question

2000

     High Fidelity (Frears, *DeVincentis-Pink*, Cusack-Hjejle)

     What Women Want (Meyers, *Goldsmith-Yuspa*, Gibson-Hunt)

Some Relevant Lists

ROMANTIC COMEDIES IN THE TOP-100-GROSSING FILMS (OVER $100 MIL)*

Pretty Woman	#36
Tootsie	#37
There's Something About Mary	#41
Jerry Maguire	#56
As Good as It Gets	#60
Runaway Bride	#67
My Best Friend's Wedding	#98
Sleepless in Seattle	#100

*In domestic release, according to *Variety* as of 2000.

ROMANTIC COMEDY WINNERS OF "BEST PICTURE" ACADEMY AWARD

It Happened One Night	1934
The Apartment	1960
My Fair Lady	1964
Annie Hall	1977
Shakespeare in Love	1998

ROMANTIC COMEDY WINNERS OF "BEST SCREENPLAY" ACADEMY AWARD

1. *It Happened One Night* (1934), Robert Riskin
2. *Pygmalion* (1938), W. P. Lipscomb, Anatole de Grunwald, Cecil Lewis, Ian Dalyrymple, George Bernard Shaw
3. *The Philadelphia Story* (1940), Donald Ogden Stewart
4. *Woman of the Year* (1942), Ring Lardner, Jr., Michael Kanin
5. *Pillow Talk* (1959), Russell Rouse, Clarence Green, Stanley Shapiro, Maurie Richlin
6. *Annie Hall* (1977), Woody Allen, Marshall Brickman
7. *Hannah and Her Sisters* (1986), Woody Allen
8. *Moonstruck* (1987), John Patrick Shanley
9. *Sense and Sensibility* (1995), Emma Thompson
10. *Shakespeare in Love* (1998), Mark Norman, Tom Stoppard

Bibliography

12 NOTABLE ROMANTIC COMEDY SCREENPLAYS IN PRINT

Annie Hall
    Allen (in *Four Films by Woody Allen*, Random House)

The Apartment
    Wilder and Diamond (Faber & Faber)

Arthur
    Gordon (in *Best American Screenplays*, ed. Thomas, Crown)

Chasing Amy
    Smith (Miramax/Hyperion)

Four Weddings and a Funeral
    Curtis (St. Martin's Griffin)

It Happened One Night
    Riskin (in *6 Screenplays by Robert Riskin*, University of California)

The Lady Eve
  Sturges (in *5 Screenplays by Preston Sturges*, University of California)

Moonstruck
  Shanley (Pantheon)

Sense and Sensibility
  Thompson (Newmarket Press)

Shakespeare in Love
  Norman and Stoppard (Miramax/Hyperion)

The Shop Around the Corner
  Raphaelson (in *3 Screen Comedies by Samson Raphaelson*, University of Wisconsin)

When Harry Met Sally
  Ephron (Knopf)

SCREENPLAY SOURCES

Published quarterly, *Scenario* is the only magazine that prints contemporary and classic screenplays in full, usually with writer interviews, averaging four per issue; *His Girl Friday* (Ben Hecht) appears in vol. 1/4.

Screenplays reprinted in their original form can be purchased on the internet (www.ScriptShop.com) and in bookstores such as Script City (8033 Sunset Boulevard, Los Angeles, CA 90046, 323-871-0707).

SELECTED BIBLIOGRAPHY

Bogdanovich, Peter. *Who the Devil Made It*, Knopf

Bjorkman, Stig. *Woody Allen on Woody Allen*, Grove

Engel, Joel. *Screenwriters on Screenwriting*, Hyperion

Froug, William. *Zen and the Art of Screenwriting*, Silman-James

Harvey, James. *Romantic Comedy in Hollywood*, Da Capo Press

Lucey, Paul. *Story Sense*, McGraw-Hill

Mamet, David. *On Directing*, Penguin

McBride, Joseph. *Hawks on Hawks*, University of California

Pope, Thomas. *Good Scripts, Bad Scripts*, Three Rivers

Seger, Linda. *Making A Good Script Great*, Dodd, Mead & Co.

Index